HOUSING IN BRITAIN

THE POST-WAR EXPERIENCE

HOUSING IN BRITAIN

THE POST-WAR EXPERIENCE

JOHN R. SHORT

METHUEN
LONDON AND NEW YORK

First published in 1982 by
Methuen & Co. Ltd
11 New Fetter Lane, London EC4P 4EE

Published in the USA by
Methuen & Co.
in association with Methuen, Inc.
733 Third Avenue, New York, NY 10017

Printed in Great Britain at the
University Press, Cambridge

British Library Cataloguing in Publication Data
Short, John R.
Housing in Britain.
1. Housing—Great Britain—History
363.5'0941 HD7333

ISBN 0-416-74290-4 Pbk

Library of Congress Cataloging in Publication Data

Short, John R.
Housing in Britain.

Bibliography: p.
Includes index.
1. Housing—Great Britain—History. 2. Housing
policy—Great Britain—History. I. Title.
HD7333.A3S337 1982 363.5'0941 82-8118 AACR2
ISBN 0-416-74290-4 (pbk.)

For Adrienne

as a small token of my love

CONTENTS

LIST OF TABLES

LIST OF FIGURES

ACKNOWLEDGEMENTS

The publishers and I would like to thank the following for permission to reproduce copyright material: the School for Advance Urban Studies, University of Bristol, for Figure 6.7; *Which* for Figure 6.8; Michael Heath and the *Sunday Times* for Figure 8.1; and Heinemann Educational Books Ltd. for Figure 10.2.

PREFACE

The title of this book captures the essence of the subject matter: it is concerned with post-war housing in Britain. Throughout the book the term 'post-war' will refer to post-1945. It is less cumbersome than 'post-Second World War' and defines the unity of the period more effectively than 'post-1945'. By Britain I generally mean England and Wales. I mean no disrespect to Scotland. Quite the opposite. Most books with Britain in the title either ignore Scotland or place it in the category of a few lines at the end of each chapter to show how Scotland compares and contrasts with England. Scotland is too important to be designated as little more than a footnote. It cannot, however, easily be incorporated into an exposition which also considers England and Wales. There is the difference in statistical base, variations in the timing of legislation and more fundamental differences in political disposition, class structure, past housing experience and present trends. The experience of England and Wales has been important in shaping that of Scotland. Scotland has been influential in certain key respects. What I have done is to separate the strands of the British experience. The book should therefore have been called *Housing in Britain: the Story of England and Wales*. This is an ugly title. A second appropriate volume may quieten the anger of those aggrieved by the inaccuracy of the title of the first.

My analysis of housing considers some items as it excludes others. My concern with housing is with an element of state policy, a commodity which has a certain market for its sale and exchange, an essential good with access and eligibility rules, and a vital part in the reproduction of social life. I have ignored explicit considerations of architecture, design, council house management, building techniques and the details of internal layout and external appearance. Others are better qualified to write on these matters and appropriate books have already appeared. The aim is to present a general exposition of the *broad* picture of post-war housing. The emphasis is on the whole of the experience rather than its constituent parts. My principal interest is with housing in urban areas. This reflects the weight of numbers and the importance of the existing distribution of political interest, legislative measures, existing research and my own research, which has been confined to analysing housing issues in urban areas.

The terms having been defined, I can say something about the exposition. The structure of the book is fourfold. In Chapter 1 I make some general remarks which aim to set the scene, outline my position and mark the reader's card for subsequent pages. This chapter is the entrance hall to the body of the book. The next three parts take up the general themes which I shall be exploring: housing and the state, the housing market, and housing as lived experience. In Chapters 2 and 3 I consider housing and the state with emphasis on the evolution of successive legislative measures and some assessment of their impact. The emphasis will be on the unfolding of events in post-war Britain. In Part 2 I consider the structure of the housing market, paying particular attention to the constellation of agents involved in the production, consumption and exchange of housing. Many of the state policies only briefly mentioned in Chapter 3 are examined in greater detail in Chapters 4–10 as they affect particular sectors of the market. There is some repetition between Parts 1 and 2, but in the form of looking at different aspects of the same phenomena. Finally, Chapter 11 looks at housing as it affects specific types of households.

This book is really one half of a whole. The other is a book I wrote with Keith Bassett entitled *Housing and Residential Structure*. In it we surveyed the different approaches to studying housing and sought to elaborate the general principles about the operation of the housing market in advanced capitalist countries. *Housing and Residential Structure* was an essay in general themes; *Housing in Britain* is a study of the particular. The former provides the arguments of why certain topics are treated in the way they are in *Housing in Britain*, while the latter elaborates with empirical material the arguments of *Housing and Residential Structure*.

Throughout the book I have sought to garnish the text with as many tables and diagrams as possible. It is a useful device to keep the reader's interest. Punctuating the text breaks up the dull monotony of pages of text and should stop the reader falling into an idle reverie. The figures also give life to statistics, while the tables of statistics give an extra dimension to the argument. Much of the argument is based on my reading of empirical material. Not to allow the reader access to this material would be to close the debate, to imply that I had incorporated all the nuances. Since I do not believe this, I have loaded the book with as much empirical material in the form of tables as possible, hoping not to sink the text, in order to keep the debate open and alive. In order to maintain the smooth flow of the exposition I have rarely used footnotes or extensive referencing. Those in the know already know, and those who don't should look to the guide for further reading at the end of the book.

Having defined the terms, explained the structure and justified the exposition it now seems appropriate to apportion blame and thanks. The former is easy – the faults are mine. The latter is more important because there is no such thing as an individual piece of work. All academic endeavours are aided by direct contact with a few close colleagues and indirect contact with the many scholars working the same street. I have drawn on the work of scores of people while writing this book, and my only hope is that I have not done any injustice to their work. I also owe a great deal to the few. I first became interested in housing at the Geography Department of Bristol University while working for a PhD and then in a post-doctoral research project. The staff there made my stay a pleasant and interesting one, and in particular I worked very closely with Keith Bassett, who is a friend as well as a colleague. In Reading, Sophie Bowlby, Andrew Kirby, Peter Hall, Lyn Davies, Alan Hooper and others have provided a great environment in which to bounce around ideas. The technical staff at Reading University Geography Department provided material assistance, and heartfelt thanks are extended to Jacqui Lewis, Rosa Husain, Sheila Dance, Brian Rogers and Christine Holland. Thanks also to Mary Ann Kernan who commissioned the work.

J.R.S.

1

GENERAL REMARKS

Housing is important. For the individual household it provides shelter from the elements, an essential base for social action, an important part of total expenditure, and a reflection of status and social standing in the community. For a whole series of agents (builders/developers, estate agents, investors, solicitors, and so on) it provides an important source of revenue. In the wider society, housing has been, and will continue to be, an important source of social conflict and political mobilization. Clearly, it is a topic worthy of investigation.

There are already many good, and some very good, studies of housing in Britain before the Second World War, but previous studies of British housing since 1945 have tended to focus on particular issues or have adopted approaches which fail to capture the totality of the post-war experience. This book is offered as an essay on the broad picture of British post-war housing. The time scale is not arbitrary. Government policy in general, and housing policy in particular, changed radically in the post-war years. The use of demand management in macro-economic policy, the creation of the welfare state and the large-scale provision of local authority housing were all elements in this (if not new, then at least different) social order. The creation of this order in the early post-war years laid the basis for further arrangements and defined the course of subsequent events. There is an essential unity in the post-war era reflected in the echoing nature of the ideological disputes, political clashes and fiscal problems. In Britain the year 1945 marks a significant break with the past and the inauguration of a new arena for political dispute. Housing issues played an important part in this discourse.

MAIN THEMES

The book looks at several themes. Part 1 considers the evolution of housing policy. Part 2 looks at the interaction between it and the agents and households involved in the production, consumption and exchange of housing. Part 3 examines in more detail the relationship between housing and households. Each of the themes deserve a few remarks in this introductory chapter.

Housing and the state

The 'why' of state involvement State involvement in housing comes about through the political demands of different agents. Three broad types of agent can be identified. First, there are those capital interests such as builders and landlords who are directly involved with housing production and consumption. They want their interests secured and they lobby government to that end. Second, there are those interests indirectly concerned with housing. Industrial capital, for example, is mainly concerned with producing commodities, but it requires a labour force which requires housing. Industrial capital thus wants a sufficient quantity of cheap, readily accessible housing so that workers' efficiency is not impaired and labour costs are kept low. Industrial capital could provide housing for the workers but this is a costly business: its demand for state involvement is mainly a demand for the off-loading of the costs of reproducing labour power on to the public sector. Third, because housing is such an important part of the individual household's life it has figured in the collective demands for social advancement and material gains. The articulated demands of working people for the social improvement of their lot has included calls for better, cheaper housing. State involvement has also been suggested by those seeking to vitiate disruptive social action. The Victorian social reformers pointed out that better housing not only produced more efficient workers, it could prevent potential social unrest caused by poor housing. As we shall see, this latter theme was an important element in the evolution of housing policy in the late nineteenth century.

The limits of state involvement There are limits to state involvement in housing matters. First, there are the self-imposed limits of a state in capitalist society which confines problem-solving to acceptable solutions. For example, the inefficiency of the house-building industry is approached through introducing methods of industrialized building and hidden subsidies, not through complete state monopoly of house construction. Then there are the politically acceptable solutions. For example, a great deal of money could be saved by abolishing income tax relief on mortgage repayments, but with owner-occupiers being a majority, this partial solution to the perceived problem of spiralling public expenditure is never seriously raised. The heat in housing-policy debates is caused by the political friction of proposed policies rubbing against these limits. Second, there is the limit of public expenditure. Public expenditure comes from government taxation. There is a finite limit to this taxation and when the state spends more than it takes it experiences a fiscal crisis. Since much of state involvement in housing matters entails state expenditure, housing is dragged into the debates on the need to reduce public expenditure. Throughout the post-war period, the quality and level of state housing have been affected by changes in public expenditure. I shall seek to identify the broad nature of these changes and the particular areas of housing provision most affected. The main conclusion drawn is that the provision of local authority housing has been worst affected.

The form of state involvement The form of state involvement in housing is shaped by three factors. First, in the medium to long term the balance of political power is important. British housing policy over the long term has been shaped in broad outline by the nature of this balance. At various times landed interests, industrial capital and working-class interests have been important in shaping policy. These interests have been mediated through the representation of political parties. At times the political parties have directly represented material interests. But because the main political parties also carry ideological baggage from previous times, memories of the past and an intellectual articulation of their position relative to other parties, they can be relatively autonomous of the interests of any one specific group. Consider the case of the Conservative party and free enterprise. Its commitment to free enterprise, expressed in terms of freeing the market from government controls, owes more to nineteenth-century debates and responses to the socialist intellectual and political challenge than a full understanding of modern capitalism. In similar vein the Labour party has a commitment to nationalization which owes more to the inter-war experience than to an analysis of how to promote industrial democracy. This observation does not lead to the conclusion that the political parties are completely independent of material interests. They are not. They express material interests through the medium of political representation.

One has to be wary of the surface expression since all parties represent their policies in terms of the national interest and universal principles. In a democracy this is the way to achieve power. In Part 1 I shall seek to show how, despite the claims of universality, housing policies in post-war Britain have benefited certain groups and constrained others. The impact of the policies has had definite redistributional consequences.

Second, in the short to medium term, state policy is shaped by the economic context: in other words, the state of the economy. This affects housing in a number of ways. In the private sector, for example, the cyclical nature of economic growth is important. Booms and slumps seem to be endemic to capitalist economies. And the roller-coaster of economic expansion and contraction is reflected in the peaks and troughs of housing starts in the private sector. In booms credit is available, business confidence is high and more houses are built. In slumps housing starts to fall off dramatically as builders find it difficult to get credit and households are strapped for cash. Net additions to the housing stock thus depend on the state of the economy and, in general, during slumps house building declines and it is more difficult for new households to obtain accommodation. State policy is affected to the extent that political pressures are generated for the state to intervene in the level of house building and to secure the entry of new households into the housing market. In the public sector the state of the economy impinges on policies most directly through the direction and level of state expenditure. Two phases can be identified. In the first, during the 1950s and 1960s, housing was used as a Keynesian regulator to increase effective demand in the economy. In the second phase, from the mid-1960s onwards, the worsening economic crisis was reflected in calls for reductions in public expenditure. Housing, and local-authority housing in particular, was badly affected by expenditure cutbacks. This two-phase categorization is crude. There were reductions in housing expenditure during the 1950s and 1960s. However, the simple division captures the essence of the post-war period, as we shall see.

The economic context does not fix set courses for state action. There is no one path set by the nature of external economic constraints. The state of the economy affects policies through the filter of political action. The constraints and opportunities afforded by the economic background will be perceived differently according to the balance of political forces. There is no inexorable policy course set by economic logic above the domain of politics.

Finally, in the short term, state policies are shaped by previous policies. Previous policies provide the legislative and political frame of reference for subsequent policies; they are the blueprint for small-scale incremental changes. Moreover, the effect of previous policies on different groups and institutions will in some measure form the shape of demands for new and revised policies. The unfolding consequences of previous policies shape the course of future policies.

The three factors outlined above can be related in a hierarchical manner to policy changes. Fundamental shifts in housing policy reflect broad changes in political power. There have been two such shifts in twentieth-century Britain. The first was immediately after the First World War and the second was immediately after the Second World War. In both periods, housing policies reflected popular demands for a higher 'social wage' in general, and for better housing in particular. These fundamental shifts placed state involvement in housing on new levels. New solutions to old housing problems were conceived. Subsequent policies after each of these major shifts were then shaped by the political response to the changing economic context. As the balance of political power changed, so did the perception of the economic constraints which in turn guided the nature of the political response to changing economic conditions; at the level of incremental change policies were shaped by the monitoring of previous policies and the lobbying of various housing agents. The general argument I put forward in Part I is that post-war housing policy in Britain represents one coherent period. The fundamental change in policy was expressed in the immediate post-war years, thereafter policy changes were of the medium-scale and incremental type.

Housing policy and housing protest A distinction can be drawn between state policies that affect housing and those policies specifically tailored to meet some expressed housing need, pacify some housing interest or placate housing protests. In the former case almost all government economic, social and planning policies affect the housing market to some extent. A recurring feature of the post-war housing story has been the way in which housing has been affected by economic policies. In managing the economy through controlling (or not as the case may be) credit rates, limiting the money supply, formulating wage and price policies, etc., the state has continually affected the housing market. In terms of the latter we can make a further distinction between policies designed to deal with specific issues and a set of linked measures which form a coherent, long-term policy. Coherent housing policies are rare; measures tend to be designed by the politics of the moment in the light of expediency. The one enduring feature of post-war housing measures has been the encouragement of owner-occupation. This has emerged as the single most important measure pursued by successive governments.

In the previous section I noted that state involvement in Britain was shaped by the balance of political power, the economic context and the unfolding consequences of previous policies. The first is self-explanatory. The second is fairly obvious and will be alluded to throughout the book. The third deserves further elaboration. Three elements are relevant. The most important has been the monitoring of previous measures by the bureaucracy. At the local level the relevant institution is the Housing Department, while the departmental responsibility at central government level has shifted. From 1945 to 1951 the department most directly responsible for housing was the Ministry of Health. In 1951 the Ministry of Housing and Local Government was established. Later, in 1970, housing came under the huge Department of the Environment. These government departments have dealt directly with housing matters. But perhaps the most important has been the Treasury, since successive economic crises in the post-war economy have resulted in Treasury pruning of government expenditure, especially in welfare sectors. The Treasury has tried to hold the purse strings of government expenditure. These different departments fill in the details of the major policies determined by the balance of political forces, and by monitoring the impact of previous policies they provide the agenda for future policy options. The process is essentially one of incrementalism. Policy measures emanating from the civil service tend to be adjustments to existing policies, fine tunings to revised budgets rather than the introduction of radically new policies.

Second, capital interests such as construction companies, landlords, etc., have sought to achieve changes in existing policies through political representation and lobbying. These interests work through both major parties, although their traditional home is in the Conservative party. There are, for example, very close ties between the major construction companies and the Tories: Sir Keith Joseph's family firm was the Bovis construction group; the chairman of the McAlpine construction company has been Treasurer of the party; and at the local level the links between builders and constituency groups are many and strong. Capital interests are represented directly by the various pressure groups (e.g. Housebuilders Federation, the Property Owners Association, etc.) and indirectly through the shared assumptions of the benefits of free enterprise, market forces and the need for profit. If successful the demands of various capital interests are mediated through the Whitehall policy machine.

Finally, housing policy changes can arise from organized household collective action. Explicitly working-class action on a wide scale has been rare. The goals and concern of organized labour in Britain have tended to remain within the factory gates; the emphasis has been on production rather than reproduction. The Glasgow rent strike of 1915 seems to have been the largest social movement combining housing demands with industrial militancy with a definite political effect. Rent controls in Britain arose from government response to the challenge from Clydeside. Much more common has been localized, small-scale, often ephemeral protest by small numbers of people. This form of housing protest has been an important element informing post-war housing policy. The protest has varied from discreet lobbying to demonstrations in the street, and the participants have ranged from the well-heeled landowner seeking the containment of new housing development to the single-parent homeless household. The form and success of the protest are related to the people concerned and the interests represented. Wealthy households rarely take to the streets, they rarely have to, while single-parent homeless households rarely have the opportunity to present their case at 10 Downing Street over coffee and sandwiches.

Three forms of housing protest have been of importance in shaping policy. First, there has been the protest about the problem of homelessness. This is the most basic of housing problems. When restricted to few people it has raised scarcely a whisper of public concern. At other times it has been masked, at least temporarily, by living with in-laws, sharing, or greater multi-occupation. When many people are affected, however, and have demonstrated, then the seismograph of political representation has registered the subterranean rumblings. In 1945 and 1946, for example, the housing shortage was sharply brought to the government's attention by the large-scale squatting in empty properties. Thereafter, throughout the late 1940s and 1950s such protest was rare. It surfaced again in the late 1960s when the continuing problem of finding decent affordable accommodation in central London was partially overcome by some households who squatted in empty properties. This protest was incorporated by most London boroughs, who handed empty property over to squatters' groups; it presented a solution to long housing waiting lists and the embarrassment of holding empty derelict property. From the 1970s the protest of the squatters worked hand in hand, in London at least, with the local authorities. The most successful housing protest did not involve demonstrations in the street: it was a television drama. In 1966 the BBC showed a powerful drama called 'Cathy Come Home' written by Jeremy Sandford about the problems of one family who had been made homeless and their tribulations in seeking temporary accommodation. The impact was enormous. Arthur Greenwood, the housing minister of the time, ordered a private showing for all his officials. More important, the housing ginger-group Shelter was established. The atmosphere of public discussion concerning 'Cathy Come Home' gave Shelter a tremendous boost. And what could have turned out to be just another ephemeral association was transformed into an important pressure group which has been an important voice in subsequent debates.

The problem of homelessness has been bedevilled by the lack of muscle of the victims. Homeless households represent a failure but not a threat. The homelessness issue has also been bedevilled by the stigmatization of the victims. At worst they are portrayed as scroungers, queue-jumpers, outsiders or, at middling, as inadequates unable to organize their lives properly. From this perspective, their problem is seen in terms of personal inadequacy rather than a malfunctioning of the housing market; like the poor (and the rich) the homeless will therefore always be with us.

A second form of housing protest is shown by the development of community organizations in certain inner-city areas which have sought to direct local authority housing plans for their neighbourhoods. In the early 1960s housing policies for the older inner-city areas consisted in the main of comprehensive redevelopment schemes which involved the demolition of existing properties and the construction of new dwellings. The newer dwellings were at much lower densities, and the schemes involved rehousing residents in new estates often miles away on the peripheral areas of the cities. Many people were glad to move out of their old, cramped, damp, bug-infested dwellings, and this should not be forgotten especially in the light of later romanticizations of slum life mainly by those who have never lived in anything worse than student lodgings. In many areas, however, a majority of the residents were unwilling to move out of the neighbourhood. But they had little choice and even less representation outside the formal channels of local politics. Protest in this case was unorganized (see Table 1.1).

Table 1.1 Housing protest and urban renewal

Forms of protest	*Place*	*Case study*
Protest unorganized	Liverpool	Muchnick (1970)
	Sunderland	Dennis (1970)
Protest blocked	Newcastle	Davies (1972)
	Sunderland	Dennis (1972)
	Newham (London)	Dunleavy (1977)
Protest partly successful	Barnsbury (London)	Ferris (1972)
	Bristol	Short and Bassett (1981)

Things began to change in the latter half of the 1960s and the early 1970s. The 1969 and 1974 Housing Acts introduced improvement as an alternative to clearance, and extended public participation exercises. Alternatives were available, channels were opened up and in some cases protest could be organized. Success, for these groups, was not guaranteed. Where the local authority disagreed with the community proposals or denied legitimacy to the proposers, then protest was unsuccessful. Successful protests came about when the local organization managed to influence the direction of local housing policy.

The catalyst groups in the organized protests have varied from committed, concerned locals, to party activists to radical community organizers. The state-sponsored community schemes have been important sources for such organizers. The largest scheme was the National Community Development Project set up by the Home Office in 1969 to send community workers to run-down inner-city areas. The initial brief was for the workers to plug the local folk into the circuit of benefits in the welfare state. The CDP experiment proved an interesting one. The reports very quickly started to eschew traditional explanations of social deprivation in proposing structural conflict models. The CDP, not unsurprisingly, was eventually closed down, but the experience was a radicalizing one for many of the communities involved as alternative planning and housing strategies began to emerge. The CDP reports have influenced a whole generation of academics and community workers. The potential and limits of community action began to be explored by the workers in the CDP schemes.

A third source of housing protest is the increasing number of residents' associations. Two general types can be identified. The first is the local authority tenants' associations. These tend to centre on individual estates and blocks of flats. Their protests concern very specific issues of rent and management. Their degree of success depends upon their level of support, the issues at stake and the receptivity of the local council. They are essentially local organizations. Attempts to form a national body have not been successful. The National Association of Tenants and Residents was set up in 1948 but its history has been one of only limited success. In 1979 the National Tenants' Organization was established to fight for a Bill of Rights for tenants. The second type is the owner-occupier residents' associations. They have sought to maintain property values and the exclusivity of their neighbourhoods. The most militant have been from the middle and upper-middle income groups. The very wealthy are able to choose residences unlikely to need the protection of pressure-group activity, and the poorer owner-occupiers in inner-city areas have little to protect. The most vulnerable are those in the middle seeking to protect their investment and social status. These groups have been active in shaping plans and housing policies at the local level.

The various forms of housing protest and their effect on housing policy is represented in a general form in Figure 1.1. Housing protest enters through political representation into the policy-making system and is ultimately expressed in new or revised policies. In some cases the protest is channelled through specific housing institutions such as Shelter and the National Tenants' Organization. In general, however, housing protest is a localized phenomenon. The degree of success depends on the scale and form of the protest, the size of the threat which it poses, the nature of the participants and their wider social and economic ties. The most successful groups have had no need to protest, since their interests are defined as the national, universal yardstick, and the least successful lack organization and

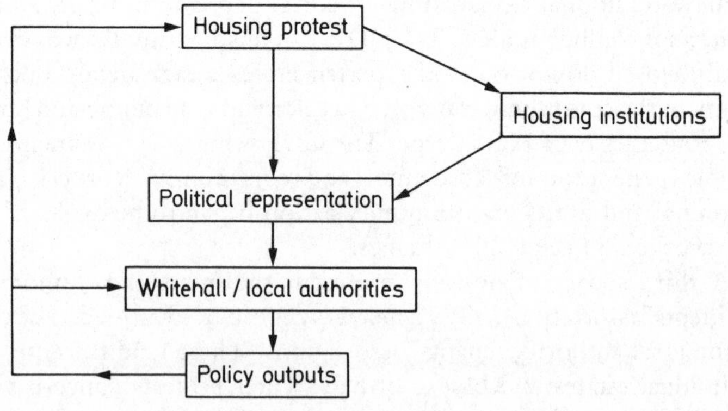

Figure 1.1 Housing protest and policy

clout; they pose no threat. Rather than simply being the expression of the underdog, housing protest is also the voice of the middle dog.

Local authorities and the implementation of housing policy Housing policies are generated by the central state, but many of them are implemented by the local authorities. Housing is one of those interesting areas of social policy which straddle the central–local government divide. Local authorities play an important part in housing matters. While the central state determines the broad context of housing policies, the local state gives shape, form and life to many of the policy directives. The local authority is the main point of direct contact between the individual and the state. The range of local government housing activities is shown in Figure 1.2.

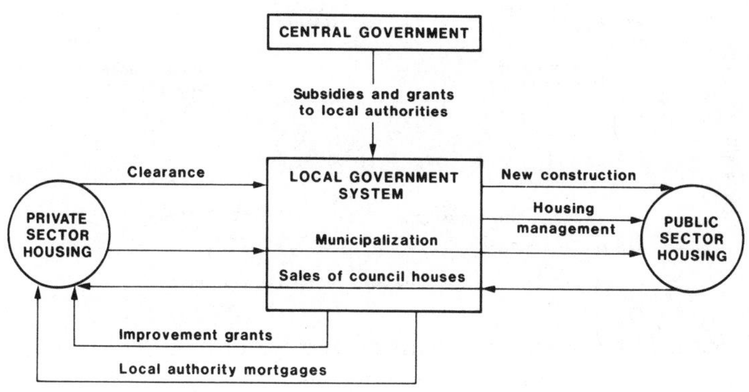

Figure 1.2 Local government and housing policies

The local authorities do more than simply take central government policies to the public. They are more than conveyor belts taking the policies of the central state to the local populace. Because of the range of policy options and the level of discretion, the local authorities have a degree of choice in policy implementation which, when exercised, produces variations in housing policy impact across the country. This variation exists in a number of forms. There is the variation in the extent to which particular policies are used. Consider the case of building and demolition. Between 1966 and 1972, for example, Manchester started to build 121 local authority houses per 1000 households. Cardiff, in contrast, started only 20 per 1000 households. In the same period Manchester demolished 152 dwellings per 1000 households, but Plymouth demolished only 3 per 1000 households. Part of this variation relates to the difference in housing stock. We would expect Manchester with its greater proportion of unfit housing to demolish more properties than Plymouth. Figure 1.3 outlines the variation in the nature of the housing stock by showing the pattern of housing starts for both inner and outer London boroughs. The Labour-controlled boroughs, on the evidence of this diagram at least, build more local authority dwellings than the Conservative boroughs even when taking location into account.

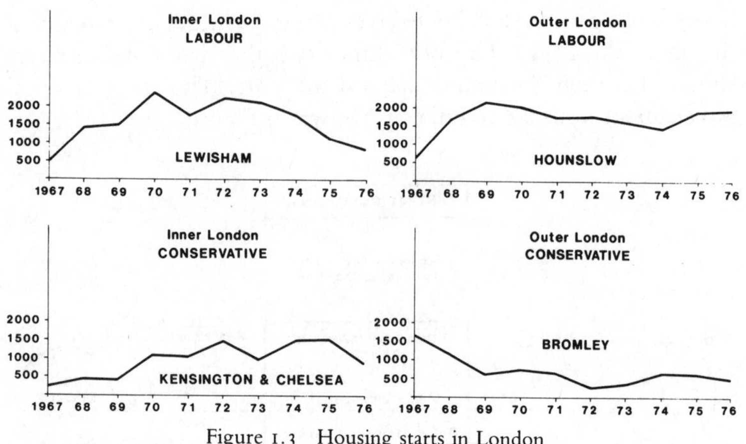

Figure 1.3 Housing starts in London

Variations also exist in the size of rents for local authority housing. In 1974, for example, while a tenant of a local authority two-bedroomed house was charged £2.95 per week in Rochdale, the tenant of a similar property was charged £4.65 in Brighton and £5.04 in Southend. In general, the big-city, Labour-controlled authorities tend to keep rents low and rely on a higher rate fund contribution, while the Tory shire counties keep rates low and tend to charge higher rents for council houses.

This book is concerned with the implementation of housing policy in post-war Britain. But since most policies are implemented to varying extents by local authorities in different parts of the country, we shall abstract only the more general trends from this complex picture. In this introductory chapter it is useful, therefore, to note the ways in which local authorities deviate from the average. There are two main sources of variation in local authority implementation, (1) the history and geography of the local authority, and (2) the political hue of the local politicians.

(1) The first reflects history and geography. Local authorities vary

in the size and nature of their housing stock. Manchester, for example, is a city with an old, outworn, housing stock. Plymouth, in contrast, does not have such a backlog of unfit housing either in absolute or relative terms. From an analysis of the 1971 Census Donnison and Soto (1980) suggested that six broad categories of urban areas can be identified in England and Wales (Table 1.2). The variations in housing and environmental economic conditions between these authorities is marked. The variation in housing policy implementation thus partly reflects the variation in the background which informs the decisions on which policies are used and to what extent. We would not expect Solihull to pursue a policy of comprehensive redevelopment on the scale of Manchester.

Table 1.2 Categories of urban areas

	Category	*Exemplar authorities*
1	London	London
2	Regional service centres	Reading, Bristol, Southampton
3	Resorts	Torbay, Hove, Bournemouth
4	Residential suburbs and new towns	Solihull, Watford, Basildon
5	Industrial towns	Rhondda, Sheffield, Bolton, Luton
6	Inner conurbations	Manchester, Birmingham

Source: Donnison and Soto, 1980

(2) Variations also reflect the political persuasion of the local authority. The physical background provides the context, it does not make the decisions; these are made by local politicians. In general, Labour-controlled authorities tend to spend more on local authority housing, place more emphasis on municipalization and, over all, tend to see solutions more in terms of state involvement than the Tories. The Conservative-controlled authorities in contrast are more responsive to the cost-cutting cries of the ratepayers and to private market solutions. The main parties are receptive to different pressure groups. While the Labour party is more receptive to council tenants' organizations and trade councils, the Conservatives pay greater heed to the needs of business and the demands of the Chambers of Commerce.

It is difficult to separate the physical and social environment of a local authority, and hence the needs of the local population, on the one hand and the political disposition of the authority on the other. Urban areas with severe housing problems tend to vote Labour. To note that Labour-controlled authorities spend more on housing than Conservative ones can be misleading without qualifications concerning the variation in need. But even when need is held constant the weight of evidence suggests that Labour authorities spend more on housing in general and council housing in particular than Conservative authorities, who in turn tend to sell more council houses.

The Housing Market

General characteristics We can characterize the housing market as a system of production, consumption and exchange. In a capitalist society such as Britain, housing is produced as a commodity; it is produced in order to make a profit for the builder-developer. In comparison with other commodities, however, the production of housing has a number of interesting characteristics. It requires land. But land is not freely available. Landowners have the power over this scarce though vital resource because of the system of private property. Land is not freely available in another sense. To build on land requires planning permission. The operation of post-war planning controls has meant that only certain types of property have been built in specific areas. There is also a long time between the assembly of land and materials, the construction of housing and the eventual sale of the dwellings. In any one cycle of production the builder-developer has to lay out expenditure for a comparatively long time before profits are realized. Credit helps to bridge the gap. But the use of credit means that the production of housing is crucially affected by the general fiscal climate and the specific nature of credit facilities. The relationship between production and finance is an important strand in the post-war story.

Housing is expensive in relation to wages. Immediate house purchase is beyond the reach of all but the wealthiest of households. We can define this *realization problem* as the difficulty of selling houses to households without the use of some mediating mechanism. The three major tenure categories can be seen, in crude economistic terms, as different solutions to the realization problem. In the case of owner-occupation the household 'buys' the property either with a lump sum or, more commonly, with borrowed money. In Britain the building societies have been the main source for financing home ownership. In the case of private renting a landlord lets out property to tenants. The tenants pay for the accommodation in a series of rent payments. In the case of council housing the state, or more correctly the local authority, is the landlord.

Housing is also exchanged. The different tenure categories have different entry procedures and allocation rules. Entry into private renting is relatively easy, if you can find a vacancy. The ability to meet the regular rent payments is generally all that is required, although for the middle and upper ranges of the market references may be required. Entry and movement within the local authority sector depends upon meeting the qualifications of need laid down by the housing department of the local authority. In the case of owner-occupation, entry depends upon raising the necessary funds; this requires a minimum income and a degree of credit-worthiness. Entry and exchange within this sector can also involve estate agents, surveyors and solicitors, the whole range of exchange professionals who make a living out of lubricating movement into and within the owner-occupied sector.

The ability of builder-developers to realize their profits and that of householders to obtain accommodation are thus a function of all the factors which affect the different realization mechanisms: in the case of owner-occupation, for example, access to the sector depends upon the position of the building societies in the money market, which determines the amount of mortgages they provide; the size of the private renting sector will reflect the relative rates of return afforded to landlords; while the size and nature of the local authority sector will be dependent on the amount of state expenditure directed towards the housing sector. The bare bones of the development of the British post-war housing market have been the decrease in the size of the private rented sector because of relatively low rates of return, and an increase in the size of the owner-occupied and local authority sector. The expansion of these sectors has been related to an increase in the size of funds directed towards financing owner-occupation and local authority housing. The implications of these trends will be examined in Part 2, where this broadest of outlines is discussed in more detail.

The different tenure categories are more than just different solutions to the realization problem. They have differing ideological connotations, and the rhythm of their development has been shaped by different sets of factors. The initial expansion of local authority housing reflected working-class demands for better housing. The rise of owner-occupation reflects state encouragement and subsequent rational economic choices by those households with effective demand. Owner-occupation has been encouraged not simply as a better solution to the realization problem, but because it is associated with certain ideological and political goals. The housing market is more than just an economic arena for the provision, purchase and consumption of a good. Social, political and ideological elements are an integral part of the housing market.

Agents and institutions There are a variety of groups and institutions with an interest in the housing market. For want of a better term we can refer to them as agents. The term is used to define those non-household actors with an interest in one or many of the various aspects of the housing market. They can be characterized with reference to their interest in the aspects of housing production, consumption and exchange. Table 1.3 highlights the main sets of agents and places them within the wider context of government policies and the socio-economic background.

Table 1.3 Agents in the housing market

		Government economic and housing policies	
Socio-economic background	*Production*	landowners, builders, financial institutions, local authorities (planning and housing departments)	*Socio-economic background*
	Exchange	solicitors, estate agents and valuers, local authority housing departments	
	Consumption	landlords, building societies, financial institutions, local authority housing departments	
		Government economic and housing policies	

It is important to study these agents in some detail in order to understand the nature of the housing market. Their actions and interactions constitute the operation of the housing market. They are the mechanisms which mesh supply and demand, the object of government policies and the generators of the mix of housing opportunities and constraints afforded and imposed on different types of households. The study of these agents will constitute an important element of Part 2 of this book.

Housing and households: Home Sweet Home

Housing is an essential element in social life. It provides shelter and comfort, a base for social action, a site of socialization, the workplace for domestic labour and an indication of social status. We can capture some of this interacting multi-faceted complexity by focusing on certain key issues.

Housing and income Housing is an important element in a household's budget. On average housing costs comprise almost 10 per cent of consumer expenditure, although this varies by income, since the poor pay proportionately more, and by tenure since young households newly entering owner-occupation pay much more than other owner-occupiers, households in local authority housing or tenants of controlled tenancies in the private rented sector. The changing proportion of housing costs in the post-war period will be examined in Part 3, as well as the consequences of these changes on different groups.

Housing and the family Since the Industrial Revolution there has been a marked separation between home and workplace. This spatial separation is overlaid by a sexual division of labour. Men as husbands and fathers travel from home to work, women as wives and mothers work in the home. The home functions as a unit reproducing the population, the labour force and the social relations within the family and in the wider society. The form of housing has come to reinforce this division. Individualized units of housing separate household from household, and this atomization increases the need for individualized domestic labour. Typically this has been the role assigned to women. A whole ideology has grown reinforcing women's role in the home and the need for family life.

The post-war years have seen tensions emerging. While housing continues to be built and communities planned which reinforce the relations of patriarchy, the growth of women in the labour force, the rise of much smaller households, including single-person households, and the development of sexual politics have proved to be powerful countervailing tendencies. Much of the tension has taken place in the home in the form of debates and struggles over the woman's role, the need for communal facilities for child care, the demand for smaller units of accommodation and the desire for dwellings which need less servicing and less use of (female) labour input.

Housing affects not only the sexual politics but also the health of a family. At a basic level, good-quality housing is an essential prerequisite to good health. Poor physical conditions can lead to the spread of disease, while poor layout, construction and design can affect morbidity, mental health and interpersonal relations: women isolated in tower blocks, families with too few rooms, and poor insulation for every type of household are all such examples. The physical nature of housing affects the very warp and weft of our lives.

The home is only one station in the journey of everyday life but an important one. The location of our home affects access to schools, jobs, recreational and shopping opportunities. Households living in different locations will have different sets of opportunities, and even within a household different locations will have varying impacts on different members. What may be a good location for the middle-aged male wage-earner may be bad for the partner, the aged parent, the adolescent boy or the very young child. In Part 3 I shall examine the changing spatial distribution of housing in post-war Britain and its effects on groups of households and their constituent members.

Housing, social structure and class Housing plays an important part in social structure and class consciousness. In terms of the former, housing is a crucial element in a person's life chances which constitute the set of opportunities and constraints afforded by their wealth, position in the job market and access to resources. Owners, for example, can accumulate wealth through their housing. In terms of consciousness, the form of housing consumption can influence political outlook. A number of writers have argued that the diffusion of owner-occupation legitimates private property and produces a large debt-encumbered section of the society with an interest in the *status quo* and an antipathy towards radical change. This is debatable. It is only just one of the points which will be examined in that section of Part 3 which outlines the role played by housing in the social stratification of contemporary Britain.

OUTLINE OF THE BOOK

Each of the three major themes will be treated in a separate section. Part 1 takes up the theme of housing and the state. The emphasis will be on examining the reasons for and the consequences of successive state housing policies. Although 1945 marked a break it is important to see what the break consisted of, the lines of fracture before 1945 and the residual elements since 1945 from previous years. Chapter 2 aims to provide such a perspective by examining the evolution of housing policy from the end of the nineteenth century to the eve of the Second World War. Chapter 3 picks up the story from 1945 until 1980. Policies are discussed in temporal succession, in order to present the sequential unfolding of the main events.

Part 2 again considers the most important post-war housing policies. But this time they are considered in a sectoral fashion. They are examined in relation to the production (Chapters 4 and 5), consumption (Chapters 6, 7, and 8) and exchange (Chapter 9) of housing. These chapters also deal with the main constellation of agents involved in the respective elements of the housing market, the form and rhythm of their interaction, and the implications for the housing chances of different groups of households. Chapter 10 considers the sub-markets within the national housing market.

Part 3 is only one chapter. Chapter 11 considers the relationship between housing and households in terms of the key issues outlined above. This is a more diffuse treatment than in Parts 1 and 2, reflecting the paucity of the available research. The study of housing as lived experience is an under-researched topic which would repay greater interest.

PART 1

HOUSING AND THE STATE

2

THE ROAD TO 1945

EARLY DAYS

Housing was an important political issue in the nineteenth century. Its housing policies, like all social policies of the time, were a response to the effects of rapid and large-scale urbanization. The Industrial Revolution inaugurated a new period in British social history. One of the most dramatic effects of this new era was the growth of towns. Throughout the nineteenth century there was a growing concentration of population in the towns and cities. In 1801 only 20 per cent of the population lived in urban places with a population greater than 5000. By 1851 the proportion had increased to 54 per cent when, almost 4.5 million people, about a quarter of the total population, lived in cities with populations greater than 100,000. By 1911 nearly 16 million people, almost a half of the total population, lived in such places. This growth was due to population increase, since people were marrying earlier, and to large-scale migration. People were leaving the land and moving to the job-opportunities in expanding towns and cities.

Housing conditions in the cities of the nineteenth century were poor, although often they were no worse than in the country areas. The idea of a rural Arcadia was more a response to the nature of the cities than a true representation of living conditions for the mass of agricultural workers. Rural dwellings were just as poorly lit, badly ventilated and ill-maintained as urban ones, but within the cities there was a concentration of such dwellings.

The poor housing conditions reflected the low wages and high rents. Most people could not afford to rent good-quality accommodation, and owner-occupation was only for the wealthy minority. Rents were high because there were limits to the outward spread of the city. People had to live close to their work and, before the introduction of the motor car and suburban railway systems, there were sharply demarcated limits to the spread of the city. As city population grew the pressure was felt in the tight spaces around the centres of work. Given the pressure of demand, landlords and landowners could raise rents. Land values increased, rents soared and high-density accommodation was the result. We can take the example of Glasgow: between 1801 and 1865 the city's population grew five times but the urban fabric remained unchanged from that in 1775. Poor housing conditions also reflected the nature of speculative building. Landowners leased the land to developers, who then subleased to small inefficient builders, who in turn sought profits from constructing narrow-frontage, high-density, poor-quality housing. As the city populations grew, dwellings were subdivided. Overcrowding and poor sanitary conditions became a serious problem. In the first half of the nineteenth century there were over 25,000 people in Liverpool living in cellars which flooded every time the tide came in. Contemporary reports read like descriptions of Dante's Inferno. Here is Engels describing St Giles in London in 1844:

> The houses are occupied from cellar to garret, filthy within and without, and their appearance is such that no human being could possibly wish to live in them. . . . The dwellings in the narrow courts and alleys between the streets, entered by covered passages between the houses in which filth and tottering ruins surpass all description.

Things were scarcely better in Manchester where the working people, according to Engels, lived 'almost all of them in wretched, damp, filthy cottages'. The subdivision of property, the minimal provision of facilities, the poor layout of dwellings and the lack of maintenance created a serious health hazard. So long as the health conditions did not affect the wealthy nothing much was done, but with the spread of cholera epidemics to the wealthy areas it became clear that the problem could not be ignored. The slum housing in the big cities was a hazard to everyone's health. The sanitary inquiries of the 1840s and the Commission on the Health of Towns pointed to the need to set up minimum standards. The Public Health Act of 1848 represented the first steps in a whole series of public health legislative measures which by 1914 had introduced street cleaning, laid the basis for the supply of good water, instituted the use of proper sewerage systems and laid down minimum space standards for dwellings. This legislation and numerous by-laws meant that the worst excesses of jerry-building and slum landlordism were, if not eradicated, then at least tempered. The right of builders and landlords to make profits irrespective of the consequences was being questioned. However, by the middle of the nineteenth century the state was still only fulfilling a minimal nightwatchman's role in domestic policy. The ideology of *laissez-faire* dominated the political scene.

Sources of reform

There were a number of impulses for change. First, some reformers tried to show the benefits to social peace of a good environment including decent housing. Poor living conditions were thought likely to provide a basis for social discontent. Good-quality accommodation on the other hand, it was thought by the reformers, would quell discontent and discipline the masses. Other reformers pointed to the debilitating effect of poor accommodation. Ill-housed workers were not efficient workers, and poor-quality accommodation would only provide poor-quality troops to defend the empire. An important element in this reform movement was the philanthropy-at-5-per-cent schemes. These were experiments by reformers at providing decent accommodation together with good rates of return to capital investors. One of the earliest was the Metropolitan Association for Improving the Dwellings of the Industrious Classes. The name gives the character of the organization, as does the Society for Improving the Conditions of the Labouring Classes founded in 1844. Organizations founded later included the Peabody Trust and the Guinness Trust. The problem was that these financial and philanthropic endeavours did not provide accommodation for the masses. Because of the high land values and consequently large costs involved in providing such accommodation and the good returns paid to capital investors, only the labour aristocracy could afford the rents. They failed to provide a solution for housing the masses, and even amongst the labour aristocracy that could afford the rents the strictly regimented blocks and the paternalistic management proved very unpopular. However, these schemes did have an important demonstration effect in providing tangible results to the arguments of reformers.

The cries of reform reached a pitch in the 1880s. In 1883 the Rev. Andrew Mearns published *The Bitter Cry of Outcast London*. It was a tract which highlighted the poor housing of the majority of Londoners and pointed to the implications of such conditions. Overcrowded housing, suggested Mearns, could lead to immorality, vice and crime. The discussion of sexual immorality in overcrowded conditions probably added to the tract's wide distribution, and its publication aroused enormous public concern. A Royal Commission to look into the housing of the working class was set up in 1884. Housing reform was coming to the fore because many social ills were associated with poor housing conditions. Better-quality housing, it was argued, could thus help eradicate poverty, social unrest, crime and violence. It was an attractive argument. By dealing with housing consumption there was no need to look at production or the distribution of wealth and life opportunities in society. Good housing for the masses became the panacea for a range of social problems.

The second main impulse came from the nascent socialist organizations and trade unions which began to develop in the last quarter of the nineteenth century. At the national level their agitation for housing legislation was only slight. The major organizations like the Social Democratic Federation and the Independent Labour Party did not develop coherent housing policies, and the Workmen's National Housing Council proved ineffective. Housing failed to provide a focus at the national level for the Labour movement: for the militants the emphasis was on changing the orientation of the entire system rather than fiddling with the housing knobs; for the labour aristocracy housing provision was relatively good. Things were different at the local level. Here, as the nineteenth century was gradually drawing to a close, trades councils, local socialist organizations and various councillors had their real say in local politics. This power was used to implement central state policies for the benefit of working people.

It was not only the reformers who were interested in housing. Other more powerful interests were at work. Chief amongst them were the large landowners, whose ground rent provided a huge source of income. They were a powerful political force with many MPs and a majority in the House of Lords. They used their political clout to aid their dealings, especially in clearance schemes. Slum clearance legislation was introduced in the 1868 Torrens Act and the 1875 Cross Act, when there was a crisis of profitability for the landowners. The implementation of these acts, introduced when there was a relative glut of accommodation, demolished large tracts of slum dwellings, reduced the supply and laid the basis for new, more profitable property development. The opportunity was quickly seized by the local bourgeoisie in different cities to make lucrative gains by slum clearance and redevelopment. The acts allowed the local authorities to clear land, gave little aid to displaced dwellers and left the way clear for future speculative enterprise in new building and railway development. These schemes did not solve the housing problem, but, like the 5-per-cent philanthropy schemes, they were not failures since they were not designed to do so. They were designed to aid certain property interests. The housing policies of the mid- to late nineteenth century gave very little help to the industrial capitalists. They wanted a well-housed labour force and cheap accommodation. Good housing could mean a contented, hard-working, disciplined labour force. Since the private market failed to provide such accommodation and the state policies only aided property interests, industrial capitalists often had to provide their own housing. Robert Owen's New Lanark was an example of such a scheme. Cadbury's Bournville provides another classic instance of a company town where the industrialists provided relatively good-quality accommodation for the workforce. But even small capitalists provided accommodation and, for example, by the end of the nineteenth century, over 150 companies in Yorkshire alone were doing so.

By the last quarter of the nineteenth century public opinion was beginning to accept the need for some form of direct state intervention. The arguments of the reformers were gaining some ground. Good housing was seen as the panacea for a range of social problems because it did not question the social and economic status quo. At the local level the actions of socialists and trades councils were giving a political dimension to these arguments. But there were limits and not everyone accepted the logic. The Liberty and Property Defence League, for example, was founded in 1882 to oppose government involvement in housing provision. Members of the League included William Torrens (of the 1868 Act) and Lord Shaftesbury. However, by the 1880s a powerful case was being argued for more direct involvement in housing provision.

Beginnings of housing legislation

The report of the Royal Commission set up in the wake of Andrew Mearns' tract, *The Bitter Cry of Outcast London*, reflected the tensions between the different interested groups: property interests on the Commission sought to temper state involvement which might attack the sanctity of profit; reformers, on the other hand, were keen to press for more legislation. The reformers seem to have won, insofar as the overriding conclusion which arose from the work of the Commission was the importance of the relationship between high rent and low wages and the need for working people to live close to their work. Philanthropic bodies were shown to have failed and private enterprise could not provide good accommodation in the right place. The Commission argued that something else had to be done. The legislative response was quick, but mediated by the different interests. In 1885 Parliament passed the Housing of the Working Classes Act. It involved central government loans at low interest rates for the provision of cheap land for local authority housing schemes. The state was now becoming directly involved in housing provision.

Subsequent acts in the pre-1914 period extended such involvement. The 1890 Housing of the Working Classes Act consolidated the earlier clearance legislation and included a section which allowed local authorities to build, convert and manage dwellings, adding that any housing built by the local authority in clearance areas had to be sold off within ten years. Later, the 1909 Housing and Town Planning Act abolished this ten-year requirement.

After a long struggle throughout the second half of the nineteenth century and the first decade of the twentieth century the notion of *laissez-faire* had been breached. The inability of private enterprise to build good-quality accommodation in sufficient quantity in the right places had been accepted, albeit grudgingly and not by everyone. The persuasion of the reformers, the arguments of the industrialists, and the agitation of the socialists had all played their part. Their success was limited, however. Between 1880 and 1914 houses built by the local authorities in each year did not exceed 1000. This was less than 1 per cent of total housing construction, and housing tenure before the First World War was still predominantly private renting (see Figure 2.1). Cash control was still imposed on municipal housing schemes and there was no central subsidy. Local authority housing schemes were obliged to run at a profit and if a loss was made it was to be charged to the ratepayers. This meant that schemes were financially hamstrung.

The case for a central subsidy, however, was being strengthened in the early years of the twentieth century as the age of imperialism and its rhetoric of chauvinism and nationalist self-interest added extra impetus to the arguments of the reformers stressing good housing for a strong workforce and a mighty army. The threat of international competition, and Britain's poor showing in the Boer War in particular, drove home these points. Over 40 per cent of volunteers for the army were rejected on medical grounds. A fighting army was not going to emerge from draughty, overcrowded dwellings. The argument was given special pertinence by the slump in house building in the first decade of the twentieth century. The house-building industry with its long lines of credit had always been subject to booms and slumps. But in the years prior

Table 2.1 Early days: legislative measures

Date	*Title*	*Brief description*
1868	Artisans' and Labourers' Dwellings Act (Torrens Act)	Slum clearance measure: allowed local authorities to demolish housing
1875	Artisans' and Labourers' Dwellings Improvement Act (Cross Act)	Redevelopment measure: allowed local authorities to demolish housing, rehouse former occupants and sell land to developers. Council housing had to be sold within ten years of construction
1885	Housing of the Working Classes Act	Building measure: access to cheap loans given to local authorities
1890	Housing of the Working Classes Act	Building measure: in consolidating and extending earlier measures this Act set the scene for larger-scale council house building and improvement
1909	Housing and Town Planning Act	Local authorities no longer had to sell newly constructed housing within ten years

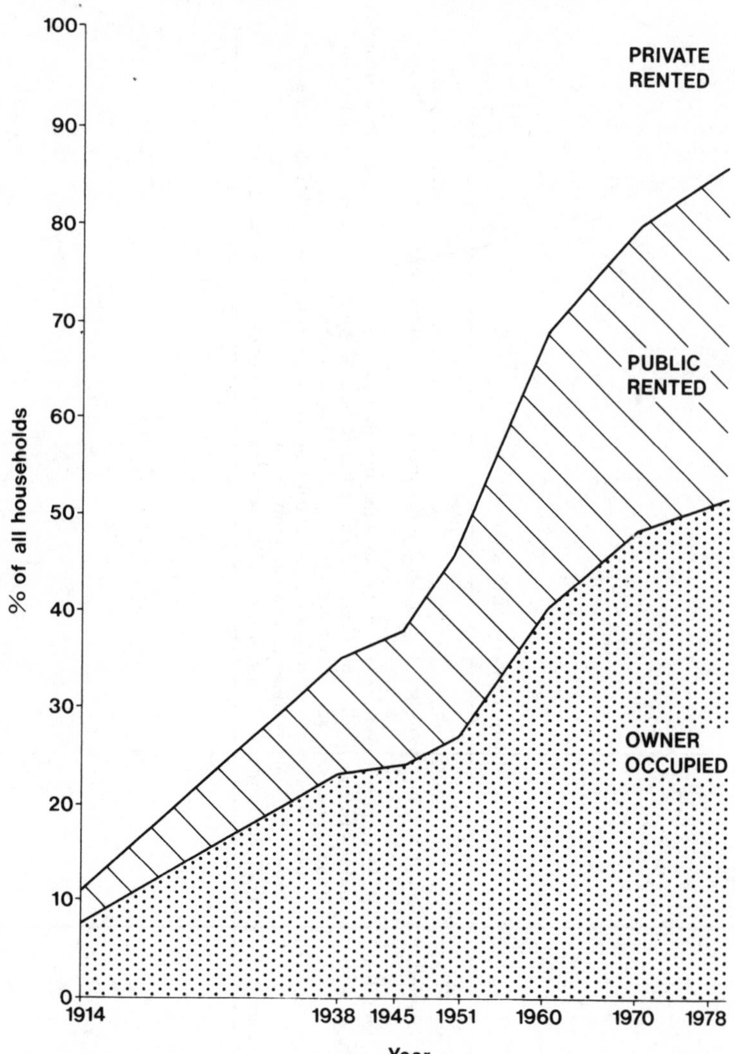

Figure 2.1 Housing tenure in Britain

to the First World War the slump was dramatic. In 1913 the amount of houses constructed was less than half that of 1900. Because working-class incomes had been falling, there was less effective demand. Moerover, capital was flowing out of the construction sector because foreign investments were providing richer pickings. The slump led to further restrictions on the housing opportunities of the mass of people, since less new housing was available and rents were taking a major share of wages. Political agitation at the local and national level increased as the private market system was now showing itself to be incapable of providing good-quality housing. On the eve of the First World War there were strong calls for more municipal housing and for a central subsidy. These were to be acted upon after the war ended.

THE INTER-WAR YEARS

The inter-war years marked a new period in British housing policy: a period differing from the pre-1914 era in the greater acceptance of state involvement in housing provision and the greater use and power of legislation explicitly concerned with housing. There was a consensus of opinion in government circles in the immediate post-1918 period which accepted that there was a housing crisis. The building slump before the war and the cessation of building during the war had dramatically cut the supply. But demand was increasing, especially after the immediate cessation of hostilities as soldiers were returning home. Estimates suggest that in 1918 there was a deficit of 600,000 dwellings. It was not simply a case of government statisticians adding up the figures and finding a deficit and suggesting remedial action. Politics rarely operate on the cold logic of arithmetic. The housing crisis had been manifest in political actions. Perhaps the most famous was the Glasgow rent strike of 1915. During the war Glasgow was one of the main centres of shell and ship manufacturing. The increase in production meant a movement of population into Glasgow's expanding factories and shipyards. Most of the accommodation was privately rented. With growing demand for accommodation and limited supply, landlords were in a powerful position, and when a rise in interest rates increased their loan repayment the landlords increased rents. Rents in the shipbuilding areas of Govan and Fairfield were increased by 23 per cent; the response was as quick as it was dramatic. A rent strike was called, industrial workers went on strike for a day and 15,000 workers threatened strike action. The threat of industrial action forced the government's hand. A bill was rushed through Parliament and it took only five weeks from the formulation of a Cabinet memorandum which urged action if the workers' demands were not to 'expand in scope and character', to the Bill's Royal Assent. The 1915 Rent and Mortgage Interest (War Restrictions) Act limited the amount of rent charged for houses with rateable values of not more than £35 in London, £26 elsewhere in England and Wales and £30 in Scotland, to that at which they were let in August 1915.

With events like the Glasgow rent strike, housing was placed on the political agenda. The Hunter committee, for example, which reported in 1917, identified inadequate housing as a major cause of unrest. Housing became part of the political parties' manifestoes and in the spirit of wartime sacrifice it held a key place in popular ideology. The slogan of 'Homes Fit for Heroes' was both an indictment of the past and a promise of things to come. Housing took a pivotal position in the immediate post-war scene. The atmosphere of the time is well-summarized in the following extract from the King's speech to representatives of the local authorities in 1919:

> While the housing of the working classes has always been a question of the greatest social importance, never has it been so important as now. It is not too much to say that an adequate solution of the housing question is the foundation of all social progress. . . . If a healthy race is to be reared, it can only be reared in healthy homes; if drink and crime are to be successfully combated, decent, sanitary houses must be provided; if 'unrest' is to be converted into contentment, the provision of good housing may prove to be one of the most potent agents in that conversion.

The weight of political and popular opinion was swinging towards an acceptance of the failure of private market forces and the need for direct government involvement.

The first major piece of legislation was the 1919 Housing and Town Planning Act, which is commonly called the Addison Act after Christopher Addison, the Minister of Health and principal architect of the Bill. Under this Act local authorities were requested to survey housing needs in their area and draw up appropriate plans. The plans were to involve local authority housing, not merely for specific needs such as slum replacement, but as part of general needs. If the plans met with Ministry of Health approval all losses in excess of a penny rate were to be met by the Treasury. Rents were to be fixed by the local authority with emphasis on need and ability to pay rather than cost considerations.

The inter-war period opened with a fine flourish. Three aspects of the Addison Act marked it out from previous measures. First, it accepted the need for a central subsidy. The costs above a penny increase in the rate were to be borne by the central exchequer, and this allowed local authority housing to be built to a high standard since cost restraints were now not so rigid as in the past. Second, local authorities now had a statutory obligation to draw up housing plans. The days of permissive legislation which allowed local authorities to ignore central government directives seemed to be over. However, within this general context the local authorities had the power to decide the number of houses they would build, the rents to be charged and the people who would live in the houses. Finally, the Addison Act involved well-planned, well-built, designed houses. The recommendations of the 1918 Tudor Walters Committee for high-quality local authority housing in a pleasant environment was incorporated into the implementation of the Act. The houses combined well-laid-out spacious accommodation in an attractive vernacular idiom, set in a pleasant almost Garden City layout. One of the main exponents of the Garden City movement, Raymond Unwin, was an important member of the Committee and his ideas proved influential. Even to this day Addison Act housing is one of the most sought-after and attractive sectors of council housing.

The Addison Act represents both the starting point and the peak of post-war housing legislation. The political circumstances in the immediate post-war period had allowed the demands of the reformers and the radical reports of government committees to be implemented. The state was now involved in building council housing, and a central subsidy had been accepted. Thereafter state housing policy in the inter-war period was influenced by three major factors.

Party politics

First, the changing balance of political power was reflected in changes in housing policy. The Addison Act was the product of the coalition government dominated by Tories which ruled from 1918 to 1922. From then on housing policy changed as political parties representing different interests with differing ideologies about state involvement in general and housing policy in particular came and went. The Tories, for example, ruled from 1922 to 1924, from October 1924 to 1929 and from 1933 to the beginning of the Second World War. Their policies were based on the fundamental belief in the efficacy of market forces. They believed that the market left to its own devices was the best method of allocating resources. They only saw a limited role for the state as provider and guarantor of social welfare. Like a fireman the state should only be called upon for short-term emergency measures. This belief in limited public expenditure and market forces was reflected in the housing policy sector by the limits they imposed on expenditure for council housing, the lack of rent controls for all but the cheapest property, and the encouragement of owner-occupation. Council housing was to be a residual tenure category, available only for the very poorest. Both owner-occupation and private renting were encouraged throughout the war and inter-war period. All this was reflected in the legislation during Conservative periods of office.

In 1923 the Chamberlain Act, introduced in a period of housing shortage, reduced the subsidies given by the Addison measures. Local authorities were allowed to build houses only if they could prove to the Minister of Health's satisfaction that it was more desirable than to leave housing provision to private enterprise. Within the context of reduced expenditure the subsidy was paid to both builders and local authorities, but was mainly used by the private sector. Over 300,000 houses were built by the private sector with Chamberlain-type subsidies, but only 74,000 local authority dwellings were built under this Act.

Although the Chamberlain Act was modified by the Wheatley Act of 1924, introduced in the period of Labour minority government, the Tory government of 1924–9 gave only slight assistance to local authority housing. Between 1923 and 1933 only 300,000 local authority dwellings were built compared with one-and-a-half million dwellings produced by the public sector. The housing conditions for the very poorest were scarcely improving.

After a brief period of a minority Labour government and then a National government the Tories gained control again in 1933. At this time they took over some of the policies formulated by the previous government but gave them the stamp of Tory orthodoxy. From 1933 to the end of the war Conservative housing policy was again one of encouraging owner-occupation, decontrolling rents and limiting local authority involvement to slum clearance. The 1933 Housing Act abolished subsidies for local authorities for general-needs housing and encouraged building societies, and an amendment Act in the same year allowed decontrol of rents in some rented property. In contrast, the Labour government, more often representing the interests of organized labour, supported the notion of more local authority housing. The Labour party sought to improve housing conditions for working people through direct state provision. The 1924 Labour government sought to halt the attack on the public sector commenced by the 1923 Chamberlain Act, and in 1924 the Wheatley Act increased subsidies to local authorities and they no longer had to prove that there would be no competition between them and the private sector. The Wheatley Act survived the fall of the Labour government but subsidies were finally disbanded by the National government in 1933. Over half a million houses were built under the Wheatley Act and, although not as good as the

Table 2.2 The inter-war years: legislative measures

Date	*Title*	*Brief description*	*Political events*
1919	Housing and Town Planning Act (Addison Act)	Local authorities given statutory duty to provide housing. Central subsidy provided by exchequer	1918–22 Coalition government
1923	Housing Act (Chamberlain Act)	Reduction of Addison subsidies. Councils had to prove that they would not compete with private sector builders, no limitations on council house rents	1922–24 Conservative government 1924 Minority Labour government
1924	Housing (Financial Provisions) Act (Wheatley Act)	Increased subsidies, fixed council house rents	1924–29 Conservative government
1930	Housing Act (Greenwood Act)	Introduced subsidies for slum clearance	1929–31 Labour government
1933	Housing (Financial Provisions) Act	Reduced subsidies for general-needs council housing	1931–39 Coalition government dominated by Conservatives

Addison houses, they were of a high standard and have proved to be popular.

Labour was once more returned to power in 1929, but again in the form of a minority government. The subsequent housing measure, the 1930 Greenwood Act, was meant to run in tandem with the Wheatley Act. Wheatley's legislation was concerned with building new housing, and the Greenwood Act was to supplement this by focusing on slum clearance. The mounting backlog of unfit houses (only 11,000 houses had been demolished between 1918 and 1930) began to impinge on the public debate. In the late 1920s popular concern over slum housing was similar to the concern of the 1880s over basic housing provision. This included such diverse phenomena as letters to *The Times* and political agitation at the local and national level. An attack on slums was an important election platform for the Labour party in the 1929 general election. The Greenwood Act introduced exchequer subsidies for slum clearance and placed a statutory duty on local authorities to rehouse displaced households. It was hoped to solve the problem inside five years.

The economic crisis intervened but by 1933 the Greenwood Act formed the basis for the government's housing policy. The Wheatley subsidies were abolished and the emphasis was now on local authority housing for the specific needs of former slum-dwellers. The housing was of very poor quality and in the major cities took the form of five-storey blocks of flats. These inter-war dwellings, built on the cheap, originally housing a stigmatized group of former slum-dwellers, constitute some of the most unpopular council housing.

Housing policy reflected political power. However, it would be a mistake to see each new government introducing brand-new legislation. What tended to happen was that successive governments adopted and modified previous legislation to their own ends. Thus the Labour government of 1923 did not abolish the Chamberlain Act of 1923, and the Tory government of 1924 modified rather than scrapped the Wheatley Act, while the National government used the Labour party's Greenwood Act of 1930. Each piece of housing legislation had a measure of legislative inertia.

Public expenditure and the crisis

The second major factor influencing housing policy in the inter-war period and one which affected all inter-war policies was the recurring economic crisis. The slump in the world economy was registered at the level of housing policy because the Treasury and many government ministers believed that reductions in public expenditure would alleviate the crisis. Welfare expenditure was particularly vulnerable to this kind of economic thinking, and throughout the inter-war period housing expenditure was cut several times. The reduction in public expenditure was not simply the result of the government's perception of economic difficulties. It reflected the balance of political power which allowed the welfare reductions to be made. The first to be affected was the implementation of the Addison Act. It was initially hoped to build in three years half a million dwellings as homes fit for heroes. The target was never achieved. The immediate post-war boom was followed by a slump in 1920. In 1920–1 unemployment increased to 18 per cent, profits dropped and production fell dramatically. The year 1921 also saw a massive defeat for organized labour. The coal-owners attempted to reduce miners' wages; an alliance of miners, railwaymen and transport workers failed to materialize, and after a three-month strike the miners had to go back to work on the reduced wage levels. The labour movement was weakened and there was very little effective protest against proposals to reduce the real and social wage. Inside Lloyd George's coalition government the hand of the businessmen and financiers was strengthened. In 1921 the Chancellor of the Exchequer put forward public expenditure proposals in which the housing programme was to be cut back. Addison resigned in protest. In July 1921 it was announced that the programme was reduced to approximately 170,000 houses to be built by the local authorities and 140,000 to be completed by the private sector. This was a far cry from half a million homes for heroes.

The second major reduction came in 1926. After the brief period of the Conservative government which produced the Chamberlain Act in 1923, and the minority Labour government which produced the Wheatley Act in 1924, the Tories were back in power by 1924. They were to rule until 1929 and during this time there was a massive confrontation between capital and labour in the 1926 general strike. Again it was the mine-owners. In 1925 they demanded wage cuts to maintain profitability. The miners resisted and the government paid the owners a subsidy to make up the difference. When the subsidy expired in April 1926 the miners refused wage cuts and were locked out. A general strike was called. It ended in defeat for Labour as the TUC leadership sold its members down the river and agreed on a return to work. The miners, now isolated, went back to work on their reduced wages, and throughout the country militants were sacked and capital had once more regained the upper hand. As in

1921, the events strengthened the hands of the financiers, businessmen, orthodox economists and right-wing Tories who wanted cuts in public expenditure. In 1926 the housing programme was affected by these cuts. Exchequer subsidies were reduced, and the Chamberlain subsidy was abolished. Although houses were still being built by the local authorities they were now of much poorer quality.

The Wheatley subsidy was abolished in 1932 in the wake of the economic crisis of 1929–32. Thereafter, housing policy was dominated by the encouragement of owner-occupation and slum clearance. The clearance programme was tailored to sharp cost constraints. In terms of rehousing, the subsidies were given on the basis of the number of people rehoused with additions for flats on inner-city sites. The result was to produce the large number of barrack-block flats common in London, Liverpool and other major cities, which minimized living space and produced a uniform ugly type of building.

The overall picture, then, is of sharp reductions in direct housing expenditure at times of economic crisis when the political balance was in favour of the Tories, against a background of general cost-cutting throughout the period of both Tory and National government rule.

Local authorities

Housing programmes were formulated by central government, but implementation was the job of the local authorities. The third element affecting housing policy was the way in which local authorities responded to central government directives. The response varied across the country. First, there were what we may term environmental factors. These included difficulties in getting land, rates of in- and out-migration, local industrial performance, the age structure of the local population and the state of the existing housing stock. Second, there were political factors. Labour-controlled local authorities tended to pursue council housing programmes more vigorously than their Tory counterparts. This was partly due to the correlation between poor housing conditions and Labour control. It was also due to the fact that house-building was an important element in the local political scene. Labour councillors were voted in for many purposes, but the most important single reason was the provision of good housing. Working-class pressure in local government was primarily concerned to achieve better housing conditions.

The building boom

The most significant feature of the housing market in the inter-war years was the private-sector building boom. Figure 2.2 shows how the majority of housing completions in the inter-war period were private-sector completions. The diagram also reveals the size of the boom. At its peak, over 275,000 houses were built in one year for the private sector, a figure which has never been equalled. What caused the boom? Government subsidies played only a minor role. Of the two million houses built, only a quarter were aided by subsidies. In essence, the boom was a private-market phenomenon.

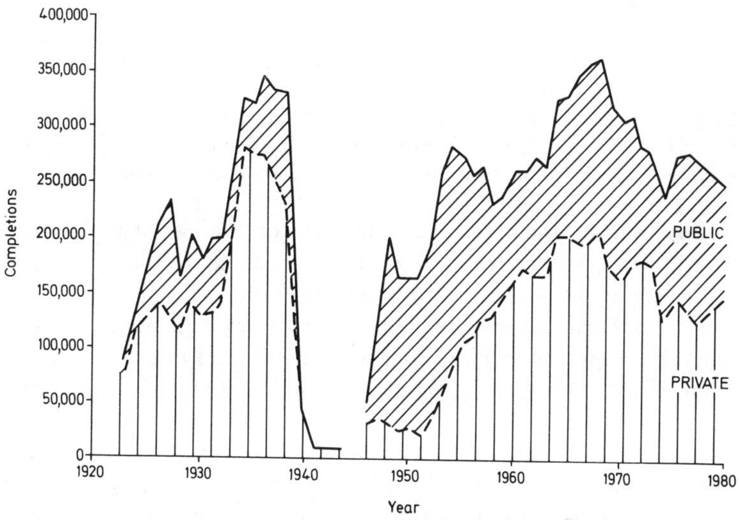

Figure 2.2 Housing completions in England and Wales

On the supply side, the fall in material costs and building workers' wages reduced the real cost of housing. On the demand side, those in employment were experiencing a rise in income. This increase in effective demand was aided by the medium of the building societies. The societies did not suffer in the depression. Compared with company shares and securities, investment in building societies provided a favourable return and, as incomes grew for those in employment, savings increased. The building societies grew and prospered as savings poured in. The deposits were used to provide mortgages for house purchase. The house-building boom was fuelled by a steady flow of building-society financing of owner-occupation.

Direct intervention by the government was minimal in the building boom. However, the state did play a part. The most important was in indirect fiscal measures. Tax relief on the mortgage interest payment was a hidden subsidy to owner-occupiers, a subsidy which cheapened the cost of buying a dwelling. The government was keen to encourage the building boom. On the one hand, it increased aggregate demand in an otherwise sluggish economy; it has been argued that the boom was a major factor in Britain's early recovery from the depression. On the other hand, it was a housing form which validated the arguments concerning the efficacy of private market forces. For the Tory-dominated National government owner-occupation was a fitting tenure type. As Viscount Cecil noted at the time,

> the ownership of property cultivates prudence. Clearly it encourages thrift, fosters the sense of security and self dependence, and sensibly deepens citizens consciousness of having a 'stake in the country', and the influence is surely one which, spreading from the individual to the community and linking all classes, must contribute appreciably to national stability.

The housing scene was very different on the eve of the Second World War to that before the First World War. Over 300,000 local authority houses had been built, a quarter of a million slum dwellings had been demolished, local authorities had amassed considerable expertise in housing management, and expectations had been raised. Subsequent observers could point to the municipal achievement of the inter-war period as an argument for more state involvement in housing provision. Private renting had declined both absolutely and relatively although it was still the largest tenure category. Owner-occupation was becoming more and more important. The inter-war building boom was really an owner-occupied suburban boom helped by a decline in the real cost of housing, increased effective demand and the entry of building societies which supplied the mortgages. Owner-occupation was becoming the tenure for the middle classes and the labour aristocracy.

Though things were better in 1939 than they were in 1914, not all the problems had been solved. Only half of the declared slums had been cleared, and housing shortages still existed. Housing difficulties were most severe for the poor. The middle classes and the skilled manual workers were increasingly moving to owner-occupation. The government's encouragement of owner-occupation was partly based on the belief that if the better-off households would move to new dwellings the rest would move into the vacancies; the housing in effect would filter down the social income scale. As Bowley (1944, p. 179) noted, 'The question outstanding in 1939 was, therefore, whether it was satisfactory that the supply of additional houses and replacement of old ones should depend for the mass of the working class population on the haphazard emigration of better-off families into new homes.'

3

THE POST-WAR YEARS: THE CENTRAL GOVERNMENT STORY

THE LEGACY OF WAR

The experience of the war years had a profound effect on post-war housing. At an immediate level there was an emerging housing crisis. Few houses had been built during the war and many had been damaged. Estimates suggest that almost half a million dwellings were either destroyed or made completely uninhabitable and a further quarter of a million were severely damaged. Almost three million dwellings had suffered lesser damage. In contrast to the supply the latent demand was increasing. Between 1939 and 1945 a million extra people had been added to the population, and the number of households was increasing even more because of the trend for household size to fall. The housing crisis was partly contained by overcrowding and shared accommodation, but demand pressed at the seams as squatting became an important phenomenon in the summer and autumn of 1946. Michael Foot (1975, pp. 80–1) noted:

> In many parts of the country, mothers and fathers, carrying their children and family belongings, invaded huts that had not been de-requisitioned by the local authorities, and set up improvised homes of their own. The idea was adopted by Communists in London who organized the Great Sunday Squat in an empty block of flats in Kensington. The Government feared widespread disorder. Eviction orders were served on the London squatters. . . . Elsewhere the squatters were sometimes victorious, retaining the primitive contests with the backing of local public opinion.

There were a number of policy responses to the immediate problems. Dwellings were requisitioned, premises converted, repairs hurriedly made to houses and prefabricated dwellings were constructed. By 1948 almost 125,000 'prefabs' had been built. Although built as a short-term solution, many of them lasted into the 1970s.

Residents' satisfaction with them was very high, perhaps because they combined the two essential qualities of the universally desired country-cottage type, namely compact inside and a large garden. Many people were sorry to leave their prefabs.

The conversions, the prefabs and the quick repairs were short-term policies; the longer-term solutions were very different from the immediate pre-war policies. The change reflected the radical shift in public opinion and political power. War had many effects, but one of its most important was that of radicalizing the population. When sacrifices are made new demands are raised. People did not believe that they were fighting the war to maintain the pre-war status quo with its two million unemployed and other social ills. The process of radicalization was reflected in many ways, from debates within army camps and long arguments in pubs to the growth of explicit left-wing solutions to public problems. This can be seen in the special issue of the news magazine *Picture Post* published on 4 January 1941. The issue put in focus what many people thought they were fighting for. The articles outlined 'a fairer, pleasanter, happier, more beautiful Britain'. There were articles by J. B. Priestley on leisure, Thomas Balogh on economic policy, Julian Huxley on health and Maxwell Fry on planning. Each of the articles pointed to the pre-war failures and looked forward to a more democratic, more planned, more just post-war Britain. The recurring themes were of the superiority of planning over blind market forces and the need for programmes of social welfare, all imbued with a tremendous sense of optimism. The tenor of the articles can be seen from the main recommendations: state control of the banks, a national economic plan, full employment, a minimum wage, comprehensive social insurance, strong land-use planning controls, new municipal services such as laundries, hot water, refuse disposal and other services, comprehensive and free education and health system and the construction of civic centres for music, drama, films and talks.

There was also intense activity at governmental level. The TUC and Labour ministers forced the war-time coalition government to prepare plans for a fairer post-war Britain. The war years saw a flurry of committees whose reports were to map out the direction of a post-war welfare state in Britain. The Beveridge Report was the basis for the 1946 Act which laid the basis for social insurance; the Norwood report of 1943 informed the Butler Education Act of 1944, which extended free public education; and the Scott and Uthwatt reports of 1942 laid the basis for the creation of the post-war planning machinery. Housing was only indirectly affected by all this activity: no national plan for housing was drawn up as for education or social services, no targets were set or allocation procedures constructed. The most important document was the Dudley report (named after the Earl of Dudley) commissioned by the Ministry of Health on the design of public housing. The report criticized previous council housing schemes, especially those under the 1923 and subsequent acts, for their cramped space standards and monotony in dwelling design. The report recommended that for new council houses the floor space of a standard three-bedroomed house should be increased from 750 to 900 square feet excluding cupboards. Kitchens should also be equipped with draining boards, larders, etc., and council estates should have a mix of dwelling types including single-storey cottages, three-storey houses and both high- and low-rise blocks of flats. The Dudley report was a blueprint for good-quality council housing.

THE COUNCIL HOUSING SOLUTION (1945–51)

The demands for improvements in social welfare were crystallized in the massive election victory of the Labour party in 1945, a party whose manifesto committed them to the reforms outlined by the war-time reports. The Labour government took these reports as the basis for their construction of a new post-war Britain.

The housing policy of the Labour government involved the short-term measures of prefabs, repairs and conversions to cope with immediate housing shortages in 1945–6, and long-term measures which placed greater emphasis on local authority housing. The Labour government announced a whole series of measures which placed the public sector in the leading role. Local authorities had already been acquiring land for building since 1943, and by 1945 there was enough land in local authority hands for over 600,000 dwellings. Under the Housing Act of 1946 the existing subsidy of £8.25 per house (£5.50 from exchequer, £2.75 from local rates) payable over forty years was raised to £22 (£16.50 from exchequer, £5.50 from rates) payable over sixty years. The local authorities were also allowed to borrow from the public works loan board (PWLB). This was a quasi-autonomous government body first set up in 1917 to lend money to local authorities at relatively low rates of interest. In the period from 1945 to 1951 most of local authority expenditure came from the PWLB, and rates of interest over this period did not exceed 3 per cent. The Land Acquisitions Act of 1946 enhanced the ability of local authorities to obtain land for public housing, and later the 1949 Act allowed the authorities to provide general-needs housing, i.e. housing for any citizen and not just the working classes or 'slum dwellers'. The houses were built to the standards recommended by the Dudley report. Given the post-war shortages of men and materials the results were impressive. As Figure 3.1 clearly shows, there was a rapid increase in public sector completions, and by 1951 over one-and-a-half million units of accommodation had been provided. The policy, however, did not achieve all its objectives. As before and as was to happen again in the future, economic crisis intervened. The dip in the graph of public sector completions (Figure 3.1) after 1948 reflects a deliberate policy decision made in August 1947 to cut the public housing programme. The crisis of 1947 was primarily due to Britain's poor trading position and the other claims on public expenditure. To overcome the balance of trade deficit, which was due to the large overseas debt and the poor export performance, Treasury officials and senior

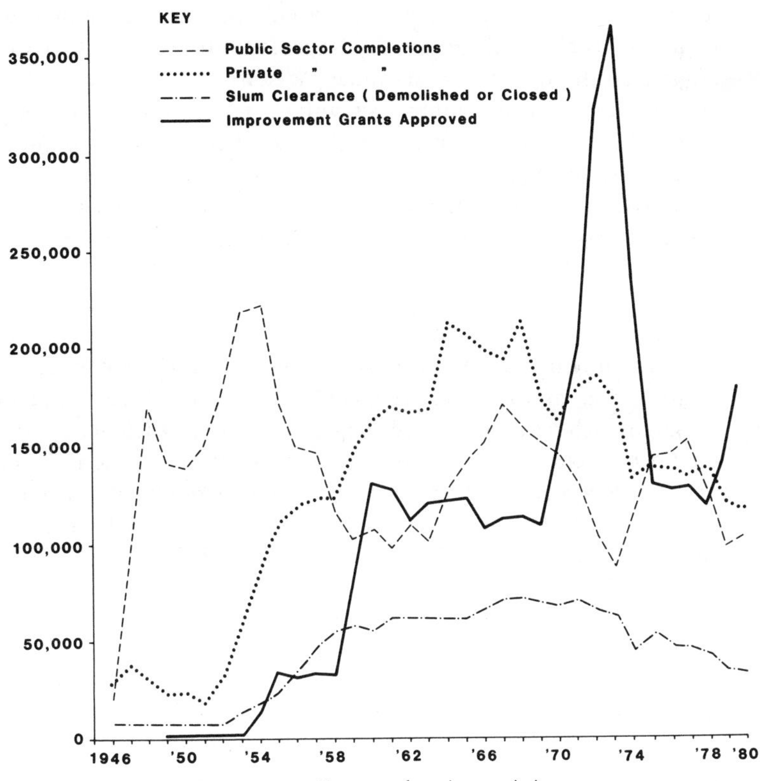

Figure 3.1 Post-war housing statistics

Labour politicians argued for more investment in export-orientated sectors. Because there were limits to public expenditure this meant a reduction in social programmes. The crisis was aggravated by the nature of the Anglo-American alliance and the heavy expenditure on armed forces. The USA had ended the war as the undisputed world power. In times of crisis, therefore, Britain had to turn to the huge neighbour over the Atlantic. In 1945, for example, Britain sought a loan of $350 million. American loans were allocated to benefit US interests. Two things were important. First, the US wanted open markets, believing perhaps rightly that the inter-war slump had been due to the closure of markets to free trade. With its strong economy the US government was eager to open up international markets. Loans and credit guarantees were therefore given on the understanding that the British and Commonwealth markets would be opened up to US goods. Second, the USA wanted strong economies in western Europe. On the one hand, this would be an important bulwark against socialist advances and, on the other, a prosperous Europe would be able to buy US goods. US foreign policy in western Europe sought to direct resources to the industrial sectors rather than the welfare programmes. Welfare did not help the US industry nor did it sit comfortably with the free enterprise ideology espoused by the Americans. The US overseers of Labour policies could report that the 1947 cuts in health, housing and education were an improvement in the Labour government's performance.

The US paymasters limited the Labour government's actions, but there were also self-imposed limits. Although there were important divisions amongst the cabinet there were enough senior Labour politicians who believed in a world-power role for Britain and the necessary military expenditure which this entailed. Defence expenditure was thus an important element in the national budget and an element which reduced welfare expenditure. In 1948 defence constituted 7 per cent of the national product. To be sure, the military presence was part legacy from the past, but there was also a significant element of socialist imperialism. The Labour party, then as later, could combine a seeming paradox of socialist goals at home and imperialist ventures abroad.

The first public housing solutions proposed and implemented by the first post-war Labour government were as much guided by circumstances as by political ideology. With the shortage of materials there was a real need to ration building materials. Bevan summed up many people's view when he stated that the speculative builder was not amenable to planning a rational allocation of resources. The onus of responsibility was thus placed on the local authorities, not the private sector. When one considers the period in retrospect there was very little explicit commitment to public housing as there was, say, for public education, a free health service or even the comprehensive welfare programme. There was no Beveridge to extol the virtues of state housing nor a Bevan to work for the creation of a national housing service. Public housing was the solution adopted because it seemed the best one in the circumstances, not because it was perceived as an inherently socialist model for building a better society. Perhaps the experience of the inter-war council estates had caused some tarnishing of the original image, or perhaps the very success of the inter-war private sector building boom was a difficult fact to square with the belief in the inadequacy of market forces. Whatever the exact combinations of reasons, Labour's formal commitment to public housing was limited. Subsequent Labour policies are easier to understand if this is borne in mind.

ENCOURAGING THE PRIVATE SECTOR (1951–64)

The Tory party, which came to power in 1951, was committed to building 300,000 dwellings. The promise had been made a year earlier at the 1950 party conference. Housing had been an important election issue and the Tories in opposition had frequently pointed to the failures of the Labour government, failures keenly felt by the population. In a Gallup Poll in 1949, 61 per cent said that they were not satisfied with the government's housing record.

The first few years of the Tory government were committed to achieving the 300,000 target. Council housing was used in this achievement. Macmillan's autobiography (he was minister in charge of housing from 1951–4) conjures up a time of feverish activity to meet the target. Local authorities were set building targets, and the 1952 Housing Act raised the standard annual subsidy to £35.60. The aggregate figures were impressive. In Figure 3.1, for example, we can see that the public sector completions rapidly climbed to over 200,000 in 1952, 1953 and 1954; this was a figure that was never achieved again in the post-war period. The aggregate figures do, however, ignore a fall in the housing standard. More houses were being built because room sizes were decreased and installations were kept to essentials. This process had been started in the dying days of the previous Labour government. The promise of the Dudley report recommendations had not been fulfilled and a generation of houses

Table 3.1 Post-war housing legislation

Date	Title	Brief description
1945–51 Labour government		
1946	Housing Act	Stimulated local authority house building: increased subsidies, local authorities allowed to obtain loans from FWLB at low interest rates
1947	Town and Country Planning Act	Nationalized development rights; plan-making powers given to local authorities
1949	Housing Act	Local authorities allowed to provide housing for everyone, not just 'working class'
1951–64 Conservative government		
1952	Housing Act	All house building stimulated: increase in subsidies for local authorities' house building
1954	Housing Repairs and Rent Act	Rent increases in private rented sector after improvement
1956	Housing Subsidies Act	Cut in subsidies to local authorities, bigger subsidies for high-rise buildings
1957	Rent Act	Attempt at rent decontrol
1957	Housing Act	Allowed local authorities to sell council houses
1961	Housing Act	Restoration of subsidies for general-needs housing
1964–70 Labour government		
1965	Rent Act	Security of tenure given to tenants in unfurnished accommodation; fair rents scheme introduced
1967	Housing Subsidies Act	Subsidy to local authorities to help against increased interest rates; option mortgage scheme introduced
1969	Housing Act	Increased level of improvement grants; introduced GIAs; emphasis now placed on improvement.
1970–4 Conservative government		
1972	Housing Finance Act	Reduced subsidies to local authorities; increased local authority rents
1974–9 Labour government		
1974	Housing Act	Level of improvement grant increased; new expanded role for housing associations; introduction of HAAs, repeal of Housing Finance Act; security of tenure given to tenants of furnished accommodation
1975	Housing Rent and Subsidies Act	Increased subsidies to local authorities
1977	Housing (Homeless Persons) Act	Duty of local authorities to provide accommodation for registered homeless
1979 Conservative government		
1980	Housing Act	Greater central government control of local authority housing expenditure; new short-hold tenancy in private rented sector; increase of rents in private and public sectors; right to buy for council house tenants

were being constructed which were to provide problems in succeeding years. The average three-bedroomed house was 1000 square feet in 1951, and this was to fall by 50 square feet in 1952.

The strong electoral commitment to the magic figure of 300,000 saved the housing programme. Macmillan reports that there were fierce attacks on his housing plans especially during the balance of payments crisis of 1951–2. He reports that the famous target figure was 'my sheet anchor, by which I could ride out the gale'.

The target was eventually reached in 1953, and surpassed in 1954. Now that the figure had been reached and the electoral promise had been redeemed, more emphasis could be placed on the private sector. The public sector was now to revert to its perceived 'rightful' role as a residual tenure category, mopping up those who could not afford to enter owner-occupation.

Encouragement of the private sector was the main theme of Conservative housing policy. The policy was outlined in a 1953 White Paper. Five issues were identified and these were to dominate Tory policy throughout their period of office until 1964:

(1) Private enterprise was to be encouraged.
(2) Owner-occupation was to be encouraged.
(3) Private renting was to be restored, allowing rent increases so that repairs could be made.
(4) Local authorities' main role was to clear slums and rehouse the former inhabitants.
(5) There should be greater emphasis on repair and improvement to the housing stock.

We can consider subsequent Tory policy in relation to each of these five items.

Lifting restrictions

To achieve the aim of encouraging private enterprise, restrictions were lifted from the private sector. Controls on the licensing system for private house building used by the previous Labour government were loosened until they were eventually abandoned in 1954. And the development charge on new building contained in the Labour government's 1947 Town and Country Planning Act was abolished by the Tories in 1953.

Encouraging owner-occupation

Owner-occupation was encouraged by government involvement in the housing demand side. In 1958 stamp duties on houses sold for under £3000 were reduced, local authorities were encouraged to sell council houses and provide funds for house purchase, the government lent the Building Societies £100 million between 1959 to 1962 to encourage lending on pre-1919 housing, and in 1962 owner-occupiers were made exempt from income tax under the schedule A tax system. Government policies were successful. Figure 3.1 shows the rapid rise in private sector completions. The annual figures steadily increased throughout the 1950s and early 1960s. The surge of building transformed the tenure distribution of the country (see Figure 2.1). In 1951, only 29 per cent of households lived in owner-occupation, but at the end of the Conservative period of government in 1964 the proportion had increased to over 45 per cent.

Helping the landlord

The government sought to improve the position of private landlords and revive private renting by lifting rent controls. Rent controls had first been introduced in 1915, reintroduced in 1939 and continued by the Labour government in 1945. The Conservatives also sought to increase the quality of the private rented sector by allowing an increase in rent for money spent on repairs and maintenance. The first measure designed to meet these goals was the 1954 Housing Act, which allowed rent increases consequent upon improvement expenditure; however, because of its complex implementation this Act was not successful. Legislation was next introduced in the 1957 Rent Act. Under this, all dwellings of a rateable value of more than £30 (£40 in London and Scotland) were automatically decontrolled. Landlords with dwellings below this value could serve a notice of rent increase if the property was in good repair. In practice the landlord could achieve decontrol and hence rent increases on a change of tenancy. The passage of the Act generated enormous political heat, with debate centring on the Conservatives' arguments for increasing the supply of rented accommodation and the Labour case for maintaining the right of tenancy. The Act itself had very little direct impact because houses which were decontrolled were generally sold for owner-occupation rather than for re-letting, and landlords carried out very few repairs. The Act's impact was not the expected one. Because decontrol and rent increases could be achieved on a change of tenancy, there was an added incentive to landlords to obtain this change. In parts of inner London unscrupulous landlords did so by evicting the existing tenants. One man in particular, Perec Rachmann, was particularly successful in this enterprise. Rachmann achieved greater notoriety, however, because of the Profumo affair. This affair, involving a heady brew of sex, scandal and corruption, went straight to the public's head and the name of Rachmann was burned indelibly in the minds of many. In the wake of the public outcry a committee of enquiry was appointed and rent controls were introduced in 1965.

Reducing council housing

The Conservatives altered the role of council housing. Under the previous government, council housing had been the major instrument of policy. After the 300,000 target had been reached by the Tories, council house building was now placed in a minor position. A new and smaller role was planned for the council house sector; rather than providing for general needs the local authorities were charged with slum clearance and rehousing, and council housing was to be mainly used for rehousing slum dwellers. This was a regression to the Chamberlain doctrine. By 1956 the subsidy for general needs was abolished and exchequer grants were only available for the special-needs categories of slum clearance and accommodation for the elderly; the pattern of subsidies favoured high-rise dwellings. The general-need subsidy was reintroduced in 1961; however, it was allocated on the formula which favoured local authorities charging the highest rents. The result was to give more subsidy to the rural authorities charging high rents than the large urban authorities with the greatest housing problem, who tended to charge lower rents.

The funding of local authority house building was also changed under Conservative administration. In October 1955 the government decreed that local authorities should use the money market rather than the PWLB. This change came about because the Treasury had been arguing throughout the early 1950s that the PWLB lending was a drain on public finances making credit control difficult. The decision to force local authorities to use the money market and dispense with the PWLB had two main effects. First, it meant that local authorities had to go to the capital market, with its much higher rates of interest, to finance their expenditure; this increased the debt charges and by the late 1950s over 60 per cent of local authority expenditure went in interest payments. Much of the problem of council house building can be seen as the unfolding consequences of the decision to make local authorities go to the money market for finance. Second, it increased rents. To meet the widening gap between increase in costs and fixed rents, local authorities either had to increase rents, increase rate contributions or reduce standards. The Tory-controlled authorities tended to increase rents whereas Labour authorities increased rate contributions. The very large authorities with ambitious programmes tended to increase rates and reduce standards, and by 1959 the size of individual council houses and the overall quality of council housing had declined. The average floor size of a three-bedroomed council house built in 1949 was 1055 square feet; the figure for a house built in 1959 had dropped to 897 square feet.

The aggregate figures shown in Figure 3.1 reveal how council house building fell steadily from its peak in 1954–5. Thereafter the new, diminished role of council housing was reflected in the fall in the numbers completed. The quickening pace of decline after 1957 was caused by another cut in housing expenditure in response to yet another crisis. This time, in August/September 1957, there was speculation on the pound and government fears of a wage-induced bout of inflation. A ceiling was imposed on public expenditure and housing expenditure was to be reduced. A 20-per-cent reduction in local authority housing expenditure was made manifest in the sharp fall in housing completions in England and Wales from almost 150,000 in 1957 to just over 100,000 in 1959.

Public housing starts were to pick up later. The years 1961–2 saw a mild recession and in line with Keynesian doctrine a series of reflationary measures were introduced. In 1963, a White Paper on housing suggested that total housing output should be increased, partly to stimulate the demand in the economy and partly to improve the Conservatives' housing record. The housing issue was crowding on to the political agenda in the late 1950s and early 1960s, and in the 1964 general election housing was a key issue. Part economics, part political strategy, the decision to build more council housing lifted the aggregate figures, and by 1965 and 1966 public sector completions in England and Wales were once again nearing 150,000 per annum.

More repairs and improvements

In the immediate post-war period the severe housing shortage precluded any demolition. There were just not enough houses to afford a careful evaluation of housing quality. As more houses were built and the housing shortage eased off, attention could turn to older, poor-quality dwellings. The inadequacy of the dwellings at the bottom of the quality scale were highlighted in the increase in housing standards.

In the years of the first post-war Conservative government there was a twofold solution to the problem of older housing. The very worst houses were to be demolished and this was the job of the local authorities, who were also charged with providing housing for displaced households. Throughout the 1950s the number of demolitions steadily rose. In 1952 the figure was negligible but in 1958 almost 50,000 dwellings were being demolished or closed. The amount of slum clearance continued because the ending of the general needs subsidy in 1956 meant that Labour councils eager to build council housing first had to knock old dwellings down.

Steps were also taken to stimulate the improvement of dwellings in the private sector. These were first taken under the Labour government, and the 1949 Housing Act made improvement grants available to both landlords and owner-occupiers. The scheme was little-used; the standards expected were high and local authorities' minds and energies were on other things. The 1949 Act did however provide the basis for subsequent legislation. The Conservatives extended the scheme under the 1954 Housing Repairs and Rent Act, which introduced improvement grants covering 50 per cent of expenditure up to a maximum grant of £400. The effect of this measure was to increase the take-up of improvement grants (see Figure 3.1) and by 1955 over 25,000 grants had been allocated. The big surge in improvement grant take-up took place after the 1959 House Purchase and Housing Act, which made it mandatory for local authorities to give grants to people improving housing up to a five-point standard. (This standard was: (1) fixed bath or shower; (2) wash basin; (3) sink; (4) WC; (5) hot and cold running water.) The maximum grant was £155, which was to cover 50 per cent of improvement expenditure, and discretionary grants were also available for the conversion of large houses, up to a maximum of £400 (£500 in a case of buildings of three or more storeys). Under the Act landlords were permitted to raise rents after improvement work had been carried out, up to 12½ per cent of their own improvement expenditure. The effect of this Act was dramatic. The number of improvement grants grew from approximately 25,000 in 1958 to almost 125,000 in 1960, with a majority of grants going to owner-occupiers. Less than a fifth of all grants went to landlords. Most landlords wanted to sell their property rather than improve it.

The Conservative years saw themes which were to dominate subsequent post-war years: owner-occupation was to be encouraged, local authorities were to clear slums and build new houses, the very poor-quality houses were to be demolished and the slightly better ones were to be improved by improvement grants. Over the course of the Conservative government the number of private sector completions increased steadily from less than 25,000 in 1951 to over 150,000 in 1964; local authorities were demolishing about 60,000 dwellings a year and the two improvement acts of 1954 and 1959 had increased grant take-up from less than 5000 per year in the early 1950s to 125,000 a year by 1964. These were the successes. By the end of the Conservative era, however, the failures were becoming more apparent. Before the election in 1964 almost three million people in Britain were living in slum accommodation. In the Greater London area alone, over 6000 families were taken into welfare accommodation. The contraction of the private rented sector and the lack of council housing was making it very difficult for those unable to afford owner-occupation to get accommodation. The housing situation varied across the country, of course, but in the big cities and London in particular the pressure for accommodation was intense. The Conservatives had failed to resuscitate the private rented sector and had not provided enough council housing. The less immediate failure was the inability to provide good-quality accommodation. The structure of subsidies had encouraged cramped space standards and cost-cutting in the council housing sector, and the result was poor-quality accommodation and the reinforcement of the stigmatization of council housing. But it was the more immediate failure which caught the political headlines. The narrow defeat of the Conservative party in the 1964 general election was caused by a number of factors; but the perceived failure of Conservative housing policy was an important element.

ECONOMIC CONFUSION AND HOUSING POLICY (1964–70)

The Labour government of 1964 did not have a coherent housing policy. What it had was short-term commitments and longer-term hopes. The commitments lay in the private rented sector. The Rachmann scandal and the publicity given to problems faced by private-sector tenants had been an important election weapon for the Labour party and it was committed to action. In 1965 a new Rent Act was introduced which gave security of tenure to most tenants in unfurnished accommodation. The Act also introduced a new system of rent determination for tenants not controlled under the old system and who were in unfurnished accommodation with a rateable value of less than £200 (£400 in London). The 1965 Act introduced a scheme of fair rents which were to be assessed by a rent officer, a civil servant, and a rent assessment committee which could review rents every three years. In theory, the fair rent was to be the likely market rent assuming no scarcity. This staggering assumption proved difficult to operate in practice and there was wide variation in rent levels between different areas. The 1965 Rent Act did halt the Tory trend of decontrol, although rent increases and often substantial increases did occur under the fair rent scheme. More of this later.

The longer-term housing plans of the Labour government were sketched out in the 1965 White Paper, 'The Housing Programme 1965–70'. The government committed itself to a massive housing drive. It was hoped that, by 1970, 500,000 dwellings would be built each year, the completions being shared equally between owner-occupation and council housing. The council housing drive was, however, to be short-lived. As the White Paper put it, 'The expansion of the public programme now proposed is to meet exceptional needs: it is borne partly of short term necessity, partly of the condition inherent in modern urban life. Expansion of owner-occupation on the other hand is normal; it effects a long term social advance which should gradually pervade every region.' Notice how owner-occupation was viewed in the White Paper as the 'normal' tenure. Public housing was a residual, a short-term expedient. In one sense this represented a complete change from the previous Labour government policies, which saw public housing as the main solution to the post-war housing shortage. Now, in contrast, council housing was to be only used in the short term. The Labour government's vision of the future now looked to a nation of owner-occupiers. In another sense, however, no radical rupture occurred in Labour party thinking. The housing policies of the 1945–51 period were partly conditioned by circumstances: few supplies, the need to get housing produced quickly and the weight of popular opinion. There was no fully argued socialist case for public housing. The benefit of a large public housing sector had not been documented or discussed to the same extent as the National Health Service, a comprehensive social security system or indeed a comprehensive education system. Housing was a policy area, not a political objective. The new Labour government was not operating principles or seeking objectives, it was simply reacting to circumstances. Between the first and second post-war Labour governments there had been the Tory encouragement of owner-occupation, and when the Labour party came to power in 1964 almost 50 per cent of households were in owner-occupation, a tenure category which had extended throughout the country and across the socio-economic categories. It was now the single most important category giving the advantages of a capital asset as well as accommodation. The issue for the Labour party was now one of extending the benefits of owner-occupation to as many people as possible.

Before the storm

In the early days of the second post-war Labour government the housing programme seemed to be relatively successful. Because of the strong election commitment, public housing was saved from the early cuts in public expenditure proposed by the Labour government in 1964–5. Thereafter, council housing construction was aided by a number of measures. First, the major urban authorities were given permission to put out tenders for work. Second, a new subsidy was introduced. Under the 1967 Housing Subsidies Act the exchequer gave a subsidy to the local authorities to make up the difference between the costs of borrowing at 4 per cent and the prevailing interest paid by the authorities. In effect it was a measure designed to save the local authority building programme from increasing interest charges and rising costs. In this respect the scheme was successful and by 1967–8 council house building was at its highest level since the early 1950s. The government had less control over the private sector, but to stimulate effective demand the government introduced the option mortgage and guarantee scheme, also under the 1967 Housing Act, to help low-income households. Under the scheme the borrowers gave up any claim to tax relief but paid less than the normal mortgage rate. The government reimbursed the building society, insurance company or local authority with the difference between the option and the normal mortgage rate. The scheme was successful: in 1972 over 20 per cent of mortgages were option mortgages. The proportion only began to fall as the tax threshold fell, and by 1976 only 7 per cent of building society mortgages and 12 per cent of local authority ones were of the option type.

The housing programme in the early days seemed to be working. Council house building was increasing, private sector starts were continuing apace, redevelopment schemes were clearing some of the worst slums and through the option mortgage scheme more people were able to become owner-occupiers. The housing programme was then upset by two things.

Economic crisis and political defeat

Economic crisis was the recurring motif in British society in the post-war period. Throughout the 1960s economic growth was faltering. The beginning of the end of the post-war boom was making itself felt worldwide, but particularly in Britain. Things came to a head in 1967 when the continuing balance of payments deficit and the run on the pound eventually led to devaluation. Subsequent deflationary measures tried to shift emphasis from welfare expenditure to private investment in order to increase exports and reduce imports. The housing programme came under Treasury scrutiny. The new subsidy arrangements introduced in 1967 were considered too expensive because as interest rates rose the subsidy increased. Prior to the new arrangement a subsidy of £24 per house was normal, by 1968 it was reaching £110. This increase was due partly to increased costs and partly to new standards in building. The Parker Morris report of 1961, *Homes for Today and Tomorrow*, had called for more space and better heating standards for new council housing, at least two day rooms and provision of two WCs in houses for five or more persons. The report also stated that the minimum space standard should be 910 square feet plus 50 square feet of storage for a five-person household. By 1965, only 20 per cent of new council housing was built to Parker Morris standards. In order to improve things the Labour government made these standards mandatory for new council housing built for new towns after 1967 and for local authorities in 1969. They tended to be implemented as maximum standards and not minimum requirements as originally proposed. It has been estimated that Parker Morris houses were one-fifth more costly than local authority houses not built to such standards. The increase in the cost of council housing made it a prime target in the scheme for public expenditure reductions; the fact that it was cut reflected the balance of political forces. The skilled unionized workers had, very largely, been housed in the better-quality public housing areas or had found accommodation in the owner-occupied sector. The people most affected by the reductions in public housing were typically the economically weak, semi-skilled and unskilled workers, the politically disorganized immigrants and the apathetic inner-city residents. The state, faced with an economically weak and politically impotent opposition, was able to prune its commitment to public housing.

The revised housing programme was announced in January 1968 as part of the post-devaluation austerity measures. The council house building programme was to be cut by 16,500 dwellings each year, but this was only the tip of the iceberg as a new era in housing policy was opened, a policy shift from the comprehensive redevelopment schemes to an emphasis on improvement. In the wake of the January measures public sector completions declined, and by 1972 their number was falling towards the 100,000 mark.

The second reason for disruption of the council house sector of Labour's housing programme lay in the realm of local politics. In 1967 and 1968 the Conservatives had made sweeping gains in the local government elections. The Tory victories were registered by the reduction in council house building. The municipal emphasis was now on private-sector solutions, and building sites were sold to developers, more council houses were sold to sitting tenants, direct labour organizations were run down and council house rents were increased. These actions had marked redistributional consequences.

A new programme

The economic crisis had wrecked the government's housing plans. Council house building was seen as too expensive in the austere climate of post-devaluation in Britain. In this new context a fresh housing policy was formulated. It was first published in the 1968 White Paper on housing, the tenor of which can be seen in the following sentence: 'The government intend that within a total of public investment in housing at about the level it has now reached, the greater share should go to the improvement of old homes.'

The implications were twofold. First, since costs and interest charges were bound to increase, the decision to restrict expenditure 'at about the level it has now reached' was in fact a decision to cut housing investment. Second, the emphasis was to change from rebuilding to housing improvement. Private rehabilitation had been touted around as an alternative to redevelopment. Three reasons were important in shaping this policy response to expenditure restrictions.

(1) The redevelopment schemes had caused the break-up of communities and the disruption of established social ties. These social costs had been ignored in the early cost–benefit analysis of the redevelopment programme, but by the late 1960s the negative effects of redevelopment were being recognized. The use of the municipal bulldozer was being questioned.

(2) The housing condition survey of 1967 had shown that approximately 0.7 million dwellings were outside clearance and potential clearance areas. As the very worst houses were cleared the remaining poor-quality houses were more widely dispersed around the inner city and not so amenable to the concentrated area approach of redevelopment.

(3) An improvement programme was reckoned to be cheaper. A

number of feasibility studies had shown that in the short run rehabilitation was a feasible and cheaper alternative to comprehensive redevelopment.

The 1969 Housing Act implemented the White Paper proposals. To encourage improvement the Act increased the level of improvement grants from £155 to £200 for the standard grant (from £350 to £450 if a bathroom required extra building) and from £400 to £1000 for the discretionary grant. The impact of the new grant system was large and immediate. As Figure 3.1 shows, the level of improvement grant take-up increased dramatically from around 110,000 grants in 1968 to over 350,000 in 1974. As new building declined and new demolitions tailed off, improvement grants were the main policy mechanism for dealing with older homes. The Act also introduced the concept of General Improvement Areas (GIA). These were to be small areas, covering between 200 and 300 dwellings, with a majority of owner-occupiers, basically sound housing and a stable population. Improvement was to be encouraged by publicity campaigns telling households of the benefits of improvement and the way in which to obtain a local authority housing improvement grant. A grant was also available to the local authorities of up to £50 per dwelling for environmental improvement, including such things as tree planting, pedestrianization schemes and the provision of recreation areas. From 1969 to December 1975 just over 900 GIAs were declared and a total of 74,165 grants had been approved out of a total of 280,000 dwellings in GIAs: this represents a 26-per-cent take-up. In comparison with national figures this is impressive, but since the GIAs were to be the most publicized and most receptive to private rehabilitation, only small comfort can be taken from the figures. The scheme had not raised housing standards to the extent expected.

THE 1970S: CHANGING POLICIES AND RECURRING CRISIS

The Conservatives and private market solutions

The 1970s began with a Conservative government. Its housing policy was similar to that of previous Conservative administrations: the emphasis was on encouraging the private sector and reducing council housing to the role of a residual tenure category. A number of policy measures were used to achieve these ends.

The encouragement of private rehabilitation rather than municipal redevelopment started under the previous Labour government's 1969 Housing Act continued. The maximum grant for environmental improvements in GIAs was raised from £50 to £100 in 1971, and in the same year the improvement grant as a percentage of expenditure was increased to 75 per cent in development and intermediate areas; these were areas which covered most of the country outside of the more affluent south-east and midlands regions. The Tories were also working on other private rehabilitation measures before they were defeated; these measures were central to the 1974 Housing Act of the next Labour government, a case of housing policy surviving political change.

Owner-occupation was encouraged by a variety of means. The Tory attitude was summed up in the 1974 White Paper: 'Home ownership is a most rewarding form of house tenure. It satisfies a deep and natural desire on the part of the householder to have independent control of the house that shelters him and his family.' To extend this 'rewarding' form of house tenure the house price limit for the 100-per-cent option mortgage was raised to £7500 from £5000, local authorities were encouraged to sell council houses and in 1974 the building societies, the main financial source for house purchase, were given a grant from the government to keep interest rates down to 9½ per cent.

The attack on council housing took a number of directions. First, there was the 1972 Housing Finance Act which aimed to reduce government subsidies and make the better-off council tenants move into owner-occupation. This was attempted by increasing council house rents to fair rent levels. The poorest tenants were to receive rent rebates, and a general subsidy would be channelled to those authorities where increased rents could not cover costs. The burden would thus fall on the better-off council house tenant – the bogeyman of the popular press, the Tory faithful and the large mass of the British public. If coals in the bath and pigeons in the spare bedroom had been the fear of the early critics of council housing, then the Jaguar in the drive was the enduring myth held by later critics. Under the Act, rents increased on average by about 50 pence per week. It was not enacted without difficulty or rancour. The legislation took away from local authorities the power to set rent levels, and Labour councils were particularly wary of imposing rent increases on council house tenants on the orders of the Conservative government. A number of local authorities chose to ignore the Act altogether, but most of the protest collapsed except in the case of Clay Cross Urban District Council, whose councillors refused to implement the legislation. The situation was partly eased when Clay Cross disappeared in the local government reorganization of 1974.

The second attack on council housing came through the encouragement of housing associations. Although the Tories had used the 1972 Housing Act to decontrol the remaining controlled tenancies in the private rented sector, there was the feeling that the demise of the private landlords was continuing apace. With the contraction of the private rented sector and the swing towards rehabilitation, there was the Tory fear of creeping municipalization in the inner city as Labour-controlled authorities gained at the expense of the private rented sector. The 1973 White Paper envisaged a greatly expanded role for the voluntary housing movement and in particular the housing associations. These were to be the third arm of housing, between owner-occupation and council housing, taking over the role of the private landlord. The Tory government was looking towards a revived voluntary housing movement to take over and improve private rented accommodation in the inner city in order to halt creeping municipalization.

Labour and economic crisis

After a three-day week, a miners' strike and a bitter general election, the Labour party came to power in 1974; they were to govern until 1979. The subsequent housing legislation can be seen in terms of three elements. First, there was the legacy from the previous Conservative administration. Labour's 1974 Housing Act incorporated many of the policy proposals previously formulated by the Conservatives. The emphasis on rehabilitation was maintained. Four different types of improvement grant were introduced: standard improvement grants, intermediate grants, special grants, and repair grants. A new area policy scheme was also introduced, the Housing Action Areas (HAAs): these were to be small areas of very poor-quality housing. The GIA policy had improved the national housing stock but not in the worst areas. The HAA scheme attempted to reverse this trend and within the HAA the voluntary take-up of improvement grants was to be encouraged by the local authorities, who in association with the housing associations were given powers to acquire and improve property. The housing associations were organized under the general guidance of the Housing Corporation. Between 1974 and 1978, 272 HAAs were declared in some of the worst housing areas in Britain, but in the latter half of the 1970s the improvement programme and the HAA scheme ran into difficulties. Improvement grants failed to keep pace with the inflation of building repair costs and the HAA programme was hamstrung by the lack of local authority resources and the restrictions on Housing Corporation spending.

The second element was explicitly Labour party proposals. The 1974 Act was by and large a housing policy legacy from the previous Conservative government. The Labour government of 1974–9 could, however, generate its own policies. It initially came to power with a number of commitments: these included the repeal of the 1972 Housing Finance Act, a halt to the automatic transfer of controlled rents to regulated rents and the extension of security of tenure to tenants of furnished accommodation. In the early days housing was given priority status. Local authority house building was increased, the authorities were given extra powers for the acquisition and improvement of old private rented accommodation, and a broad-ranging review of housing finance was started. To revive council house building, which had fallen under the Conservatives (in 1973 council house building was at its lowest since 1947), the government introduced the 1975 Housing Rent and Subsidies Act, which abandoned the notion of 'fair' rent levels and placed the setting of rent levels in the hands of the local authorities. New subsidies were introduced under the Act, with the aim of keeping rents down and protecting local authority housing from the worst ravages of spiralling costs. The goal was partly achieved. Between 1973 and 1978 the average weekly unrelated council rent in England and Wales rose from £3.70 to £5.95. If we take inflation and wage increases into account, this represents in real terms a 25-per-cent reduction. Council house building also picked up (see Figure 3.1) and the number of public sector completions began to climb from its 1973 level of under 100,000 per year to over 150,000 by 1977.

The review of housing finance was eventually published in 1977. The Green Paper, *Housing Policy* (DOE, 1977), represents the most ambitious report on housing matters to date. The result was disappointing. Although the three technical volumes provided a comprehensive set of statistics, perhaps the best single source for any discussion of housing in England and Wales, the conclusions drawn from the study were predictably bland. The emerging themes of post-war housing policy were reiterated:

(1) Owner-occupation was to be increased. The Green Paper noted that 'owning one's own home is a basic and natural desire'. So as not to tamper with 'natural desires' the government decided not to alter the existing arrangement governing tax relief on mortgage interest and option mortgage subsidy. Electoral weight was firmly on the side of maintaining the status quo.

(2) Public housing was to remain in the hands of the local authorities but a new system of housing investment programmes was to be

drawn up. The local authorities were to construct these while the central government was to provide the single block grant. This new system gave local authorities some flexibility but introduced a strong element of central government control. A new subsidy scheme was suggested but never achieved, and many of the other proposals for the public sector were lost in Labour's electoral defeat of 1979.

The Labour government had already been following through policies to encourage owner-occupation. In 1974 a £500-million loan from the government had enabled the building societies to stabilize the flow of funds. The government also introduced in 1975 the support lending scheme under which the building societies agreed to relax the lending criteria for applicants referred to them by the local authorities. But perhaps Labour's biggest boost to owner-occupation was given by not intervening. The Green Paper argued that subsidies to owner-occupation through income tax relief on mortgage interest payments, which by 1975–6 were costing the Exchequer £1100 million at 1977 survey prices compared with £1353 million for the general local authorities subsidy, should not be changed. The government agreed. As owner-occupation continued to be such a desirable form of tenure, its attraction continued to exercise its effect. By 1976, 55 per cent of the dwellings in England and Wales were owner-occupied.

Labour's plans for housing in general and the public sector in particular were undermined by another economic crisis. This constitutes the third element in the evolution of housing policy under the 1974–9 Labour government. The crisis loomed in 1976, although it had been present throughout the early 1970s as unemployment steadily grew and economic output faltered and in key sectors stopped almost completely. Things were not helped by the oil price increase in 1973–4 and the slump in world trade in 1974. Soon after taking office the Labour government sought a deflationary solution to the problem. The emphasis of government policy was on public expenditure control, and in the April Budget of 1975 the Chancellor of the Exchequer, Dennis Healey called for a £1 billion cut in the public sector borrowing requirement (PSBR) in the financial year 1975–6, and a further £3 billion cut for 1976–7. By reducing public expenditure Healey hoped to transfer resources away from social welfare to the regeneration of British industry. Further cuts were announced in July 1976 after loans from the International Monetary Fund had been agreed, which cuts amounted to a £1 billion reduction in government spending for 1977–8. Housing expenditure was to bear a cut of £150 million with the main retrenchment occurring in the fields of local authority acquisitions, local authority mortgage lending, local authority improvement grants and new local authority building. Local authority housing investment fell from £2580 million in 1975–6 to £1934 million in 1977–8.

The effects were rapid. First, housing improvement grant take-up fell as improvement grants did not keep within inflation and local authority resources for GIAs and HAAs were thinly stretched. Second, some people on the border line were denied access to local authority mortgages. New council house building declined. The effects were most directly felt by those seeking housing and unable to obtain a building society mortgage or quick entry into a good local authority dwelling. By 1979 Labour's housing plans were in a mess. For the party of planning it was unmitigated disaster. As Peter Townsend (1980, p. 23) noted, 'a long term public expenditure cut was substituted for socialist planning. . . .'

ENCOURAGING THE PRIVATE MARKET . . . AGAIN

The Conservative party which came to power in 1979 was in many ways a different political beast from the previous Conservative government. Under the later Heath government the centre and left wing of the party had been ascendant. But after Heath's defeat the belief in the corporate state and the consensus with Labour over the scope and limits of the welfare state began to fade. Throughout the 1970s the right wing of the party gained intellectual sustenance from such men as Friedman, Hayek and Joseph. The new monetarism, a belief in market forces and an attack on the welfare state fitted into a broad ideology encompassing a variety of intellectual and popular opinions which emphasized 'the restoration of competition and personal responsibility for effort and reward, the image of the overtaxed individual, enervated by welfare coddling, his initiative sapped by handouts by the state' (Hall, 1979, p. 17).

Within this ideology, housing took on some significance. The encouragement of owner-occupation and the attack on council housing fitted in with the new ideas: a house of your own encouraged independence and thrift, while a large council housing sector with its supposedly huge subsidies was both a drain on the nation's resources and an unacceptable extension of state control. The concept of liberating the council house tenantry almost took on a religious fervour within the Tory rank and file. There was a belief that housing market forces left to themselves could find the right solution. According to the Tories the private rented sector had shrunk because of the deadening hand of rent controls; if only the controls could be lifted or at least eased, the market would respond. The basic housing tenets of Conservative policies were: owner-occupation is good; the housing crisis is over; the public housing sector is over-subsidized and the private rented sector can be revived. These became the main goals of the new Conservative party and they were mediated by previous policy proposals and the available legislative measures.

The 1980 Housing Act

Almost as soon as the Conservatives came to power a new housing bill began to make its tortuous way through Parliament. The bill received royal assent in August 1980. The 1980 Housing Act formalized the new Tory thinking on housing. Two separate elements of this Act can be considered. First, there was the legislative legacy from the previous Labour government. The continuity took shape in the tenants' charter planned for council housing subsidies. Part of the charter gave security of tenure to council house tenants and allowed them some basic freedoms such as the right to take in lodgers, have pets, paint their doors, etc. Most of these amendments to the status of council house tenancies had been proposed by the previous Labour government but there was a subtle change of emphasis in the new Tory measures. The previous proposals had stressed the rights of tenants' groups and organizations, whilst the Conservative proposals in contrast focused on individual as opposed to collective rights. In terms of council house financing, the 1980 Act's subsidy arrangements took on the form first outlined in the 1977 Green Paper. A new deficit subsidy was to be introduced, composed of two elements: a base element calculated on last year's subsidy, and a housing cost differential element which was to cover the difference between reckonable costs less local contributions from rents and rate fund contributions. Again there was a subtle difference between the previous Labour proposals and the present Conservative plans. Whereas Labour had suggested that council rents were to be adjusted according to the increase in average earnings, and local authorities were given some control over rent fixing, under the new Conservative legislation it was the Secretary of State who was to determine reckonable costs, subsidizable expenditure and rent levels. Financial control was shifted from the local authorities to central government. The new Act also carried forward the commitment to improvement as opposed to redevelopment. It made provision for the allocation of repair grants which previously had only been available to dwellings in HAAs and GIAs and made the procedures for applying for improvement grants much easier.

Second, there were the measures seemingly unmediated by previous policies. The most important was the statutory right to buy conferred on council house tenants and tenants of non-chargeable housing associations. Under this scheme tenants with three years' occupancy had the right to buy at 33 per cent of market value, with up to a 50-per-cent discount for tenants who had lived in a dwelling for twenty years or more. Local authorities were also obliged to provide a mortgage for those households seeking to buy their council house. The sale of council houses proved to be a hot issue. The Tory commitment to selling council houses had been an important element in their election victory and there was a broad appeal for the scheme. There was also heavy criticism from council house managers fearful of the loss of good-quality housing stock and from those who argued against a further residualization of the council house sector. Some local authorities refused to implement the scheme or at least did all they could to dissuade would-be buyers. The revolt was not restricted to Labour-controlled authorities as many Conservative ones, especially in rural areas, were fearful of the consequences. In the early months of the scheme the sales were disappointing, reflecting both local government resistance and high mortgage rates. In the early 1980s, perhaps the biggest single housing issue was the question of council house sales, with the central government committed to extending the right to buy and many local authorities fighting against the loss of local control.

The attempt to 'free' the private rented sector took a number of forms:

(1) A short-hold tenancy was introduced in which security of tenure was assured for more than one year but less than three years, after which time the landlord could repossess.
(2) Fair rents were to be registered every two years instead of three, thus allowing more frequent rent increases.
(3) Wider grounds for repossession were introduced and tenants no longer would be able to apply to rent tribunals for suspension of notice to quit, but the courts were given the discretion to postpone a possession order for up to three months.
(4) Controlled tenancies were to be changed to regulated tenancies.

The overall aim of the act was to stop the decline of the private sector by allowing higher rents, a shorter time period between rent increases and a reduction in the security of tenure afforded to tenants.

Expenditure cutbacks

Housing was a key feature of Conservative policies in the early years of the Thatcher government. Apart from the Housing Act, housing shouldered a large proportion of the public expenditure cuts. The Conservatives had come to power convinced that cutting public expenditure and particularly the PSBR was an essential prerequisite for stimulating the British economy. Too much expenditure led to too much taxation and hence, so their argument went, to the fettering of enterprise. Besides, a PSBR meant high interest rates which crippled British industry. Imbued with Friedmanite economics, Joseph's philosophy and Thatcher's determination, the government sought to swing the axe on public expenditure. It was not a random butchering. Welfare schemes came under heavy scrutiny but aid to industry was less savagely treated.

Cuts in housing expenditure were first announced in June 1979, nearly four months after Thatcher came to power. Expenditure on housing, which was then totalling £5000 million, was to be cut by 6 per cent. Then in early 1980 the government announced basic expenditure plans from 1981 to 1983/4 (the extent of the cutbacks proposed by the document can be seen in Figure 3.2). The size of the cuts was substantial. While the White Paper forecast a 4-per-cent reduction in public expenditure, 92 per cent of total savings were to come from the housing budget.

Local authority housing plans, as expressed in their housing investment programmes (HIPs) submissions, were heavily pruned. The process had already been occurring under the Labour government but, as Table 3.2 shows, the cutbacks in the HIPs block grants after the Conservatives took over was substantial. The cuts had immediate impact. The city of Bristol will illustrate the point. In the financial year 1979/80 the city of Bristol asked for £19.8 million under its HIPs, but spent £16.5 million. In the next year, 1980/1, the city asked for £19.3 million (at 1979/80 prices); it received only £11.8 million. To cope with these costs the council had to cut its existing house-building programme by 53 per cent, council house renovations by 32 per cent and improvement grant allocations by 36 per cent. No new house building was envisaged for the foreseeable future despite a rise in the waiting list from 3900 in 1977 to over 5000 in 1980.

It is difficult to estimate the overall impact of the cuts but a House of Commons Select Committee made some estimates in 1980. Their conclusions suggest that the cuts would lead to public house build-

Table 3.2 Housing investment programmes of English local authorities

	£ million		
Year	*Amount requested*	*Amount allocated*	*Allocation as % of requests*
1978/9	5173	3431	66
1979/80	4564	3167	69
1980/1	4532	2199	49

ing being reduced by half in 1984, a 16-per-cent rise in council house rents and a shortfall of 500,000 dwellings by 1983/4. Council house building was then stopped completely by the moratorium announced by Heseltine at the end of 1980.

The Conservative plans for expenditure reductions concentrated on council house building. They were based on the belief that the state was featherbedding well-off council tenants. The bulk of the cuts would be in the form of reduced subsidies for council housing, and the effect would be to increase rents by about £3 a week. Public expenditure cutbacks in the early days of the Thatcher government

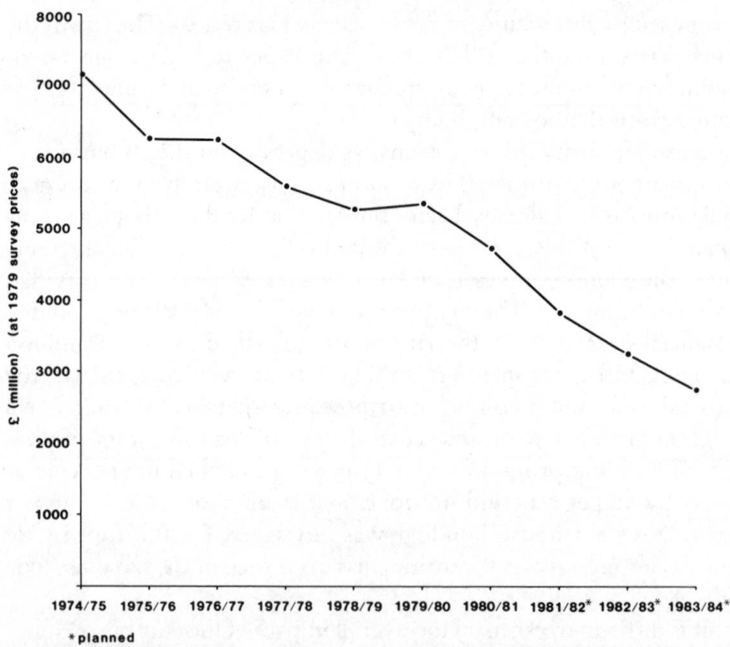

Figure 3.2 Public expenditure on housing (expenditure includes loan charges, council-house subsidies, improvement grants and new council-house building)

were basically housing expenditure cutbacks, which in turn were essentially cutbacks in council house building. The £1000 million subsidy to owner-occupiers in the form of tax relief was never seriously considered as a candidate for expenditure reduction. It was not simply a case of cutting public expenditure but of cutting 'undesirable' public expenditure.

At the beginning of the 1980s it seemed that another housing crisis was looming. Council house building was decimated by cutbacks, the take-up of improvement grants had fallen throughout the 1970s, and there was a slump in the private housing market caused by lack of effective demand and a general recession in the economy. Statistics were telling a sorry tale: housing starts had fallen to their lowest level for thirty years and the likely shortfall of 500,000 dwellings by 1984 was already making itself felt. The Tory-controlled London Boroughs Association, for example, had 100,000 new waiting-list applicants over the period from the end of 1978 to the end of 1980. In 1981 there were 1.2 million households on council house waiting lists, and estimates suggested that by 1985 this would rise to two million. Improvement activity had also fallen. As both public and private improvement activity was declining, the overall quality of the housing stock was deteriorating. In 1970, over 600,000 dwellings needed major repairs but by 1980 this figure had increased to over one million. Although public debate and political discourse were dominated by the economic crisis at the beginning of the 1980s, the sharp elbows of the housing question were beginning to force themselves on to the political agenda.

PART 2

THE HOUSING MARKET

4

LAND CONVERSION

The production of housing involves land. And land involves a variety of agents including landowners, developers and planners, all with differing and often conflicting interests. In this chapter I shall consider the nature of these agents in the form of their interaction. Before doing so it is important to consider the policy context which provides the background to this interaction.

THE POLICY CONTEXT

Early reports

Prior to 1947 there had been very little explicit land-use planning. The question of land and land taxes had exercised various minds, notably those of Henry George and John Stuart Mill, who formulated plans for betterment levies on private gains made from public actions. In Britain the government's main concern was with compensating landowners for government action. The landowning interests are well-represented in Westminster, and the sanctity of private property was enshrined as a fundamental political tenet. The first real change came with the Liberal government's Housing and Town Planning Act of 1909, which gave local authorities power to charge a levy on sites where values were raised by local authority planning schemes. The levy was to be 50 per cent of the increase in value. Property interests continued to be maintained by government actions, and in 1919 local authorities were made to pay compensation to landowners denied planning permission. The compensation was to be at full market value. So although there had been some incursions into private property rights before 1947, private interests were strongly guarded. The changes came in wartime. The radicalizing effects of the war were crystallized in a succession of reports which sought to lay the foundations for a new and better Britain.

The cornerstones of the planning system were two reports published in 1942: the Scott report on land use in rural areas and the Uthwatt report on compensation and betterment. The Scott report's main conclusion was that agricultural land should be protected. Underlying the Scott report was the wartime experience of reliance on home-grown produce, the inter-war surge of house building which took huge chunks of the countryside, and the belief firmly held by most English people that cities were in effect blemishes on the landscape. It was the duty of the present generation to preserve present scenes and the landscape of the past for the benefit of future generations. The Scott report underwrote the post-war planning-system goal of containing urban growth and protecting the countryside from unplanned urban sprawl. The Uthwatt report accepted the principle of national land-use planning. The main problem involved in such planning arose from compensation and betterment. The pre-war legislation had made it difficult for effective planning because of the heavy compensation costs demanded by developers who were refused permission. The committee considered that

> the problem arises from the existing legal position with regard to the use of land, which attempts largely to preserve, in a highly developed economy, the purely individualistic approach to land ownership. That . . . is no longer tenable in the present stage of development and it operates to prevent the proper and effective utilisation of limited land resources.

The report sought to overcome these problems by suggesting taking over land outside urban areas into public control when public purposes merited it or where a change of use was proposed. The report was basically asking for rights of development to be shifted from the private to the public domain. The report also tackled the problem of gain from public action. A landowner, for example, with a holding next to public land which had had money spent on improvement such as infrastructure investments, tended to gain in the process. The land increased in value and this betterment by public action benefited private individuals. The Uthwatt approach sought to change this by charging a betterment levy. It was thought difficult to identify the specific contribution of betterment by public action, and the report therefore recommended a 75-per-cent levy on all increases in annual site value.

The 1947 framework

The post-war planning system was enacted by the 1947 Town and Country Planning Act. This legislation carried out most of the wartime report recommendations and the Act effectively nationalized development rights. This involved buying out the development rights from landowners, and a sum of £300 million was set aside for the purpose. A final figure of £387 million was paid to them. With this new power the Act thus did three things:

(1) It required planning permission for any change of land use (there were agricultural exemptions).
(2) It meant that no compensation was payable to landowners where planning permission was refused.
(3) It charged a betterment levy of 100 per cent on the gain in value before development took place. The levy was charged by the central land board.

The Act also set up the machinery to implement these proposals. Plan-making and development control were given to the counties and county boroughs. These planning authorities were to draw up twenty-year development plans showing the present and future configuration of land uses. The plan was to be submitted to the Minister of Housing and Local Government for approval and reviewed every five years.

The 1947 framework has existed in broad outline throughout the post-war period, with the subsequent development and land-use planning revolving around the contentious issue of compensation/betterment. The 1947 Act collected a betterment levy and paid compensation at existing use value. This was the main bone of contention between the political parties. When the Conservatives came to power in 1951 they were committed to limiting the role of the state and they looked at the private sector to meet housing needs. The existing system as they saw it gave no incentive to landowners to sell their land. The betterment levy was dropped in 1953 and the role of the central land board was restricted to calculating and paying compensation. In 1959 compensation paid to landowners was estimated on the (higher) basis of full market value rather than existing use value.

The Tory changes made land development more profitable. The upsurge in population, producing a huge increase in housing demand, also made housing construction a profitable enterprise. The result in the early 1960s was a building boom and a bout of land speculation which caused a Tory reappraisal of their pure market-force ideology and strengthened Labour's commitment to changing the Tory framework.

The Labour government of 1964–70 made a second attempt to tax gains. The precarious government of 1964–6 had little room for new manoeuvre, but with the larger majority in 1966 it could tackle the problem. Under the 1967 Land Commission Act a betterment levy of 40 per cent was charged on development gain, and the Land Commission was given powers to acquire a bank of land which could be released to developers. The Commission would then sell relatively cheap land and be involved in indicative planning insofar as land would be released to fit in with the existing planning proposals. The scheme was a failure. There was confusion and friction between the local authorities and the Land Commission, the Commission had too small a budget and the betterment levy led to a land shortage, and house prices increased because landowners withheld land from development hoping for a change of government.

The incoming Tories scrapped the Land Commission in 1971 and repealed the betterment levy legislation. During the period in opposition the Tories had outlined a position of minimal intervention. As they saw it, there was no need for the state to be directly involved in taxing land gain. The gain could be taxed by the traditional methods of capital gains tax. The Tory response could not cope with the property boom and the huge surge in land and house prices in the early 1970s. Vast profits were made and there was widespread social concern about the level of private gain from public planning measures.

The political response of the Labour party was a third attempt at positive control and betterment levy. The 1974 White Paper produced by the Labour government was committed to the principle that all development land should be held by the community. The White Paper envisaged local authorities buying up parcels of development land at existing use value and then benefiting from any increase in value resulting from planning permission. In the transition before all development land was brought under public control, the White Paper also envisaged a land tax of 80 per cent charged on the difference between the disposal price and the current value. The powerful property lobby worked against the scheme, and between the promise of the White Paper and the reality of the 1975 Community Land Act numerous concessions were given to the property sector. The scheme was hamstrung from the start. Conservative local authorities were against it, and the initial level of funding was small and further reduced in December 1976. Expenditure was further reduced from £76.7 million in 1976/7 to only £38 million in 1977/8. The political uncertainty over the Act's future did little to aid its implementation.

The Tories scrapped the Community Land Act in 1980 and their Local Government, Planning and Land bill sought to change the emphasis of land use in favour of the private sector. Under legislation proposed, local authorities were directed to release more land for development, and public holdings in land were to be further reduced. The 1980 Act represented a shift in the balance of power away from public authorities and towards the private sector.

The consequences of the 1947 framework

It was difficult to assess the consequences of the 1947 system. What was caused by the system and what by other factors is one of those difficult questions for which there are no ready answers. However, we can identify a number of broad influences of the 1947 framework.

First, the planning system did contain urban growth and residential development. Planning controls were used through such schemes as Green Belts to restrict urban encroachment on agricultural land. This was achieved through building at higher densities, especially in the urban renewal schemes of the 1960s, and by concentrating new building outside the major cities in selected towns and villages in the least attractive rural areas. Containment was achieved, but at a price, and this price has been the increase in land costs. Containment has involved releasing only small amounts of land for development, and the scarcity value of land given planning permission and the costs of zoning land for development have led to the increase in land prices. This has been passed on to consumers by builders in the form of more expensive housing or in the form of higher-density, poorer-quality housing. At the upper end of the market, land costs were directly translated into house prices, but at the lower end increased land costs were absorbed by building housing of reduced size, space and quality. Discussing new housing, commentators on the post-war planning system have stated:

> many of the 850 square feet bungaloid development in exurbia could easily be confused with being the equivalent of late nineteenth-century industrial slums with their poor architecture, repetitive and unimaginative design and totally inadequate space standards for a consumer society about to enter the last quarter of the twentieth century
>
> (Hall *et al.*, 1973, vol. 2, p. 401)

Second, the operation of the planning system has led to a growing separation between home and workplace. The framework could not halt the growing suburbanization of the population, but the development plans discouraged the suburbanization of such facilities as offices, shops, hospitals and so on. Local authorities were not keen to lose the valuable tax base of commercial and industrial premises, and industrial location policies of central government were implemented at the interregional rather than the intraregional level. The planning system thus had a differential impact on houses and jobs which led to separation between centres of employment and residences.

Third, the operation of the planning system has had marked redistributional consequences. Rich rural residents have had their peace and tranquillity preserved and their house prices maintained by a planning system which has blocked new developments in prime areas of the shire counties; they have gained from containment. Lower-income housebuyers in contrast have had the worst deal. They have been segregated in selected sites often far from work, and given poor-quality, high-density housing because of the large cost of land. These lower-income households have paid the price of containment.

Fourth, the planning system has been a system of negative controls. The local authority planning departments indicate where development can take place but they do not generate such development. The abuse of planners in the pseudo-radical literature is misplaced. It criticizes the planners as active agents. But planning in Britain is more of a context than an agenda for action; it is a system of negative controls within which private market forces operate. The style and pace of residential development has been shaped more by the agents in the private sector than by the wishes of planners. This lack of positive action by the planning system is most sharply brought to light when market forces are at their strongest. Such a time was the property boom of the early 1970s, when investment flowed into the property sector. The effect was felt in most cities in a commercial office-building boom. In some cases local politicians were eager to see such developments. Many local authorities were eager to attract such job-creating, rate-paying establishments. In other areas loose alliances of community groups and councillors fought against such developments. Planning tended to play only a minimal role in the whole process. What tended to happen was that planning did not stop the process, rather it placed conditions on the character of the development. What did emerge was a series of arrangements whereby applications for planning permission for property developers were subject to conditions which have subsequently been termed planning gains; local authorities asked developers to make contributions to the provision of roads, public open spaces, recreational facilities, land for schools, etc. The extent of the planning gain was shaped by the attractiveness of the site in question, the resources of the planning authorities, the extent of local political commitment and the ability of the developer to get less onerous terms elsewhere. In general, however, the gains in the development process went to developers, and the costs were paid by the local residents.

In the control of residential development the planning system has been much more successful. Throughout the 1950s and early 1960s all new private residential developments in the suburban areas were subject to strong planning controls. County planners were successful in guiding development to the less attractive areas, organizing development in large units and imposing comprehensive plans for estate design and layout. A working relationship was established in local areas between planners and developers, each knowing the desires and constraints of the other. This cosy relationship was severely dented in the 1960s and 1970s as population grew and land release could not keep pace with demand. In the pressure points of the Midlands and south east there was greater lobbying for more land to be released, and the number of appeals to the Minister by developers against refusals of planning permission increased. In designated areas of growth, such as the Reading region, central government ordered more land to be released than initially allowed in the development and structure plans. Here, the power of local planners was curtailed while the system struggled to control and guide population growth.

LANDOWNERS

Landowners have an important role to play in the production of housing because they control the scarcest of resources: the landowners control the overall supply of building land. In simple terms the landowners release land for development if the proceeds from the sale are greater than opportunity costs. There are, however, other considerations; it is necessary to consider the structure of the landownership. Massey and Catalano (1978) identified three types of landownership in Britain. The biggest single group, which they term *former landed property*, include the Church, the Crown Estates, the landed aristocracy and the landed gentry. This group owns almost 36 per cent of the acreage of Great Britain. Like all landowning groups in a capitalist society, it conducts its operations on the basis of maintaining profitability. However, for this group other considerations are important. For the landed aristocracy, which owns almost 31 per cent of all land in Great Britain, land is not simply a commodity to be sold to developers to realize higher profits. In the rural landholdings in particular, economic calculations are mediated by social and historical ties. Particular plots of land are considered as heirlooms and as a binding agent of wider social relations and connections. In the urban holdings of the very large estates the emphasis is on the maximizing of returns, and in many cases the proceeds and dealing in urban landholdings have subsidized the agricultural operations. For the smaller gentry, cross-subsidization from other more profitable holdings is difficult. In these cases, when times are hard, land is sold off for development but, again, the psychological costs of selling are very high. Landholdings also constitute an important part of the Church of England's wealth. The Church owns residential and commercial property as well as agricultural land. To finance the highly profitable development of its urban holdings the Church has sought to sell off much of its other land. This is because the Church cannot work on borrowed money: further developments can only come from the sale of existing assets. Throughout the post-war period the Church has sold much of its land to developers and local authorities. For the Crown Estates, basically the land area owned by the royal family, land rents are a major source of revenue. Rents from the holdings in London alone accounted for 75 per cent of the income generated in 1974–5 for the Crown Estates. The Estates have no liabilities and no shareholders. This lack of financial pressure means that there is less need to sell off land for more profitable development. The Estates in London have been developed at a relatively slow pace and there has been very little sale of agricultural land for residential development.

The second category identified by Massey and Catalano is termed *industrial land ownership*. For this group land is an essential element in the operation. The owner-occupier farmers own almost 35 per cent of British land, and throughout the century this percentage has increased as the great landed estates have sold off much of their landholdings. In the post-war period the size of the owner-occupied farms has steadily increased, as farms of over 500 acres now constitute over 50 per cent of Britain's agricultural acreage. It is this group which is of crucial importance in the land conversion process because the owner-occupier farmers tend to predominate around the cities and towns where future residential developments will take place. The owner-occupier farmers lie midway between the aristocrats, who have long ties with particular plots of land, and the property companies, who have land simply as a commodity to be bought and sold. For the owner-occupier farmers land is both a means to an end, an essential prerequisite for production, and of wider significance. The decision to sell will thus depend on a range of factors including short-term financial considerations and longer-term social ones. The sale of land in the owner-occupied farming sector frequently occurs on a change of ownership. Often the death of a farmer leaves the heir with an opportunity to make more money by selling the land. Farmers in periurban areas may be able to sell off parts of their holdings; they will thus be able to make short-term profits whilst still retaining their agricultural interest.

Table 4.1 Landowning types in Britain

Category	*Predominant land use*
Former landed property	
Church	Urban, agricultural
Landed aristocracy	Urban, agricultural, sporting estates
Landed gentry	Agricultural
Crown Estates	Urban, agricultural
Industrial landownership	
Owner–occupier farmers	Agricultural
Manufacturing industry	Industrial
Construction companies	Residential
Financial landownership	
Financial institutions	Urban, agricultural
Property companies	Urban, industrial

Note: Urban refers to both residential, shops and commercial office properties

The third category of ownership they term *financial land ownership*. It includes finance institutions such as insurance companies, pension funds and banks, and property companies. The financial institutions have grown enormously in the post-war period. Rising real incomes have meant that the pool of savings has been growing in size. Moreover, the growth of pension schemes, contributory and non-contributory, have channelled much of these savings into pension funds and insurance schemes. Over the period 1961–73 the extent of insurance companies' holdings increased from £675 million to £2932 million. These institutions seek profitable investment, but the need for long-term security outweighs the need for short-term liquidity. Because they do not pay out large parts of their assets in short periods, they do not need to invest in areas where they can quickly get their money back. They can thus afford long-term investments. As the funds of these institutions have grown and inflation has increased, many of the funds have been invested in land

and property to provide a long-term asset which is all but inflation-proof. The financial institutions now want key city-centre sites where commercial redevelopment has taken or can take place; and, increasingly, agricultural land. In 1975 the pension fund of the Post Office bought nearly £700,000 of agricultural land alone. Urban landholdings furnish higher rates of return than agricultural holdings, but the latter provide a long-term investment without the uncertainty common to commercial development projects. The financial institutions invested in land and property increasingly throughout the 1970s, since this provided high and secure rates of return. The level of investment reached a peak in the early 1970s but declined markedly, reflecting the decline in relative yields. The property companies differ from the financial institutions insofar as they specialize in land and property: over 90 per cent of their assets are in this sector. The property companies also differ from financial institutions in that the short- to medium-term criterion of maximum returns for investment predominates. The companies are less concerned than the institutions with long-term appreciating assets.

Each of the three groups of landowners thus have a differing mix of secondary considerations in their land operations, and even within each of the groups different agents have differing temporal perspectives. The most significant feature of the post-war period has been the development of property companies, especially over the period 1950–74, and the growth of financial institutions in land dealings. The institutions have been particularly important in buying up prime city-centre sites, absorbing property companies and more recently in buying agricultural land. Another important development has been the land-buying behaviour of the large construction companies. The creation of land banks by the large builders is a topic which will be discussed in the next chapter.

RESIDENTIAL DEVELOPMENT IN THE PRIVATE SECTOR

The pattern of landownership determines the extent and timing of land conversion. All landowners are primarily concerned to increase their yield; however, some, especially in the former landed category, have strong psychological and social barriers against selling particular plots while others, the financial landowners, are particularly sensitive to even small changes in relative yield. If a decision is made to sell, then the landowner is involved in bargaining with the developers and builders. The terms of the bargain depend on the location of the plot of land. There is no single market in land.

Through the operation of planning permissions the planning system restricts the supply of land for development. By granting planning permission in some areas rather than others the planning system enhances the value of particular plots of land. The landowners of these plots thus have a stronger bargaining position; they not only own the scarce resource of land but the even scarcer resource of land zoned for development, and a higher price can be charged for the latter. A rough threefold distinction can be drawn for non-urban land:

(a) Land which has been granted outline or detailed planning permission for residential development.
(b) Land which has the possibility of obtaining planning permission for residential development.
(c) Land which has no possibility of obtaining planning permission for residential development.

Land type (a) is the most expensive because of its scarce nature. In the case of (b), land is cheaper, but for the developer there is more of a risk. The prospective gain in buying land cheaply and then developing it has to be outweighed by the costs of servicing the land-purchase loan with the associated delays and possible refusal of planning permission. It is only the larger developers and builders who can afford this gamble.

The price for land which the developer can pay is generally determined by two methods: the *residual method* and the *selling rate method*. In the residual method the developer calculates from an estimate of the likely number of houses that can be built on a particular plot, the total selling price of all the houses (A) (see Table 4.2). From this sum the developer subtracts the building costs (B), a profit element (C), say 15 per cent, and the difference (A – (B + C)) is what the developer can bid for the land. In the residual method it would appear that increases in land prices are in fact caused by house price increases. In the residual method it is the effective demand for housing which pulls up land prices.

For the larger developers, especially those dealing in the mass market, profits on individual dwellings are low. The emphasis is on rapid sale and the aim is to maximize capital turnover. For these

Table 4.2 The residual method of land pricing

A: 10 houses selling at £15,000 each	=	£150,000
B: Total building costs, of £10,000 each house	=	£100,000
C: Profit	=	£22,500
∴ Land bid (A – B + C)	=	£27,500

developers the selling rate approach is used in calculating land prices. Their concern is rather with the speed of sale than with estimating selling prices. The greater the speed of sale, the higher the land bid. For example, if the houses shown in Table 4.2 can be sold within ten weeks, then more money can be paid for the land than if the total selling time was twenty weeks. As with the residual method, this method seems to suggest that land prices are pulled up by demand for houses. In the period 1955–62 this occurred, but throughout the 1960s and especially in the early 1970s land costs increased more than house prices (see Figure 4.1), and the land cost component constituted an increasing proportion of house prices: for a typical house in West London, for example, the land cost in 1960 constituted 12 per cent of the final selling price but by 1970 this proportion had increased to 50 per cent. What was happening in these periods was that demand was outpacing supply. This was due to rising real incomes and the building societies fuelling effective demand. In these circumstances, if we use the figures in Table 4.2 as an example, the land-

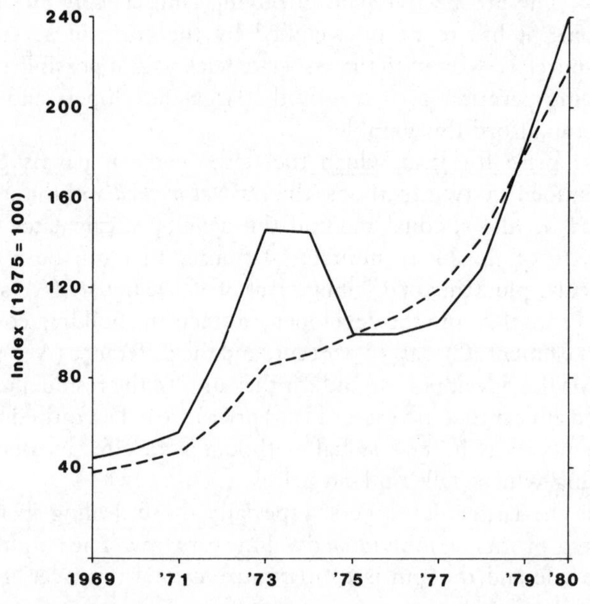

Figure 4.1 Housing and land prices

owners of a plot with planning permission would ask for more than £27,500. Since new houses were scarce a number of things could happen:

(1) The total selling price could be increased from £15,000 to, say, £17,500, and the extra £2500 per house could be directed to the landowner.
(2) A developer could accept a lower profit level, reducing from, say, £22,500 to £15,000. The larger builders would be able to accept this temporary reduction in profit in order to sustain their operations. The smaller builders would be hard-pressed.
(3) The diversion of more income to the landowner could be met by the developer by reducing construction costs and increasing plot densities, perhaps by squeezing an extra house on to the site in order to cover some of these increased land costs.

During boom periods, landowners with land having planning permission can use their monopoly power to increase profits made on land sales. The net result is an increase in house prices and/or a reduction in the quality of new housing.

The extent of land conversion

The principal aim of the post-war planning system has been to preserve and maintain agricultural land. The relative success of the policy has been the subject of intense debate and hinges on the relative assessment of the extent of conversion. The optimists, exemplified in the work of Robin Best (1976, 1977), argue that the pessimists exaggerate the extent of urban encroachment. The extent of land use conversion has remained steady in the post-war period at about 16,000 hectares per year or approximately 6000 average-sized football pitches per year. This figure is well below the 25,000 hectares converted each year during the inter-war building boom (see Figure 4.2). Half of this encroachment is taken up by housing. The optimists also argue that this conversion has not led to substantial loss of agricultural production, because developments and productivity have far outweighed loss of land and, besides, the most fertile areas of Britain, the rich lands of East Anglia in particular, have been less affected than the rest of the country by land use conversion. Estimates by Best suggest that if present trends continue, even by the turn of the century only 14 per cent of land in England and Wales will be urban. The term 'urban' is used by Best to cover built-up land with its associated urban space (see Table 4.3).

The pessimists, exemplified by the work of Alice Coleman (1976), suggest that these aggregate figures conceal substantial levels

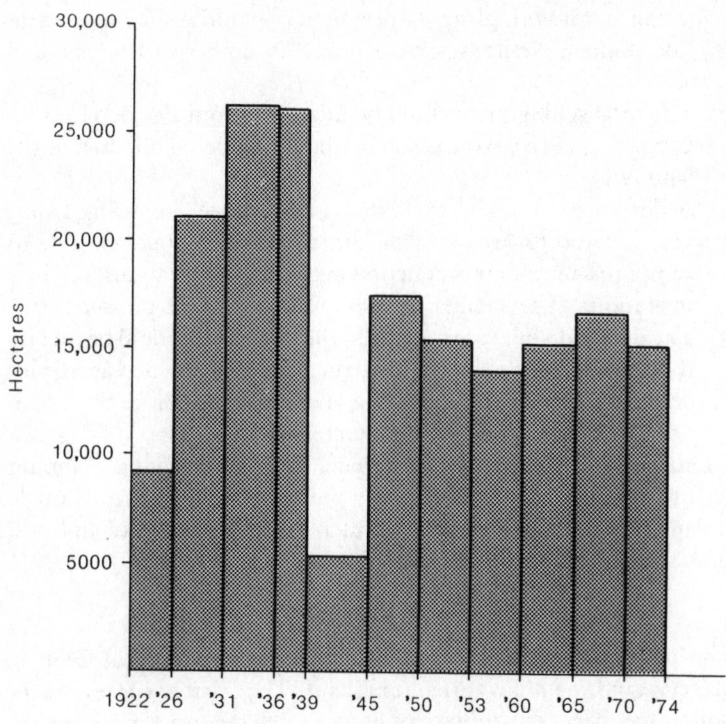

Figure 4.2 Conversion of agricultural land into urban land use

of encroachment. Coleman's work in Berkshire, for example, has shown how the level of waste land has grown substantially over a ten-year period (see Table 4.4). She suggests that planning has done little to halt the spread of low-density urban spaces, such as areas

Table 4.3 Population and land use in England and Wales

	Population (millions)	*% urban land use*
1939	41.5	8.0
1951	43.8	8.9
1961	46.1	9.9
1971	48.6	11.0
2001	54.9	14.1

Table 4.4 Land-use changes in the Thames estuary (km²)

Land-use type	*1962*	*1972*	*Change 1962–72*
Residential	396.5	415.0	+18.5
Improved farmland	138.5	98.0	−40.5
Waste land	33.0	63.5	+30.5

around new flatted factories, extensive fringe areas beside roads, etc., all of which constitute semi-public waste land.

To some extent the argument is one of scale. Best's work shows that at the national level, rates of land conversion do not seem to threaten agricultural production. Coleman's work, however, was based on an area of growth. Here the pressures of residential development may be causing local problems. A thumbnail sketch of the post-war scene would show a steady rate of residential development, land conversion averaging 16,000 hectares per year with a national average of 0.1 per cent of land converted from agricultural to urban land each year. In the growth areas stretching from Liverpool and Manchester through Birmingham to London and the south-east, the rate of conversion is higher – almost 0.3 per cent. The extent of conversion has had an obvious visual impact on the landscape, but the fears of land conversion debilitating British agriculture have been swept aside by dramatic bursts of productivity in the agricultural sector and by the lack of residential development in the most productive farmland areas of eastern England.

The framers of the 1947 Act thought that agricultural land was worth preserving. The main danger they saw was from urban land uses and especially from residential development. Planning controls were introduced to slow down and modify the process of conversion. For the farmers there were very few planning controls. But perhaps the most important change in agricultural land use has not been from outside pressures but from within the agricultural sector. The post-war years have seen the rise of agriculture as big business. Agriculture is an industry with profit-maximization as its criterion and land as its raw material. To improve profits farmers have increased levels of mechanization and adopted very intensive methods of livestock rearing and crop production. These changes have affected the landscape as field sizes have been increased by the removal of trees, hedgerows and walls; new farm buildings have been built; moorland areas have been cleared of bracken and heather, and ugly regimented conifers have been planted. The result has been a dramatic change in the landscape, a change which traditional land-use planning has not been able to control. As one of the more committed commentators on this process has noted,

> the English countryside has been turned into a vast, featureless expanse of prairie. Its surface is given over either to cereal growing or to grass monoculture fuelling intensive stock clearing. This new English landscape can offer little delight to the human eye or ear. It cannot sustain our traditional wild flowers, birds and animals. But each year it takes over

hundreds more square miles of England. Already much of the east of the country looks disappointingly familiar to tourists from the American Mid-west and unless something is done to curb agricultural intensification, virtually the whole of the countryside will be no more than a food factory by the early part of the next century. (Shoard, 1980; p. 10)

Here speaks the voice of commitment, but with an argument which is basically sound. The agricultural lobby is one of the most successful pressure groups in modern British politics. The level of subsidization is high (Shoard estimates that on average each farmer receives £8500 per annum subsidy), and the controls on operations are few. The receipt of public money should be associated with the shouldering of public responsibility.

The land-availability debate

Land-use planning involves the release of land for residential development. For planners, this release is associated with short-, medium- and long-term plans for the location and form of settlement patterns. For the builders, land is an essential element and the release of land is a vital determinant of their operations. We have already seen that throughout the 1950s land prices rose steadily, but between 1962 and 1974 land prices increased dramatically. The house builders responded by asking for more land to be released – the problem as they saw it was that the planners were not releasing enough land; moreover, getting planning permission was a long, tortuous business. The builders blamed the planners and the planning system for the rapid increase in land prices and house prices.

In the 1970s the house builders acting through their representatives called for more land to be released. The demand was heeded because a Tory government came to power in 1970 which was committed to stripping away many of the land-use controls. Circulars from the Conservative central government called on local authorities to make sure that enough land was available for house building, a number of land-availability studies were commissioned and a report was commissioned in 1973 to see if the planning system was meeting current needs, i.e. the needs of the builders.

The land-availability studies gave some interesting findings. The finding of the study in the south-east, which reported in 1975, suggested that land availability was not the single most important determinant of residential development. The crucial factor was found to be the availability of building society mortgages which allowed households to buy the houses. A study of land availability in the West Midlands during the period 1968–73 also suggested that while the planners might not have released enough land, delays were also caused by the inability of the construction industry to adjust to boom conditions; manpower and material shortages contributed to delay. This study also argued that additional land released in the short term made little contribution in a short-lived boom because of the two-year time-lag to developers' responses; houses would be constructed in the boom but available for sale in the slump. The findings of these studies did not merge with the interests of the builders and so the land-availability debate continued. The House Builders' Federation, in particular, lobbied central and local government into releasing more land, and another government circular appeared in 1978 which called on local authorities to hold discussions with private house builders about their land requirements. To show how this could be put into practice, the House Builders' Federation in association with the Department of the Environment conducted a survey of land availability in Manchester for the period 1978–80. This study, unlike the previous ones, concentrated on the needs of the house-building industry, not unusual given the fact that the House Builders' Federation was involved. For the first time the needs of developers were met insofar as:

(1) The study excluded land which had been granted planning permission but for which there would be marketing problems.
(2) A degree of slack in land availability was included.
(3) The developers' request for land available for each of three broad types of up-market, middle- and down-market housing was met.

The hand of the house-building lobby was further strengthened by the Tory government of 1979. This government was committed to less planning and to the freeing of private enterprise, and with its strong links with the Conservative party private house building was a favourite enterprise. A government circular asked local authorities to cooperate with house builders in making site assessments of land available, in order to ensure a five-year supply of private house-building land in line with structure and local plan policies. From the time of the circular, given to local authorities in 1980, housing land-availability studies have been conducted with planning authorities and the House Builders' Federation very much on the lines of the Manchester study; this ensured that the needs for the private house builders were being met. The needs of the private house builders were strengthened by the 1980 Local Government, Planning and Land Act, which charged local authorities to make a register of land owned by them and nationalized industries available at council offices, and called upon both central and local government to dispose of more land.

Behind the land-availability debate lies a clash of interest. The planning system is geared to containing urban growth and directing residential development. The house builders, on the other hand, want a ready supply of cheap land with little interference in their activities. Their demands are best articulated in a discussion paper prepared by a working party of the House Builders' Federation (1979). This paper calls for more land to be released for residential development, less interference in their building and design proposals, and the continuation of the policy under which facilities such as water and sewage have been paid for out of local taxes rather than by the builders. To cloak their interests in the guise of arguments about general benefits to the community is to mislead. Their case is perhaps strong enough not to need fake support. The builders have been successful in getting land-release policies which more closely suit their needs. The house builders have a very well-organized pressure group with many friends in central and local government, and the 1970s have seen a steady growth in the appreciation of developers' land-availability needs. For the builder-developers this is growing realism; for the more radical planner it signifies a loss of planning control; and by some commentators it has been seen as the distortion of the planning system for the benefit of the builders at the cost of the community.

5

THE CONSTRUCTION OF HOUSING

THE HOUSE-BUILDING INDUSTRY

It is difficult to obtain accurate information on the house-building industry. Statistics are only available for the construction industry as a whole. This in part reflects the ability of construction companies to diversify their operations across the range of activities from civil engineering projects to house building to repair and improvement. The government statistics provide a rough fourfold division between the value of output by housing subdivided into public and private, other new work subdivided by public and private, repair and maintenance, and work done by officers employed by public authorities. Figure 5.1 shows the change in distribution of output by these different sectors from 1955 onwards: new house building constituted between 20 and 30 per cent of output by value over the years 1955–80; repair and maintenance of housing another 10 to 20 per cent. Total housing activity thus accounts for between 30 and 50 per cent of all construction activity. Figure 5.1 also shows the change in distribution of the different sectors. The change reflects macroeconomic policy, as successive governments have used the construction sector to regulate the economy in Keynesian fashion. More recently, building programmes have been cut back as part of a strategy to reduce public expenditure. The construction sector has been particularly affected by government policies since between 28 and 40 per cent of total output (at current prices) is in the public sector programmes.

The general state of the economy also influences the construction sector. When business confidence is high and credit is easy, residential and non-residential construction is increased as in the early 1960s and early 1970s. Alternatively, when interest rates are high and credit is difficult to obtain, construction activity tails off. Since 1976

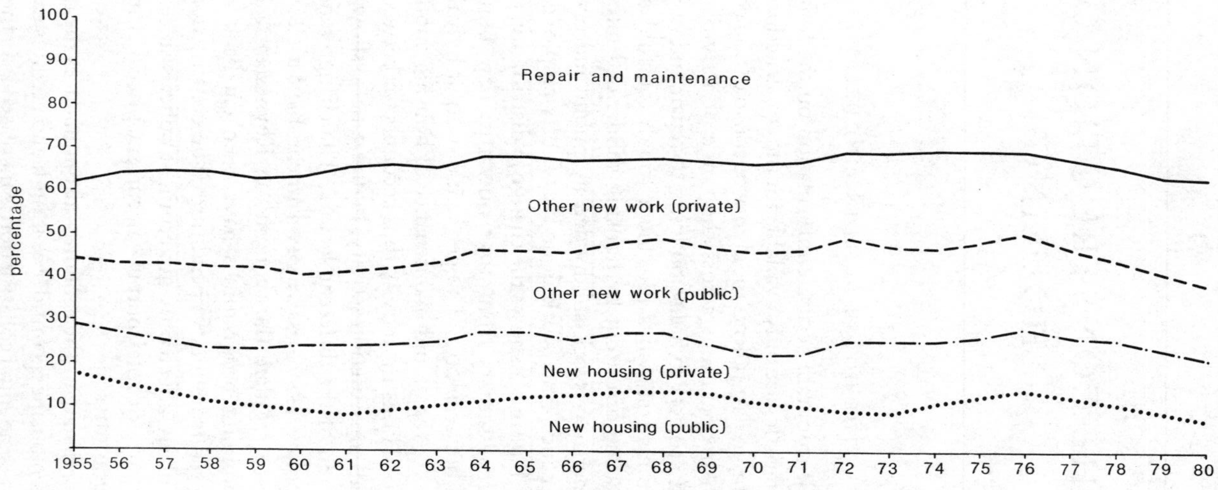

Figure 5.1 Value of construction output by sector

both the public and private new housing sectors and other work categories have declined.

The fluctuating demand has created a number of problems for the construction industry. When demand is low, skilled workers leave and many companies go out of business. When demand picks up there is often a shortage of skilled personnel and a shortage of materials. Because of these rapid fluctuations in the post-war years there is a lower than average investment in plant and machinery (as companies do not want to buy expensive plant which may lie idle), discouragement of technical development and a low level of training for the work force. All these characteristics are heightened by the contract system, which is the arrangement whereby a company tenders for a one-off job. The contract system exacerbates the tendency for low technical development and low productivity as companies have no guarantee of winning the contract, the future of the workload is difficult to plan and the emphasis is on maximizing the profit on each single contract. The net result is to make the construction industry one of the least productive industries and ultimately to make housing more expensive.

A great deal has now been written about the low productivity of the construction industry. The low productivity reflects a number of factors:

(1) Fluctuating demand which leads to lack of investment in plant and machinery;
(2) The contract system;
(3) Separation of design and construction: architects design buildings but builders construct them, and there is very little pooled experience between architects, structural engineers and builders, while the building represents the wishes of the client often without reference to cheaper methods of construction;
(4) The form of calculation in the contract system: pricing is done for finished work and, given the large number of items, there is considerable scope for huge variations in the quoted price; the form of pricing does little for effective cost control.

Factor (1) affects both private and public house building, while factors (2), (3) and (4) mainly apply to local authority housing.

Because of the fluctuating demand there is a great deal of sub-contracting in the construction industry and a lack of investment. This allows opportunity for small firms that rely on sub-contracting and need little by the way of large capital investment to start up. This is reflected in the structure of the construction industry: in 1978 it was composed of no less than 91,520 firms. The number has varied over the years but, unlike in other industrial sectors, there has been no marked long-term decline in the number of firms. In 1935, for example, there were 76,112 building firms; in 1954 there were 88,535. Activity is unevenly distributed and Table 5.1 shows the picture for 1978. There are a large number of small firms, but most of the work is done by the medium-sized and large companies that employ most of the building workers. The overall structure has changed little in the post-war years, and this reflects the lack of technical innovation and the fluctuating demand which have not led to the concentration of production in a small number of very large industries that has been a feature of other sectors of industry. There is a very important role in the construction industry for small firms either involved in their own contracts or sub-contracting for the main firms. The small firms require little capital and despite the high bankruptcy rate they continue to be numerically important.

Table 5.1 The structure of the construction industry

Size of firms (number of operatives)	*Number of firms (%)*	*% of numbers employed*	*% of output*
0–1	28,551 (31.2)	2.6	1.7
2–24	56,881 (62.2)	31.2	25.5
25–114	5032 (5.5)	21.8	22.1
115–599	957 (1.0)	26.5	23.7
+600	169 (0.1)	23.9	26.9
Total	91,520 (100.0)	100.0	100.0

THE BUILDER-DEVELOPER: HOUSE BUILDING IN THE PRIVATE SECTOR

In the construction of non-residential property (offices, shops, banks and factories) a distinction can often be made between the construction company which builds the premises and the development company which assembles land, hires the builder and sells or leases the property. In the case of house building this distinction is less easy to make. House builders invariably assemble land and sell off the houses. I will thus use the term builder-developer with reference to the construction firm in the house-building industry. Although all builder-developers are involved in the same process of land assembly, production and sale of housing, there are differences between them. These differences refer to the opportunities conferred and the constraints imposed on the builder-developer with differing resources and investment strategy. The differences can be conveniently described with respect to the size of the firms, and the private house-building industry can be subdivided into three major size types.

Small builders

The small-scale builders are very important in the private house-building sector. Over 40 per cent of the value of work done in private house building in 1978 was done by builder-developers employing less than twenty-four operatives (see Figure 5.2). The small builder-developers require little capital, borrowing most of their money. They cannot afford land speculation and thus they mainly deal in small sites with planning permission. They cannot afford to speculate on land without planning permission or afford the delay costs of obtaining such permission. Since the greatest profits are made on larger houses, it does not cost much more to build rooms with an extra 15-square-foot floor space, but the selling price and the profit are much higher, the small-scale builder-developers tend to concentrate on the upper end of the housing

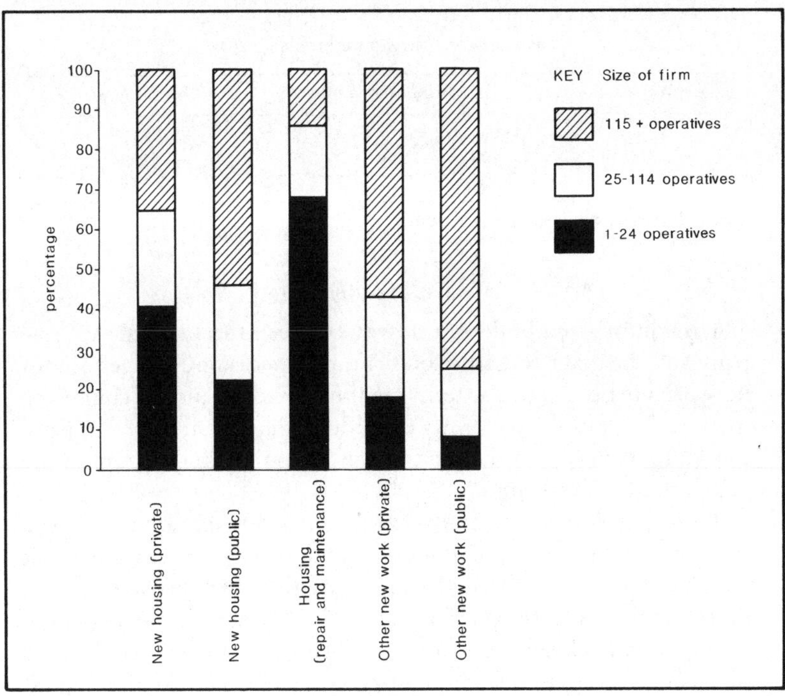

Figure 5.2 Sector output by size of firm

market. A typical small-scale builder-developer constructs higher-quality detached housing on small in-fill sites in favoured residential areas, and tends to use labour-intensive rather than capital-intensive methods. The two most important considerations are (a) the price and availability of land, and (b) the effective demand for the houses.

(a) The builder will tend to buy a small plot of land, assemble the materials and manpower and seek to build as quickly as possible. The houses will very often be sold before they are complete. The sale will be direct to the public and only sometimes through an estate agent.

(b) The small builder is dependent on external sources of finance. The extent of self-financing is small and thus changes in credit facilities and mortgage opportunities are crucially important.

The profitability of the small-scale builder-developer is determined by the price and availability of land on the one hand and by effective demand on the other. The builder-developer needs ample supplies of relatively cheap land and to be sure of selling the houses as quickly as possible since credit is difficult to maintain over the long term. When credit lines are over-extended, bankruptcies occur.

Table 5.2 Private house building, 1974

Average number of houses started each year	*No. of firms*
1–20	7037
21–200	1363
+200	143

Source: National Housebuilding Council

Medium-sized builders

The medium-sized builder, midway between the small-scale company and the giant construction firm, produces about 26 per cent of new private housing. The term medium-sized should, of course, be used with caution, covering as it does the expanding company thrusting its way into the big time and also the likely victim of the next round of bankruptcy.

The essence of the medium-sized company is that it builds more than twenty houses, its activities are mainly local or regional and it has had experience of growth. This growth, which involves capital investment, can be the platform either for further sustained growth or for extended lines of credit which throttle the firm when demand drags and prices rise. Medium-sized companies, unlike the biggest companies, need to grow and do not have internal sources of finance;

they have to rely on external financing, and their reliance on credit, especially during boom periods when they respond to increases in effective demand, makes them susceptible to subsequent slump. They cannot move easily into other branches of production and because they are highly geared (i.e. they have a high proportion of external financing) they are vulnerable to take-over by other firms.

The medium-sized companies need a steady supply of land. On average two years' supply is required to maintain steady production and regular work. The companies obtain land through a number of methods: contacting estate agents and surveyors; personal contact with local solicitors and banks to deal with landowners; contact with area planning officers; by auction; by buying land from other companies. The larger the company, the greater the ability to buy land without planning permission. The smaller the company, the less ability to finance land speculation.

Like the small builder the medium-sized builder is affected by the extent of effective demand and the availability and price of land. During the 1950s and early 1960s land-price increases matched the general trend, as demand was limited though secure. In the latter half of the 1960s as land became scarce, land prices increased and demand fell. The medium-sized developers responded in two ways. First, some of them, like the small builders, switched their attention to the more expensive up-market housing where land price increases could be readily absorbed; this option was not open to the larger builder-developers who relied on turnover of a larger number of houses. Those with relatively big sites found it difficult to market the more expensive housing. In this case the builder-developers responded by increasing densities and reducing the quality of housing. The serried ranks of poorly finished town-houses and semi-detached dwellings which were built after 1965 were the nadir of post-war speculative house building. Builders did little landscaping work on the estates, while the standard of internal design was poor, storage space was limited and the finish not up to high standards. More recently, the relative price of land has fallen, but effective demand has also fallen as the slump in the economy and the difficulty of obtaining a mortgage has made it difficult for people to buy houses. The medium-sized companies in the less prosperous regions are finding it particularly difficult.

The large builder

The large-scale builders – those building more than 200 houses a year and employing more than 100 people – built about 35 per cent of new private housing in 1978. The proportions change. The larger-scale builders have the ability to shift funds within the different sectors of construction in response to relative rates of return. During the commercial property boom of the early 1970s, for example, the large construction companies invested heavily in the office-building boom. The big companies have also turned their attention to overseas and in the wake of OPEC price rises and the gush of oil money they have competed for work in the Middle East (see Table 5.3). This is a volatile market; after the boom of the early 1970s there was a slowing down of growth, and an absolute decline after 1978.

Table 5.3 British construction work overseas

	Value of contracts obtained (£ million at current prices)			
	1968/9	*1974/5*	*1977/8*	*1978/9*
All countries	232	1084	1645	1299
Middle East	37	519	793	619

The main characteristics of the big companies are their access to sources of finance and their institutional connections. The big builder-developers have internal reserves which can finance their activities; they are not so 'geared' as the small and medium-sized companies. The public companies can also tap credit sources from the stock market and other institutions. But in order to continue to attract investment the big builder-developers have to present a picture of growth and dynamism. Further growth is dependent on more investment, and levels of investment are determined by growth records and growth potential. The big builders are in the mass market where there is a rapid turnover of capital and relatively high rates of growth. In the mass market, although there are low profits on individual houses, this is compensated by the large volume of sales.

The big builders have links with other institutions. In the early post-war years construction companies in general kept their activities within the sphere of construction, but with the commercial property booms of the late 1950s, late 1960s and early 1970s very large companies became involved in property development, not only constructing premises but buying and selling the land and either selling or leasing the premises. The very large companies are now huge enterprises with a sprawling presence across the activities of house building, construction, property development, land and property dealings.

The big builder-developers concentrate on the mass market in the private house-building sector, building low- to medium-priced housing. They tend to assemble large tracts of land, since it is more profitable to build 2000 houses on one site than 100 houses on twenty different sites. Their land requirements are heavy but they have the necessary finance to buy and hold large tracts of land both with and without planning permission. The big companies have sought to build up their stocks of land in land banks. These banks ensure their continuing operation. A study of twenty-four house builders in the early 1970s show that between them they held an 18,400-acre land bank comprising over 170,000 housing plots.

As land prices increased dramatically in the late 1960s and early 1970s the large builder-developers with land banks held a steadily increasing asset. The big builder-developers now span the two land-owning categories of industrial land ownership and financial landownership. They are in the former insofar as they use land as an element in their production process. They are in the latter insofar as the land holdings can provide speculative gains. The larger the company, the larger the land bank and the greater the possibility of speculation. The big builder-developers with land banks have gained when land prices have increased. The extent of the gain is limited by two things. First, there are limits to house price increases and/or reductions in housing quality. Thus there is a limit to the extent that land prices can be passed on to the housing consumer, especially in the mass market. Second, the gain on land without planning permission is only realized if planning permission can be obtained. This is an important reason for the lobbying of local planners and councils by builder-developers to get more land released for residential development. Particular pressure is exerted through appeals on unsuccessful planning decisions, while general pressure has been exerted through the House Builders' Federation and other institutional bodies lobbying central government and informing public opinion.

There is a tension within the house-building industry between the land speculators and those with long-term commitments to house building. Some builder-developers may be able to time their land purchases conveniently, buying cheap and selling their houses when land is much more expensive, but this is not true of all developers. Some will have to buy land when it is very expensive, and, if they are in the mass market, there are limits upon the extent to which they can pass these increases on to the final selling price of the houses. Land price increases and associated land speculation benefit some builder-developers but not all.

The large builder-developers need to sell their houses quickly. Empty houses are idle capital. The sale of houses is crucially dependent on mortgage facilities; when building society mortgages are readily available, people buy houses, and builder-developers realize their profits. When mortgages are much more difficult to obtain, effective demand falls and profits are not realized. The big builder-developers can avoid the worst excesses of a fall in demand through their preferential arrangements with building societies; many large developers have arrangements with building societies in which the societies keep a proportion of their mortgage allocation to lend to households purchasing the builder-developers' new housing. If the mortgage squeeze is not too hard then the builder-developer will still have customers (the policy of the building societies to grant mortgages for the purchase of new housing aids the builder-developers). When the squeeze is hard, as in 1974 for example, effective demand falls and builder-developers have unsold houses on their hands and thus build less housing; but when credit again becomes available builder-developers cannot react sufficiently quickly, since the response time of house production is approximately two years. After a mortgage famine, in the first eighteen months of a mortgage boom, there tend to be too many mortgages chasing too few houses – the classic recipe for a house price spiral. Since the mid-1960s there has been a series of such spirals in the private housing market, which have become particularly marked because of the volatility of building society receipts and their mortgage allocation, which determine the effective demand for housing.

The large builder-developers gain from conducting large-scale operations on single sites. They benefit from the economies of scale. As the big builder-developers have grown in size, they have been able to conduct very large-scale operations almost extending to building new towns; we can see this from the development of Lower Earley in Berkshire and in Yate outside Bristol, where one or more very large-scale builder-developers have been building total environments. In these places the concept of the master builder who builds houses and then sells them is being replaced by that of the community builder, the very large-scale developer who not only builds houses but creates a total environment of shops, schools and all the other infrastructural elements which make up the total urban environment. These are the new towns of the 1980s.

HOUSE BUILDING IN THE PUBLIC SECTOR

I have already noted in Chapter 3 how council house building was determined by macro-economic policies and other central and local government policies. The roller coaster of public sector completions shown in Figure 3.1 corresponds with the output of the construction industry shown in Figure 5.1; there have been three main waves of council house building: 1947 to the mid-1950s, 1964 to 1970 and 1974 to 1977. In comparison with the private sector, house building in the public sector is dominated by the large construction companies (see Figure 5.2).

Site acquisition

Local authorities have the power to acquire land for council housing. From 1947 to 1959 local authorities were able to purchase land on the basis of existing use value, which meant that land costs were only a small component of total costs. In the early 1950s land costs were less than 5 per cent of the total cost of a dwelling. The Tories' Town and Country Planning Act overturned the principle of buying land at existing use prices, and their 1959 Act marked a return to the inter-war methods of landowners being able to charge compensation at the full market value. The result was an increase in land acquisition costs. In the 1960s land costs increased to almost 10 per cent of the total cost of council dwellings, and by the mid-1970s almost 20 per cent, as the spiralling land prices in the private market affected local authority land acquisition and ultimately the standard and quality of council housing. In association with high interest charges the very high land prices of the later 1960s led to an increase in the cost of local authority housing. The housing cost yardstick introduced in 1967 was an attempt to stem this increase by limiting expenditure.

Financing of council housing

Local authorities rely on external sources to finance their house-building programme. In the immediate post-war years the local authority house-building programme was funded almost entirely by the Public Works Loan Board (PWLB) who gave loans at low interest rates (approximately 3 per cent was charged for loans in the period 1945–51). The Tory government of 1951 sought to bring the Board's interest rate in line with those of the market, and local authorities now went directly to the money markets to secure long- and short-term loans. Access to the PWLB was also restricted after

1955 as part of an attempt to reduce government spending, but the restriction was lifted after 1964 and now PWLB loans constitute between 30 and 50 per cent of the finance of local authority house building.

Because council house building is financed from loans it is influenced by interest rates. Figure 5.3 shows the relationship between local authority capital expenditure on housing (which includes site acquisition and rehabilitation as well as new building and interest rates charged by the PWLB). The diagram has to be seen in relation to Figure 3.1, which shows public sector completions. A comparison of the two figures reveals that increases in capital expenditure do not mean an increase in the number of new houses built. The most rapid increase in expenditure was over the period 1969–74, and the number of public sector housing completions actually fell from approximately 150,000 to under 100,000. The very marked increase in capital expenditure has been caused by factors other than interest

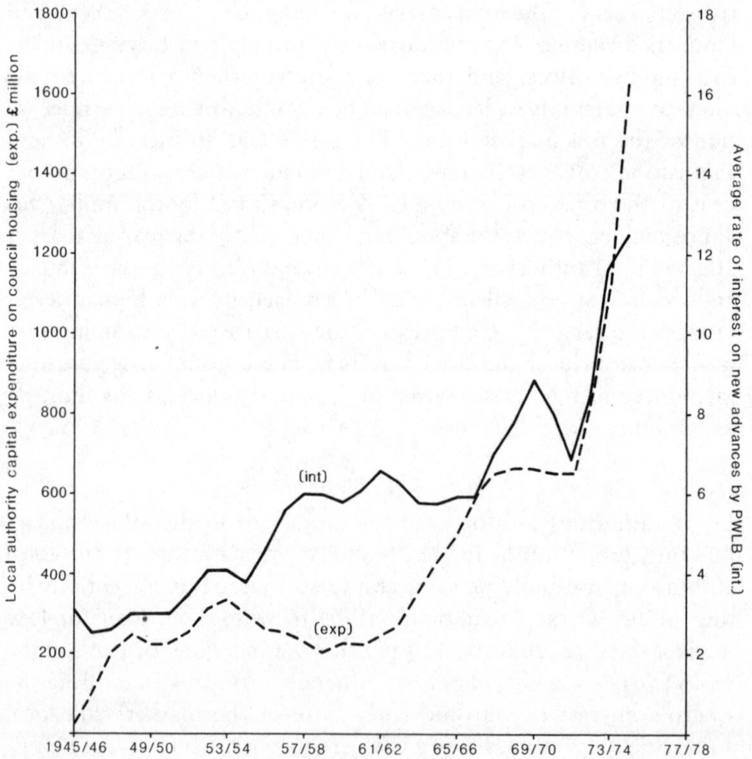

Figure 5.3 Interest rates and local authority capital expenditure on housing

rates. Inflation pushed up prices and in the construction industry price increases have been even more marked. But market interest rates have been the single most important external factor influencing the extent of local authority capital expenditure on council housing.

Construction

House building in the public sector is commissioned by local authorities. The housing and planning departments of the authorities will have made some rough estimates of need and the availability of cash and land. When the plans for building are passed by the local council and approved by central government, then architects are employed to prepare plans. Most local authorities use their own architects, but outside architects, especially the big names, are sometimes used for prestige projects.

The scale of individual projects in the public sector tends to be much larger than in the private sector. Information for the late 1940s and 1950s is difficult to obtain but Table 5.4 gives an indication of the experience since then. From 1960 there was an increase in the average size of schemes; the modal group in 1960 was between twenty-six and fifty dwellings, but in 1968 it was over 100 dwellings per scheme. This trend reached its height in the mid- to late-1960s and this reflected the construction of very large-scale, high-rise blocks. Since then there has been, sometimes in the literal sense, the rise and fall of the big multi-storey development. The position in 1978 was one in which less dwellings were approved and the big developments were less important. The larger the projects, the greater the use of the large-scale builder-developers.

When projects are approved, tenders are invited. Tenders can either be open or selected. In open tenders any contractor can bid, irrespective of his/her capability. In selective tenders invita-

Table 5.4 Council housing projects

Tenders agreed by number of dwellings in each scheme		*% of all dwellings*		
		1960	*1968*	*1978*
1–10		6.6	2.7	3.5
11–25		13.6	6.4	10.8
26–100		40.3	24.2	48.2
+100		39.5	66.7	37.5
Total*		100.0	100.0	100.0
	n =	100,508	154,884	72,620

* Figures rounded up to 100
Source: HCS

tions are limited to a small number of 'reliable' firms. Other types are negotiated tenders and package deals formulated with just one company. Government circulars have suggested to local authorities to make greater use of selective tendering. The trend towards selective tendering is apparent in Table 5.5. Open tendering has declined on the advice of central government and on the basis of bitter experience. The negotiated and package-deal arrangements have also declined in importance as the tower-block industrialized building phase has passed its peak. Selective tendering is now the most important form of tender: it involves competing contractors being given the site plan and details of material requirement with specification and completion date. Up to two months is allowed for a reply. Selective tendering allows local authorities to choose competent builders and it also allows less room for corruption than in the negotiated or package deal, but those builders who receive an invitation to tender, obviously gain an advantage. Builder-developers thus seek to maintain close and friendly ties with the local authority representatives. The ties can range from normal lobbying to explicit corruption. The level of corruption shown in the Poulson case, for example, was considerable. Other cases have also come to light. In Birmingham, for example, the long association between Birmingham Council and Bryants Construction Industry (between 1961 and 1973 Bryants took 40 per cent of all housing work, most of it in the form of negotiated contracts) was ended when three directors from Bryants were gaoled for a total of twelve years after admitting charges of bribery and corruption.

Table 5.5 Types of tendering in local authority building projects (%)

	Open tender	*Selected tender*	*Negotiated tender*	*Package deal*	*Total**
1969	16.0	48.0	23.1	12.1	100
1978	4.8	90.7	4.4	0.2	100

* Figures rounded to 100
Source: HCS

The overall density of council housing has been conditioned by the operation of planning controls and the division of government. As we have seen in the previous chapter, land-use controls operated to contain urban growth. The containment of residential development put a brake on council housing in suburbia and rural areas. Moreover, the pre-1974 division of county boroughs and shire counties often marked the division between Labour-controlled and

Tory-controlled authorities. The latter did not want big new council estates upsetting the rural calm or the political balance, and it is not incidental that when slum clearance programmes were given more impetus in the early 1950s the Tory government also gave support to the concept of green belts round big cities and the building of council estates at high densities. In the post-war period, densities have been in the order of between sixty and seventy persons per acre in England and Wales. The highest figures were recorded in the mid- and late 1960s (70.4 persons per acre for tenders approved in 1966). But in the 1970s there has been a steady fall from 65.2 in 1970 to 61.4 in 1978. The decline reflects the lack of large high-rise developments which often had more than 200 persons per acre.

Internal space specifications have been guided by standards set down by central government. In the immediate post-war period relatively generous standards were set. The Dudley report of 1944 had the enthusiastic support of the first post-war Minister of Housing, Aneurin Bevan, and provided the basis for high space standards. Thereafter, and especially throughout the 1950s, standards were allowed to drop as economies were pursued (see Figure 5.4). The decline in standards did not go unnoticed and a committee was set up in 1959 under Parker Morris, whose report in December 1961 called for better space standards. In the year it was published the average size of a five-bedspace dwelling was 83.4 square metres – a decline from the 97.8 square metres of the late 1940s. The Parker Morris report urged local authorities for a minimum of 910 square feet for a five-bedspace dwelling. The report's suggestions were not made mandatory and no subsidies were given for their implementation. Standards did improve, however, as some local authorities did try to implement some of the Parker Morris suggestions. The Labour government of 1964 urged all local authorities to implement the

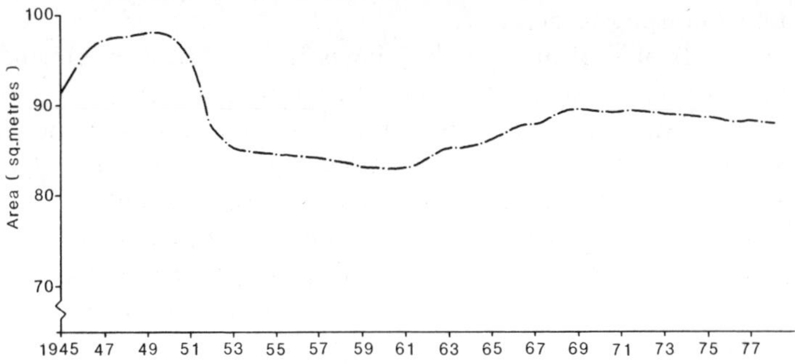

Figure 5.4 The average floorspace of a five-bed local authority dwelling

report's recommendations, and in 1969 the Parker Morris standards were made mandatory. Thereafter space standards remained at a constant level throughout the 1970s.

Local authorities were advised to use Parker Morris standards in a government document, Circular 36/67. The same circular also introduced the housing cost yardstick. If local authorities were now obliged to build better housing, a limit was now to be placed on their expenditure. Subsidies were only to be paid on costs which fell within the yardsticks, and local authorities were not allowed to borrow money for tenders which exceeded 110 per cent of the cost yardstick. The yardstick proved a real problem, since it failed to keep pace as tender prices rose substantially after 1966 in response to rising land and interest rates. In 1969 the average cost of a one-storey house built by the local authorities was £2223; in 1974 this had increased to £5311. The authorities responded by designing cheaper housing to stay within the yardstick, and the result was ill-designed, shoddy buildings where the high cost of maintenance and repair are still being paid.

The most recent development has been the removal of standards but the retention of cost control. The Conservative government announced in 1981 that the Parker Morris standards would now no longer be obligatory, and regulations designed to maintain the living standards of council housing would be reassessed. This was part of the Conservative government's strategy towards local authorities, giving them freedom to spend the amount of money which is set by central government. In one sense it meant less government intervention or, to be more precise, less central government intervention, but in the more important sense it is a spurious freedom because in the climate of the time the freedom given to local authorities was where to make expenditure cutbacks or reductions in the quality of service. Throughout the 1980s we can expect the space standards of council housing to decrease.

The bulk of local authority housing is built by private companies. There is a relationship between the size of company and the size of project, with the very large companies competing for the big projects. After the plans have been drawn up and tenders invited, the building companies compete for the contracts. A pamphlet by the Direct Labour Collective (1978) has examined the contracting system whereby firms compete for specific projects. The authors assert that it is a wasteful system: it encourages builders to maximize profits on each contract and it discourages innovation and increased efficiency. For the contractors the aim is to get the contract, not reduce costs. Costs will be reduced if there is fierce competition, but because of the close ties between local authorities and specific firms and the operation of price-fixing rings there is very little real competition. The pamphlet goes on to argue that the contract system is loaded in favour of the contractors and local authorities have little control over quality or excess costs. They present a convincing argument as the pamphlet chronicles the saga of building failures, time overruns and shoddy workmanship in local authority house-building in the 1970s. It makes sorry reading as scheme after scheme is shown to be a catalogue of expensive errors. Not all contracts end in failure or in shoddy buildings but a significant proportion do.

Flats and high-rise buildings

The most important single feature of post-war council housing has been the use of flat construction, particularly high-rise buildings. Figure 5.5 shows how the percentage of flats (buildings of three-storeys or more) has grown in the post-war period from less than 25 per cent in 1953 to almost 50 per cent in the 1960s and 70s. This relative increase also reflects an absolute increase. Flat construction has been aided by central government subsidies; the subsidies were used to encourage new industrialized systems of construction. Flats were also seen as solutions to high land prices. But most importantly it was thought that by building at higher densities and lower space standards substantial savings could be made.

Within the growing use of flats in the council house sector there has been the rise and decline of the high-rise block. Figure 5.5 shows how flats of more than ten storeys were increasingly being used from the mid-1950s, peaking in 1964 and from then on showing a rapid decline. This relative change was also reflected in absolute terms: in 1964, 27,557 dwellings in blocks of more than ten storeys were approved in England and Wales, but by 1973 this had fallen to 643 and by 1978 to only 37 dwellings. The reasons and chronology behind this phenomenon have been examined by Cooney (1974). The initial impetus for the use of high-rise buildings came from various architectural movements in the inter-war years. The modern movement saw high towers as a tight, compact solution to the problems of providing lots of housing. In this architectural ideology the aggressive, confident towers of the planners were the markers of a new utopia. People figured very little in the drawings, the schemes or the ideology. The ideology was given substance in the early post-war period. The Dudley report put new emphasis on variety in local authority estates and encouraged a mixture of low- and high-

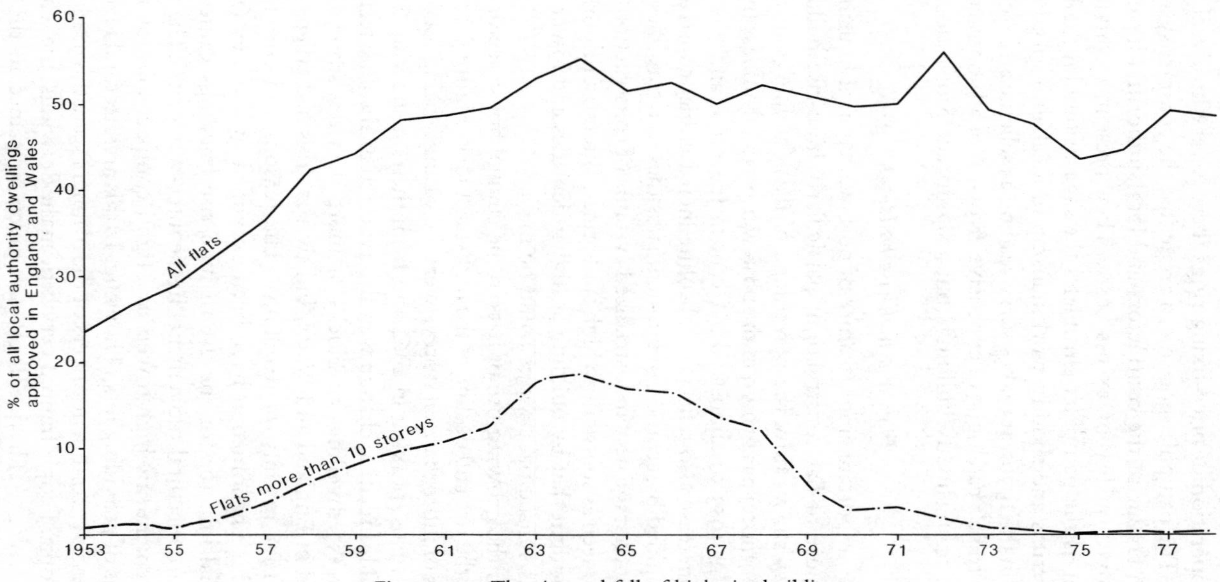

Figure 5.5 The rise and fall of high-rise buildings

rise blocks. The first of such schemes in Roehampton, built by the London County Council, was widely regarded as a success. During the 1950s other authorities began to consider high-rise buildings as a means of dealing with land-availability problems. Denied the ability to incorporate chunks of suburban land, the big city authorities had to rehouse the people affected by the slum clearance schemes within the local authority boundaries. High-rise blocks were seen as a method of achieving big rehousing programmes within the constraints of lack of land.

The central government aided the construction of high-rise blocks by granting subsidies. Between 1956 and 1967 government subsidies increased with the height of the block. A series of government circulars called on local authorities to look favourably at the high-rise solution to problems of land availability. The pressures on local authorities from central government were matched by the pressures from the large construction companies, who were keen to obtain a steady market for the new industrialized systems of building. The local authority council housing sector was a large market. And if contracts could be obtained the contractors had an effective demand for the new building systems. The industrialized systems of building were being developed by the large contractors because they lessened dependence on labour and weather, and increased profit.

Suggested by architects, promoted by central government and pushed for by the big contractors, the high-rise blocks were touted as the solution to problems of land availability and as a panacea to modernizing the construction industry. Some individual authorities, such as Birmingham, led the way, but throughout the early 1960s more local authorities began to use high-rise blocks. The high-rise tower was a potent phallic symbol of municipal virility and aggression. There was no more visible sign of an authority's housing achievement than a row of gleaming concrete towers puncturing the sky.

The rapid rise was followed by a rapid decline. After 1964 the proportion of high-rise blocks began to fall. The fall was especially steep after 1967–8. Cooney suggests a number of reasons for the decline. First, the Housing Subsidies Act of 1967 reduced the subsidies for blocks of flats of more than six storeys. Local authorities were now less keen to commission high-rise towers. Second, the expenditure reduction announced after the November 1967 devaluation constrained the local authority house-building programme. Since high-rise blocks were expensive they bore the brunt of cutbacks. Third, the Ronan Point disaster was a powerful argument against the high-rise block solution. On 16 May 1967 part of a twenty-two-storey block in Newham, London, collapsed. Four people died and seventeen were injured. The media gave it massive coverage, and the inquiry set up in its aftermath highlighted a number of substantial defects in the design and construction of the building. The publication of the findings had a major impact, and a substantial amount of informed public opinion was mobilized against high-rise blocks. Finally, there was mounting criticism at a variety of levels and from a number of quarters against tower blocks. They were increasingly seen to be unpopular, expensive and ugly.

The high-rise saga is an important tale in post-war council housing. The use of tower blocks affected the cost, location, design and, in fact, the whole character of council housing in the post-war period. The shiny towers, initially the sign of achievement, became the sign of failure and incompetence. The failure was not one of general principle. High-rise blocks *per se* are not bad. The experience of western Europe has shown that high-rise living is not inherently unattractive. The failure was more particular. Shoddy, ill-designed and badly built high-rise blocks were constructed. The quality of finish in most blocks was terrible, ventilation was poor and levels of housing dissatisfaction were high. Most major local authorities now have their high-rise problem blocks which are falling apart through neglect and building failure. They are so unpopular, partly because of the design faults, especially the problems of dampness and condensation, that most tenants try to move out as soon as possible. The real failure lay in the fact that no-one paid much attention to what the tenants wanted. There was the implicit assumption that the architects, the builders, the housing departments and the central government knew what should be built for people. The fact that most council tenants wanted a house with a garden seems to have been ignored. Blocks of flats are often ideal for young childless households who do not want the responsibilities of gardens or maintenance, but for the majority of council house tenants high-rise blocks were totally unsuitable. Parents could not keep their eye on the children, the lack of defensible space meant vandalism was rife, and community ties were difficult to create, let alone maintain. The high-rise solution was a building solution, a design solution, it was not a people's solution. The ultimate failure lay in the failure to consult the tenant either before or during the process of construction.

Direct labour organizations

Direct labour is a workforce employed by local authorities for construction work. The very first direct labour organization (DLO) was set up by London County Council in 1892 after a public outcry over shoddy housing work, amid stories of widespread graft and corruption and also in response to building workers' union demands for better conditions. The continued inability of the private sector to meet the demand of local authorities has maintained a need for DLOs. The DLOs quickly grew after the two world wars when the private sectors could not meet the demand of the large council house-building programmes and excessive tendering led to some authorities setting up their own building departments. After the Second World War the size of the council house-building programme and the strength of the building workers' union led to most local authorities establishing some kind of DLO. By 1969, 86 per cent of local authorities had a DLO of some description, and by 1979 this figure had increased to 96 per cent. The size of DLOs varies by authority. The Labour-controlled local authorities, especially the Inner London boroughs and the Metropolitan Districts, have large DLOs involved in new building as well as repair and maintenance. In the Tory-controlled shire counties, DLOs are small and do very little housing work; they are restricted to small-scale repair and maintenance work. The position of a DLO within an authority changes not only in response to national directives but also to the rhythm of local political change. Conservative control is followed by a reduction in DLOs as Labour victories are signalled very often by the expansion of DLOs.

By 1979 DLOs in England and Wales were employing 134,862 operatives compared with 674,000 working for private contractors, and the value of work done was £346 million compared with the £3500 million in the private sector. The breakdown of DLO activity is shown in Table 5.6, where it can be seen that the majority of work is in the repair and maintenance sector. New housing work constitutes only a small proportion of DLO operations.

The size and operation of the DLOs has been shaped by national and local political pressures. At the national level the pressure of private builders has been important. In a very real sense the DLOs represent a direct challenge to the private sector. When business is booming, the challenge is lessened because there is enough work for the private contractors. The DLOs expanded during the early 1970s, for example, since the property boom was more profitable for

Table 5.6 DLOs in England and Wales, 1979

Type of work	*Value of work done (%)*
New work	*13.5*
housing	6.8
non-housing	6.7
Repair and maintenance	*86.5*
housing	39.8
non-housing	46.7
Total	100 (£346 million)

contractors than the local authority projects; and because many local authorities found difficulty in obtaining reasonably priced tenders, DLOs expanded and moved into new housing construction. By contrast, when there is a slump, contracts are scarce and DLOs represent a threat to the private sector; the history of DLOs in Britain has been a succession of attacks by private contractors in times of slump. In the post-war period the first attack came in the late 1950s as the building industry slumped. The then Conservative government introduced a number of contracting requirements and wage restraints on DLOs. Criticism also rose in the late 1960s, but the most sustained attack has come since the end of the building boom in 1973–4. The severity of the attack reflects the size of the problem to the private sector. Public expenditure has been slashed and the house-building sector has been reduced. DLOs were taking valuable trade in both the new housing and the repair and maintenance sectors. As we have already seen, DLOs are heavily involved in the repair and maintenance sector, and the relative size of this sector has increased in recent years. There are two reasons for this. First, in times of slump large capital cost construction projects are most immediately affected, but in the short to medium term the relatively small-scale current expenditure of repair and maintenance can be shielded from the axe of public expenditure reduction. Second, the emphasis in government housing policy has swung from the redevelopment schemes of the 1960s to the improvement strategies of the 1970s. The 1969 and 1974 Housing Acts signalled the growing use of rehabilitation of existing buildings rather than the construction of new dwellings. The net result has been for the repair and maintenance sectors to form an important part of construction work (see Table 5.7). The private builders have attempted to prise loose the hold of the DLOs on local authority repair and

Table 5.7 Repair and maintenance work

Year	*Repair and maintenance as % of total construction output*
1969	12.2
1970	12.4
1971	12.5
1972	13.5
1973	14.4
1974	14.9
1975	14.5
1976	14.2
1977	15.3
1978	16.2
1979	17.6
1980	18.2

maintenance work as well as on the new housing sector. The most recent attack on DLOs started in 1975 when the National Federation of Building Trade Employers (NFBTE) started an extensive campaign against the DLOs involving publicity and the lobbying of government ministers and opinion-makers. The NFBTE spent £250,000 in 1976–7 pushing their campaign. Their argument reflected not so much the builders' interests but focused on the inefficiency of the DLOs and the high cost to the taxpayer. The efficiency argument provides no real basis for a reasoned argument, but their claims for allowing free enterprise to flower found a receptive response in the Conservative party. The Tory government elected in 1979 acted quickly in reducing DLOs. They introduced new rules for DLOs in 1981, under which the DLOs must earn a 5-per-cent rate of return on capital employed. This compares with the 2-per-cent average for British industry as a whole. DLOs will now have to compete against private-sector firms with the dice heavily weighted against them. The complaints of many local authority leaders that DLOs will be slimmed down drastically and that councils will be entirely at the mercy of the private sector when the slump ends, have been ignored. The building industry's lobbying has been successful.

REPAIR AND IMPROVEMENT

Housing tends to last for a long time. A typical house is expected to last for at least sixty years. The long life of housing has two consequences. On the one hand, a particular unit of accommodation may be overtaken by rising standards and rising expectations and may fall into the category of 'unfit' or unsuitable. As standards rise, older housing may require improvement work. On the other hand, housing needs regular maintenance. The passage of years and the work of the elements, natural and human, all take their toll on the appearance and quality of housing. Housing, especially older housing, thus needs repair work.

The bulk of housing repair maintenance is done by the small building firms. Almost 70 per cent of such work is done by firms with less than twenty-four operatives. Exact proportions will change over time. When the economy is growing and there is a building boom, then the large and medium-sized companies switch to new building work. Conversely, when new building declines the repair and maintenance sector may provide some work and profit.

In the housing sector a distinction can be drawn between grant-aided and non-grant-aided improvement work. There are statistics for the former but not for the latter.

Grant-aided improvement

As the name implies, this form of improvement work is done in conjunction with a grant from the local authority. The level of such improvement primarily reflects the ease of obtaining, the size, and the purchasing power of the grant. In Figure 3.1 we can see that in the post-war period the level of grant take-up has had a definite pattern of rapid growth followed by levelling off, repeated three times. The first surge took place after 1954 when the Housing Repairs and Rent Act of that year allowed the local authorities to allocate a 50-per-cent grant up to £400 for improvement of a dwelling up to a set standard. Grant take-up grew in response, and each year between 1954 and 1958 almost 30,000 grants were approved. The second surge occurred after the 1959 House Purchase and Housing Act, which introduced standard grants (maximum £350) and discretionary (maximum £400) grants again covering 50 per cent of expenditure. Grant take-up shot up to over 100,000 by 1960, as many households in the older residential areas used the standard grant to install new bathrooms. A plateau of approximately 100,000 grants approved each year continued until the 1969 Housing Act, which increased the standard grant to £450 and the discretionary to £1000. The effect, as Figure 3.1 clearly shows, was dramatic. Improvement grant take-up rose to 200,000 in 1972 and over 310,000 in 1973. Since 1974 grant take-up has fallen, despite the 1974 Housing Act which increased improvement grants to £1600. The rapid decline since 1973 reflects the fall in the real purchasing power of the grant, and expenditure cutbacks. Since the mid-1970s the improvement grant has failed to keep pace with the inflation of building repair costs, and local authorities have also cut back their allocation of improvement grants as a response to central government's fiscal screw-tightening.

The distribution of improvement grant take-up has not exactly matched either housing need or housing quality. Improvement grants have tended to go to the basically sound turn-of-the-century terraced housing. During the period 1969–73 there was also much activity by landlords and speculators using improvement grants to upgrade property and then sell to higher-income households. This was effectively discouraged by the 1974 Housing Act, which placed restrictions on immediate resale. It sought to redirect grant-aided improvement to the poor-quality inner-city areas, but the scheme was undermined by lack of resources.

Non-grant-aided improvement

We know very little about non-grant-aided improvement. We can only comment from the standpoint of the slippery footholds of aggregate figures. Such improvement is not a random occurrence. The majority of improvers are households with a younger than average head of household that have recently moved into their accommodation. Older households, and especially those that have lived a long time in the same accommodation, are less likely to undertake improvement. A significant factor is the lack of perception of the need for maintenance and/or repair the longer one stays in a place. This form of subliminal perception leaves the household unaware of any need for improvement or repair. There can in some instances also be a demonstration effect whereby improvers in a particular street or particular neighbourhood demonstrate to their neighbours the ease and the advantages of improvement. In certain favoured inner-city areas this demonstration effect combines with the in-movement of young and mobile households to produce a fertile climate for further improvement work. In other areas by contrast, conditions militate against improvement. Where traditional sources of housing finance are limited and local authority municipalization schemes are few, householders and owners have very little incentive to improve their property. What happens can be termed the prisoner's dilemma, whereby it is in the interest of each household to improve less than their neighbour. By this action they will spend less on repair and improvement work but gain from the externalities of their neighbours' higher level of improvement expenditure. Certain inner-city areas would seem to be caught in a downward spiral of decreasing improvement, and are thus unable to attract building society finance, which in turn leads to lack of further improvement.

Do-it-yourself improvement and repair is now a major hobby and important industry. With more leisure time and the increase in owner-occupation, which both allows and necessitates individual improvement work rather than the collective maintenance of local authority housing, do-it-yourself has increased in the post-war period to become one of the most important if largely unrecorded elements in housing repair and maintenance. Not all households can do-it-themselves. The very old and incapacitated may find it very difficult indeed and they either have to pay builders or rely on friends and helpers.

Repair, improvement and maintenance expenditure can be a significant element in a household's housing budget. The poorer the household, the greater the significance. As repair and maintenance costs have increased, some low-income owner-occupiers have responded by reducing such expenditure. Landlords have also reduced on this expenditure to maintain profits when faced with fixed rents. The net result is a worsening in the overall quality of the housing stock. Over the period 1971–6 there was a 20-per-cent increase in dwellings needing repairs costing more than £500, and a 43-per-cent increase in those requiring more than £1000 repair work (at 1971 prices). As the slum clearance programmes have ended and the recession bites into the public and private improvement programmes, the deterioration of housing is continuing apace.

6

OWNER-OCCUPATION

One of the most important changes in the post-war British housing scene has been the rise of owner-occupation. In 1945 26 per cent of households could be described as owner-occupiers, but by 1978 this figure had increased to over 53 per cent. The majority of British households can now be described as owner-occupiers, and owner-occupation is now the single most important tenure category.

THE STATE AND OWNER-OCCUPATION

A number of reasons lie behind the change. In subsequent pages we shall note how funds have been channelled very efficiently into the purchase of housing. For the moment we shall examine the role of the state in facilitating the increase in owner-occupation. The state has encouraged this tenure form by aiding the building societies through the adoption of favourable fiscal policies. There have been a number of times during the post-war years when the building societies have been helped by the government. Between 1959 and 1962 the Tory government lent them £100 million to encourage lending on property built before 1900; in 1974 the societies agreed with the Tories on a three-month bridging grant in order to keep the mortgage rate below 9½ per cent; the societies received a £500 million loan from the incoming Labour government in the same year. A variety of fiscal policies have evolved to make owner-occupation an attractive proposition. First, there is tax relief on mortgage interest. The ability of building society borrowers to claim tax relief against interest payments was first formalized in 1951, and tax relief is now a major subsidy to house purchasers, amounting to over £1260 million in 1977–8. Since 1974 tax relief has been restricted to loans up to £25,000. Second, owner-occupiers receive an imputed rental income. Before 1963, under Schedule A income tax, owner-occupiers were taxed on the imputed income from property, but since then this has been abolished. Boddy (1980) reports that the total imputed rental income in 1975 was £2383 million. Third, the government have helped lower-income households to purchase property through the option mortgage scheme, which was introduced in 1967 to provide the equivalent of tax relief for those with incomes too low to qualify for income tax. Finally, sales of residences are exempt from capital gains tax. The profit made from the sale of a house is the difference between the sale price minus the purchase price and the loan repayments. Estimates by Shelter suggest that in 1975 capital gains tax of 30 per cent would have yielded about £500 million.

The net result is to make the owner-occupier a privileged investor, one who borrows money at subsidized rates of interest to purchase an asset for which no imputed rent is paid and which can be sold without paying any capital gains tax. The financial incentives to owner-occupation are both large and clear.

The reasons why the state has encouraged owner-occupation are many. Owner-occupation has been an important part of Tory ideology. Even before 1946, when Eden noted that the Conservative aim was a 'nation-wide property-owning democracy', encouragement of owner-occupation was a central plank of Tory housing policy. Their periods of office in post-war governments have been characterized by endeavours to facilitate owner-occupation. This tenure forms an important part of the Conservative strategy of ensuring social harmony by widening the basis of property ownership and legitimating the concept of such ownership. Moreover, owner-occupiers are seen as potential Tory supporters. It is believed that the encouragement of owner-occupation assures both social stability and future political support.

In the immediate post-war period Labour were committed to seeking the solution to housing problems within the public sector. When they next gained power their previous radicalism was blunted by a much more pragmatic approach. By 1964, almost 45 per cent of households in Britain were owner-occupiers and the balance of advantages was clearly in favour of owner-occupation. Most people who could afford it thus sought to become owner-occupiers. The weight of popular demand swung Labour towards an approach not dissimilar to that of the Tories, and since the mid-1960s both major parties have been committed to widening the extent of owner-occupation. The owner-occupiers, now a majority, constitute a powerful political force which make governments responsive to maintaining the position of owner-occupiers. The fiscal structure makes owner-occupation a continued attraction to new households seeking accommodation.

The increase of owner-occupation is seen as more than just a reflection of the fiscal pattern. A whole series of government documents point to the 'naturalness' of owner-occupation: 'home ownership is the most rewarding form of house tenure. It satisfies a deep natural desire on the part of the householder to have independent control of the house that shelters him and his family' (White Paper, 1971); 'for most people owning one's home is a basic and natural desire' (Green Paper, 1977). In this kind of thinking the encouragement of owner-occupation takes on a duty of satisfying innate desires. There is a neat logical trick involved here: people desire owner-occupation as it is more financially attractive because state policies have made it so; this desire is seen as natural; it is thus up to the government to meet this natural desire. What could be more natural?

For the Conservatives and parts of the Labour party, promoting owner-occupation is more than encouraging a particular tenure form; it is associated with saving, thrift, hard work, independence – the very best qualities for a hard-working, stable population. To encourage owner-occupation is thus to foster these very qualities and its promotion becomes almost a social duty which any right-minded government should pursue. The other tenures recede into the background as deviations, second-best alternatives to the right and true housing path. The right-wing *Daily Express* can thus herald the 1979 Tory government's commitment to selling off council houses as an act of freeing the council tenancy. In contemporary Britain owner-occupation is more than just one of three tenure forms, it is an emblem, an image rich with meaning and full of wider social and political significance.

Owner-occupation has also been encouraged by the policies and practice of council house sales. The sale of council houses has been one of those key housing elements which have informed political debate in post-war Britain. Council house sales were first encouraged in the post-war period by the Conservative government in 1952; a circular in that year allowed local authorities to sell houses. At this early stage, however, council house sales did not have an important position in Tory ideology and the issue was not debated at any Conservative annual conferences between 1953 and 1967. Later, in 1957 a housing Act contained measures for allowing local authorities to sell off council houses, and between 1957 and 1964 approximately 60,000 council houses were sold. At the central government level, with Labour's return to power in 1964, official encouragement was limited. However, at the local level council house sales continued apace, especially in those authorities where the Conservatives had gained control. Between 1959 and 1972 approximately 150,000 council houses were sold. The Labour party response was to debate the issue at the 1967 conference and to reaffirm their opposition to the policy; a government circular in 1968 tried to reverse the trend of selling off council houses. On returning to office in 1970 the Tories reversed these restrictions. The sale of council houses has now taken an important position in Conservative housing policies. The experience of Conservative local authorities had shown that the issue was an electoral winner and it also had a broad ideological appeal within the party. When Labour came back to power again in 1974 there was a repeat of their earlier performance in that council house sales were discouraged. Again, however, they continued apace at the local level. Council house sales were becoming an important issue throughout the 1970s, especially as the gains to owner-occupiers were becoming obvious. The issue formed an important part of the 1979 Conservative election strategy, and many have argued, quite convincingly, that their support of council house sales was an important element in their election victory. The Conservative policy towards council housing and towards owner-occupation is crystallized in their 1980 Housing Act, which gives to local authority tenants the right to buy their accommodation. The actual practice of council house sales in post-war Britain has tended to reinforce the advantages of owner-occupation. The council houses which have been sold have been some of the best of the council house stock. The majority of housing sold has been the best-regarded, better-quality housing on favoured estates. As the best housing is sold off, what remains is the residue of poor-quality, high-rise housing. This process of residualization leads to a further stigmatization of council housing and a further reinforcement of the appeal of owner-occupation.

THE FINANCIAL INSTITUTIONS

The outright purchase of housing is beyond the reach of all but the wealthy. For most people owner-occupation implies borrowing money. In a few cases the money can be raised from informal sources. Communities, especially tight communities which have a strong extended family system, can borrow money from within an informal nexus of friends and relatives. For many first-time purchasers family finances can provide an important source of house purchase finance, especially in the form of help with payment of a deposit. The most important sources of house purchase finance are the formal sources, the financial institutions. There are four main such sources: building societies, local authorities, banks and insurance companies. We shall examine each of these sources in turn.

The building societies

The building societies are the biggest single source of house purchase finance in Britain. Throughout the 1970s they contributed more than two-thirds of the total amount of money lent for house purchase (see Figure 6.1). They are major financial institutions: in 1980 they held assets of almost £54 billion, ranking in importance only after the banks and insurance companies. They are also one of the largest institutions in the personal savings sector: their share of total personal savings in Britain has varied between a fifth and a quarter since 1970.

These modern-day financial giants had humble origins. They grew as self-help organizations out of the experience of workers in the expanding towns and cities of the late eighteenth and early nineteenth centuries. Then, council housing was not provided and some of the better-paid and better-organized workers responded by establishing societies whose members paid regular contributions. In the early societies the members saved together and when enough for one 'share', which was a specified amount, was raised, this was allocated to one of the members to buy, rent or build accommodation. The members, including the person who had benefited the last time, continued to pay their subscription. When enough funds were raised this was allocated again to one of the members. And so the process went on. The system was a means of mobilizing collective savings for individual benefits. The early societies were small. From 1775 to 1825, 250 societies were involved in the construction and purchase of 2000 houses, and activity was concentrated in the Midlands and the North where skilled artisans had the commitment and necessary income. These early societies came from the same roots as the Cooperative Society and the Labour party. The societies were temporary, and disbanded after each initial member had received his/her share.

From the mid-1850s permanent societies were founded. Now members could withdraw their money at any time and borrowers paid back their loan over a set period. In this framework the communality of investors and depositors was broken as building societies

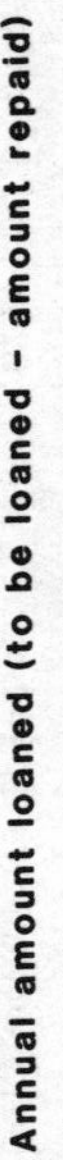

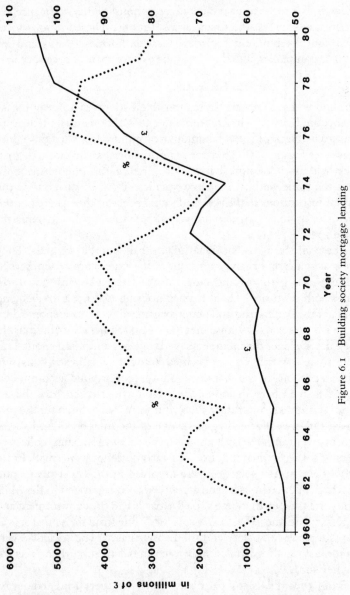

Figure 6.1 Building society mortgage lending

became the link organizations between investors seeking returns and borrowers requiring mortgages. The societies were eventually given corporate status by the 1874 Building Societies Act, which restricted the investment of surplus funds to mortgages or government-guaranteed securities. With the 1874 Act the building societies were legally constituted as economic agents; they had become institutions.

The real change for building societies came after the First World War. In the last quarter of the nineteenth and the first fifteen years of the twentieth centuries the building societies went through a rough time as the house market slumped and a number of scandals shook public confidence. After the war, however, it was rapid expansion time. In the twenty-year period from 1920 to 1940 the number of share accounts increased from just over three-quarters of a million to over two million, and the total assets grew from £87 million to £756 million; the scale of expansion was impressive. How did the societies escape the inter-war slump felt in many other sectors? There were a number of reasons. First, the societies offered competitive rates of return in comparison with the banks, securities and shares. The building societies were an attractive proposition for those with savings, and it is important to remember that even during depression the income of those in employment tended to rise in real terms and savings levels increased. The sharp end of the depression was felt by the unemployed; for those in employment and especially the middle-income, middle-class groups, rising incomes were associated with the falling prices. Investment poured into building societies and the demand for housing, especially in the affluent south-east, was high since the real cost of housing was falling because of the depressed wages of the building workers and the fall in price of building materials. The societies lubricated the inter-war building boom.

Table 6.1 Building societies: summary statistics

Year	No. of societies	No. of share accounts	No. of mortgage accounts	Advances during year numbers	Advances during year amount (£m)	Total assets (£m)
1900	2286	585	–	–	9	60
1940	952	2088	1503	43	21	756
1950	819	2256	1508	302	270	1256
1960	726	3910	2349	387	560	3166
1970	481	10,265	3655	624	1954	10,819
1979	287	27,878	5251	1040	9002	45,789

Source: BSA

After 1945 the scale of building society activity increased. Rather than simply being a savings and mortgage institution for the middle-income groups the societies extended their operations. By 1980 almost a half of the adult population had savings in building societies, and more than five million households had borrowed money from them. The long post-war economic boom saw rising real wages for the majority of the population, and some of this money found its way into building society accounts. The growth of the societies was also part and parcel of the post-war rise in owner-occupation. The rise of the societies was part cause and part effect of the rapid increase in owner-occupation. Ultimately, of course, the societies' growth reflected their strong position in the savings market, a position guaranteed to some extent by a state eager to promote owner-occupation.

The growth of societies has involved a concentration of activity. In 1890 there were 2579 societies, but by 1979 this figure had dropped to 287. In 1970 the largest twenty societies held 77.4 per cent of all society assets, but by 1977 almost 83.3 per cent. The corresponding figures for the largest ten societies were 63.4 and 69.2 per cent. This concentration has occurred by amalgamation as the largest most successful societies have incorporated the smaller ones.

The societies as financial institutions Societies operate as non-profit-making financial institutions by attracting savings and lending mortgages. Their operations rest on their ability to attract investments. The post-war rise of societies reflects their competitive position in the savings market; they offer a combination of 'security and liquidity with an assured and highly competitive rate of return'. Investments in building societies are considered as safe as bank deposits or government securities, and the societies have carefully nurtured the image of thriftiness, careful investment and sound management. They have a well-earned reputation for financial soundness. As we shall see, translated into mortgage allocation this has definite repercussions on housing markets. It is relatively easy to invest in the building society and deposits can be withdrawn at short notice, although if you pledge to keep savings for long periods the rate of interest is higher. The competitive rates of return have been aided by the privileged position afforded to the societies by the government. The return afforded by societies to savers is after tax has been deducted. Tax is charged at a composite rather than a basic rate, which helps the societies to keep a competitive edge over banks and other savings institutions, where the tax on savings is at the generally higher basic rate. Moreover, societies have been sheltered from the various financial constraints operated by the government. Compared with the banks, for example, the societies were not subject either to strict reserve: asset ratio rules or the various monetary policies such as the corset. The net effect has been for societies to be able to offer competitive rates on savings which are secure and which are easy to get at.

The greater the relative rate of return afforded by the societies, the more investment is attracted. Conversely, when more competitive rates are offered elsewhere, then money is withdrawn. The changing position of the building societies in the savings market and the effect on net receipts in the 1970s is shown in Figure 6.2. The wide fluctuation of interest rates apparent in this diagram reflects the explicit operation of fiscal controls by the government through the manipulation of interest rates. Successive economic crises have been attacked through varying the interest rate. Change in interest rate affects the banks' competitive position, and the societies have re-

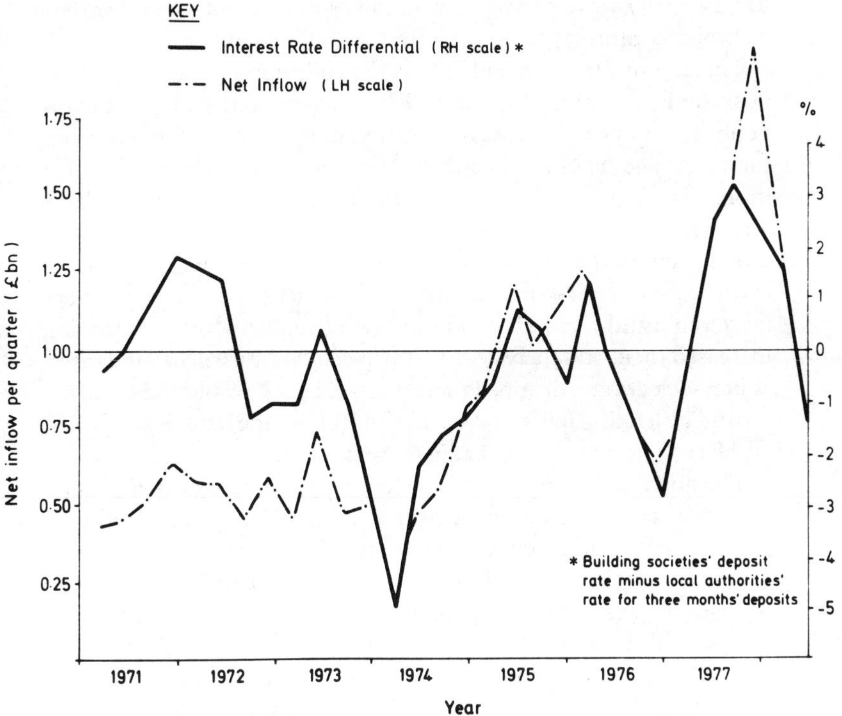

Figure 6.2 Interest rates and building society deposits

sponded in order to stop a haemorrhage of savings. Savings have flowed in and out so quickly in response to changes in relative rates of return because the societies have offered such good rates that they have attracted the big investors. In 1977, although only 20 per cent of accounts were in holdings over £2000, these constituted almost three-quarters of the total balances. The competitive position of the building societies has attracted these big investors, but the latter are very sensitive to small relative changes. A one-per-cent difference in return is scarcely noticed by the small saver, but for the big investor it is most important. The very success of the building societies has brought its own problems as the hot money flows in and out, upsetting net receipts and ultimately affecting net lending.

The societies as lending institutions The main lending business of building societies is mortgages for house purchase. Over 80 per cent of building society funds are used as loans for mortgages, with the rest going to investments in the local authorities and government securities. The net lending of building societies depends on two things: their intake of savings and the proportion of these that they dish out as mortgages.

The amount the societies take in depends upon their competitive position in the savings market. When rates of return are less competitive, investors withdraw their holdings and there are less funds for mortgage lending. The fluctuation of net lending has become more pronounced throughout the 1970s as the societies have attracted the big investors sensitive to the rapid changes of relative rates of return. The most dramatic change in net lending came in the early 1970s. In 1971 and 1972 the societies' rates were very favourable and there was a net inflow of funds. Mortgage lending increased then, and there was a 20-per-cent increase in net advances. When society rates dropped there was a net outflow of funds, and net mortgage lending fell in real terms throughout the latter half of 1972, all of 1973 and reached a nadir in early 1974.

The flow of savings is only one element, albeit the most important one, affecting net lending. The other is the liquidity ratio, which is the ratio of liquid assets to total assets. A high ratio indicates that more receipts are being placed in liquid investments rather than in mortgages. An increase in liquidity ratio suggests a build-up of reserves. In the 1950s the liquidity ratio was averaging about 15 per cent; throughout the 1960s the ratio was increasing to an average of 16 per cent. The early 1970s saw an increase as savings poured in, but a decline in 1973 to 15.8 per cent as savings were withdrawn. The general trend in the liquidity ratio since 1973 has been upward and by 1977 it was 21 per cent. The ratio fell in 1978/9 to 19.1 per cent in 1980 as a response to large withdrawals. Although the societies have reserves which can be drawn upon in times of net withdrawal of funds, these reserves do not provide a perfect buffer against very large-scale fluctuations and withdrawals. If the fluctuations are large enough, then net lending is affected in two ways. First, when the number of mortgages declines, the level of effective demand is reduced. This eventually feeds through to the house-building industry as builders find it difficult to sell housing. The decline in building society mortgages is reflected in the fall-off in new housing starts. The competitive position of the building societies thus has a direct effect on the number of houses constructed. Second, the rapid increase in the volume of funds will, holding everything else constant, tend to lead to house price increases. When there are many mortgages chasing fewer houses, conditions are ripe for inflation in the price of new houses. This was well-illustrated in the house price explosion of the early 1970s, when a net intake of funds by the societies led to record mortgage lending and ultimately to a house price spiral. The converse is also true. When there is a reduction in mortgages, effective demand falls and less mortgages are chasing more houses. As in the mid-1970s the result is for a slowing-down of house price increases.

Patterns of mortgage lending When building societies allocate mortgages they tend to avoid risky propositions. Mindful that their ability to attract savings is dependent upon the security of their investments they tend to adopt the policy of risk-minimization. Since there always seem to be more applicants than mortgages the societies are in the position of being able to pick and choose to whom they give mortgages. And they choose those applicants who meet the requirements. Let us consider the allocation of mortgages by households, by dwellings and by residential areas.

Households An important consideration is income; societies are loath to give a mortgage worth more than two-and-a-half times a household's annual income. A household with a total annual income of £8000 may receive a £20,000 mortgage. Allowances are sometimes made for households where there are two wage-earners. A typical case is for the society to give two-and-a-half times the man's income and a sum equal to the woman's; thus a man earning £8000 and a woman earning £6000 are able to get a mortgage up to £26,000.

Income is not the only requirement: the societies are also concerned with its stability. Good risks are those in salaried positions with regular employment and security of tenure with good clear prospects. Bad bets are those not on salaries with fluctuating incomes. Actors, for example, find it notoriously difficult to get mortgages. The figure of two-and-a-half times income is only an average and conceals wide variations.

The net result is for building societies to favour non-manual salaried workers. This bias has changed throughout the 1970s, however, as unionized manual workers, especially skilled manual workers, have achieved better working conditions and more secure employment contracts. Although the bias exists, in absolute terms the number of manual heads of households receiving mortgages is greater than non-manual heads of households. Building society allocation of mortgages does, however, operate against low-income non-manual workers. Their income is often insufficient to enter the housing market, and their poor security of employment and limited job prospects make them a bad risk in the eyes of the building societies. The overall distribution of mortgages by different socio-economic groups, and the resultant bias towards non-manual workers, is shown in Figure 6.3.

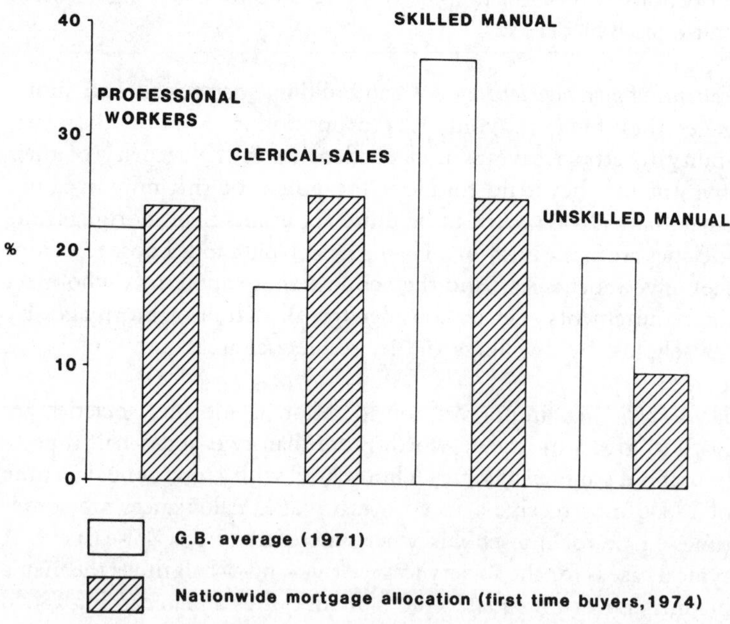

Figure 6.3 Mortgage allocation by socio-economic group

Building societies are also concerned with the age of applicants. Building society loans are typically for a twenty-five-year period; 60 per cent of loans made in 1977 were of this length. Older households, those with the head of household over forty, receive shorter terms with higher repayments. The societies are particularly eager to attract young heads of households, especially first-time buyers. Throughout the 1970s the proportion of mortgages going to such households was greater than 40 per cent. The figure fell from 61 per cent in 1971 to 47.3 per cent in 1978. As owner-occupation has become more important, the existing owner-occupiers seeking second and third mortgages are beginning to dominate the societies' waiting lists. The allocation of mortgages to individual households is also affected by a range of wider considerations. The building society managers' main task is to secure investments. Mortgages are often allocated in order to lubricate the continued inflow of investment. Solicitors, estate agents and other financial agents who help in this process are aided in return by favourable treatment of people they recommend for mortgages. The best way to gain a mortgage is to be young, rich, and very friendly with a solicitor who plays golf with a building society manager.

Dwellings Building societies are concerned with the security of the loan. In the event of foreclosure they want to be able to resell the property quickly. Their ideal property is a detached or semi-detached new house in a quiet residential area. They are not so keen to lend on non-standard property, e.g. converted property, older property or property in mixed residential/industrial areas. Societies lend more mortgages on newer properties (see Table 6.2). When lending on non-standard, older property they require larger deposits, 25 to 30 per cent of purchase price rather than the 5 to 10 per cent for newer properties, and shorter repayment periods, between ten and fifteen years rather than the twenty to twenty-five years' repayment period for newer, standard properties.

Table 6.2 Age of dwellings and building society mortgage allocation

	Age distribution all o–o dwellings (%)	*Mortgage allocation (1976) (%)*
Pre-1919	33.5	20.0
1919–45	29.9	18.0
Post-1945	36.4	61.0

Residential areas Because of building society lending rules there is a definite spatial expression to building society lending. Very crudely, we can characterize it as a flow of funds to the suburbs and a mere trickle to inner-city areas. The outer and inner suburbs contain the newer property in predominantly residential areas, and the typical purchaser is the middle-income household. In the inner areas by contrast, the housing is older, often terraced and sometimes non-standard. The land use is mixed with industrial premises and major traffic groups, and since the housing is cheaper it attracts the lower-income purchaser. The operation of building society lending rules biases mortgage allocations away from inner areas.

In some areas explicit policies of minimum lending have been discovered. Certain inner areas are seen by building society managers as bad risks and very few mortgages are allocated to them. The term 'red-lining' has been used to describe this practice. The name is supposed to derive from the experience of a reporter in Boston, Mass., who was investigating the lending patterns of financial institutions and found one that had a map of the city with a red line round the area within which it would not give mortgages. The name has stuck. My own research experience confirms that it is practised in British cities: during an interview with a branch manager of a major building society the term red-lining came up. The manager stated categorically, 'we do not red-line'. Later in the discussion he pointed to the St Pauls district of Bristol on the map and said that 'there are certain areas in the city, however, where we won't lend'.

Building society policy can become a self-fulfilling prophecy in respect of these inner-city areas. The societies refuse to lend because they consider the areas to be too run-down. But by their very action of withdrawing the life blood of mortgage finance they hasten deterioration. Existing owners cannot sell, few can buy, and property maintenance declines. The lack of building society finance may vitiate policies which seek to improve the older neighbourhoods of our major cities. Policies of rehabilitation and improvement are predicated upon the existence of finance for owner-occupation. If this is lacking it is difficult to stop further deterioration.

Building society lending policy varies through time as net receipts vary in size. When the building societies have a strong position in the savings market, investment is attracted and net lending increases. The societies can advance a higher proportion of purchase price, give a higher mortgage-to-income ratio, and more money is available for the 'marginal' properties of older dwellings, converted flats and inner-city properties. When the societies' competitive position falters, investments are withdrawn and net lending may decline. Societies ration their mortgages; first in line are savers with the society, first-time buyers and those having to buy another house because of a change in job which requires household relocation. After this demand has been met the societies tend to give lower advances, with a smaller mortgage-to-income ratio, and the marginal cases are reconsidered. There is a drawing in of lending as less mortgages are granted to marginal properties, and very large mortgages are no longer allocated. A reduction in net lending involves a concentration on the middle-income households buying standard property.

Throughout the 1970s a number of changes affected building society policy. First, the shift from redevelopment to improvement and the decline of house building introduced a subtle change in the supply and demand for housing. There are now more mortgage applications for older, inner-city properties. The societies have been slow to respond. Their traditional bias against such property in general, and certain inner-city areas in particular, have continued despite the emerging trends. There is now pressure in the form of demand and political prompting for societies to lend more on older inner-city properties, and especially properties in GIAs. Second, family structure has changed. There are now more single-person households and adults living together outside marriage. The traditional nuclear family of mother, father and two children is dissolving into smaller households. This has involved greater demand for smaller flat-type properties and introduced complications in assessing household income. Again, the building societies have been slow to respond, and the picture of a desirable borrower held by most building society managers is of the steady man in a steady job with a steady family. Third, there is more pressure on the building societies from other savings institutions. The banks are hustling for trade, and the government through national savings schemes is eager to attract savings. The building societies are now facing stiffer competition. Their response has varied between different societies, and the result is for the traditional uniformity of society policy to change as the more vigorous societies have responded to this new competition by offering different interest rates and more attractive propositions for the small-time savers, and, in general, adopting a more aggressive stance. We may well be witnessing a period of change in the building society movement as the smaller, less innovative societies go to the wall in the face of this new competition.

The local authorities

Mortgages are also granted by the local authorities. There is a long history of local authorities' mortgage lending. Under the Small Dwelling Acquisition Acts of 1899 and 1923 advances could be made on property within the local authority area for a maximum loan period of thirty years, and interest rates were set at 0.25 per cent above the current rate charged by the PWLB to the local authority. These Acts were an early attempt to encourage owner-occupation. At the time of their implementation owner-occupation was a minority tenure and building societies were small fry. The Acts had very little impact.

The most significant increase in local mortgage lending came with the Housing Financial Provisions Act of 1958. Under this Act authorities were allowed to lend mortgages to any person acquiring, instructing, converting, enlarging or improving housing. Unlike in previous legislation, no limitation was placed on the location of property, no maximum repayment period was defined and no particular interest rate charges were suggested. The Act has to be seen as part of the post-war Tory attitude towards encouraging owner-occupation and, more particularly, as a response to a short-term decline in building society receipts and net lending. In 1955 the net advances of building societies amounted to £180 million, but this had declined by 1957 to £155 million and to £149 million in 1958. The 1958 legislation was a means of further encouraging owner-occupation at a time when building society lending was falling.

The absolute and relative amounts of local authority lending is shown in Figure 6.4. In the early 1960s, when local authorities were advancing between £50 million and £150 million, there appeared to have been very few direct controls by central government on the amount or the direction of lending. From 1965 onwards central government controls became more important. They took two forms. First, there were restrictions on total lending. The graph of subsequent lending is a useful barometer of economic crisis in the British economy and subsequent public expenditure cutbacks. The cuts in lending in 1968–9 and 1976–7 were part and parcel of exercises in public expenditure reductions. Against this overall background of lending being an element used in the pursuit of macroeconomic policies, mortgage lending has been used by central government as a response to housing problems and in pursuit of housing objectives. Thus, lending was allowed to increase in the early 1970s as building society lending was falling, and it was expanded

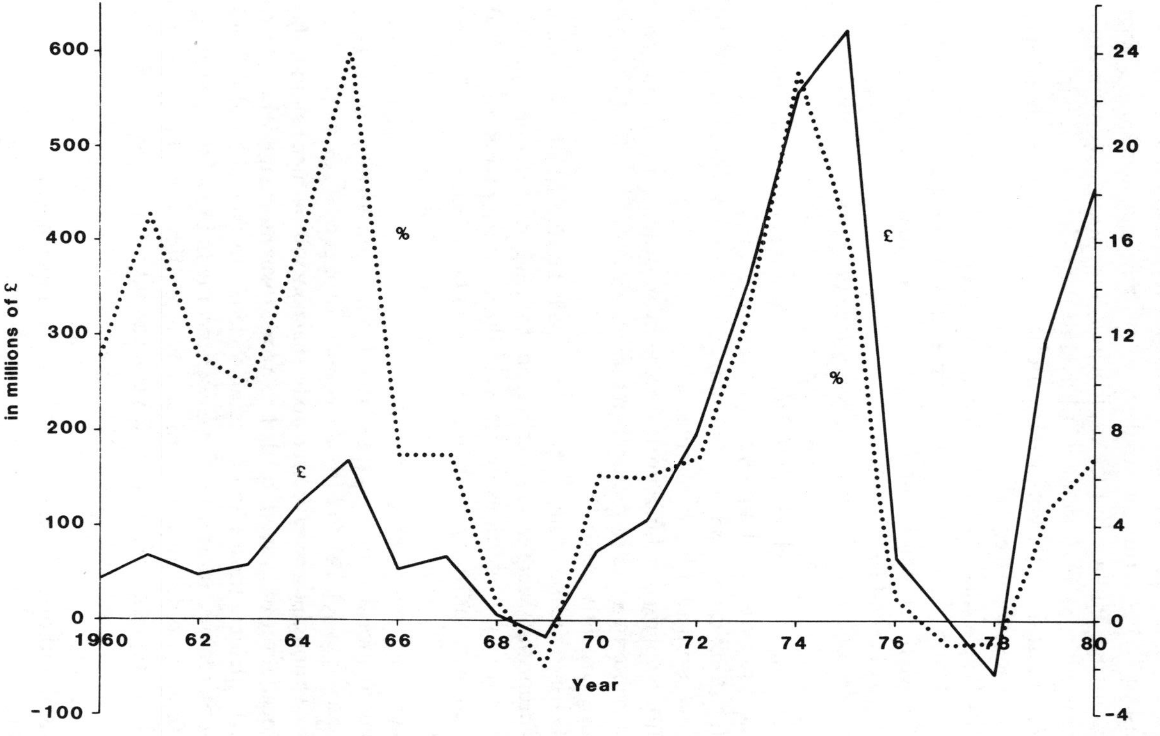

Figure 6.4 Local authority mortgage lending

again in 1980 as part of the Tory policy to encourage the sale of council houses. Second, central-government controls also extended to the direction of lending. From 1965 local authorities have been asked by government circulars to provide information on their mortgage lending. In 1971 explicit guidelines were laid down. Local authorities were encouraged to lend to the following groups:

(a) Existing tenants of local authorities, people on the waiting list or those displaced by slum clearance.
(b) Applicants who are homeless, threatened with homelessness or living in overcrowded and unhealthy conditions.
(c) Members of self-build groups who want to occupy the premises as individual owners.
(d) Applicants who want to buy older property or property that could be improved with improvement grants.
(e) Applicants who wish to buy older and smaller property but are unlikely to get a commercial mortgage.
(f) Applicants who wish to purchase larger property for partial occupation by themselves.
(g) Applicants taking up residence in or around a development, intermediate or overspill-receiving area.
(h) Urgently needed staff.

During the building society mortgage famine of 1973–4, local authorities were also encouraged to lend to first-time buyers purchasing new housing. It was during this period that local authority mortgage lending increased in both relative and absolute terms. When the building societies recovered their position, the local authority quota was reduced and the mortgage lending of the authorities declined sharply after 1975. From 1976–7 to 1978–9, categories (c), (g) and (h) above were dropped.

Although there have been no formal controls on such lending, the local authorities have tended to work their mortgage schemes to complement those of the building societies. In general, local authorities provide mortgages for lower-income households purchasing cheaper, older property; these characteristics are highlighted in Table 6.3. The figures are taken from a study of mortgage lending in Bristol during 1977, and the building society figures relate to a major building society. Notice two things about the figures: first, how local authority lending tends to go to lower-income households, older property and inner-city areas; second, that although relatively more important in these areas the absolute size of building society lending is important. For example, while 92 per cent of local authority lending went to dwellings built before 1919 and only 47 per cent of building society loans, the respective absolute figures are 115 and 231. Throughout the country, while the local authorities made 62,000 loans to pre-1919 dwellings in 1975, the building societies in total gave 126,000 mortgages.

Table 6.3 Mortgage lending in Bristol, 1977

Characteristic of applicants	*Local authority*	*Building society*
Average income	£3449	£4830
Average age	30	30
% in professional and managerial jobs	13%	26%
% in semiskilled and unskilled jobs	24%	19%
Loan characteristics		
Average loan	£5718	£8354
Loan as % of amount requested	97%	77%
Average repayment	20 years	24 years
Property characteristics		
Loans on pre-1919 dwellings	92%	47%
Average purchase price	£6441	£10,800
Neighbourhood characteristics		
Loans in inner city	72%	30%
Total number of mortgages	125	492
Total amount of lending	£0.7 million	£4.11 million

Source: Bassett and Short, 1980b

Local authority mortgage lending varies across time and space. The variation in time reflects the peaks and troughs of overall mortgage lending. When there are more funds, more mortgages can be allocated and most of the priority groups ((a) to (h) above) can be considered. Indeed, there is some evidence that local authority mortgage lending extends beyond these categories during boom periods. When total lending is reduced, most authorities respond by restricting lending to the priority cases. In Bristol, for example, a comparison of local authority mortgage lending in 1975 and 1977 reveals that the decline in lending over the period was accompanied by a greater concentration on priority cases and on households less likely to obtain a building society mortgage because of income, age or the nature of the property. The variation in space is a function of the variation in lending practice between local authorities. Although there are basic similarities, local authorities vary in the details of their lending policy. Some give loans up to a maximum of 90 per cent, others 95 and 100 per cent in special cases; some have a maximum of twenty-five years' repayment period, others thirty years'. The authorities also differ in the price limit on dwellings. A study of local authority lending in the West Midlands found that the limit varied from £5000 in Wolverhampton to £12,000 in West Bromwich. These variations have important consequences for the housing opportunities afforded to households in the different local authority areas.

Although local authorities lend to lower-income households more than building societies, they do not service the whole of the lower end of the market. The poorest households seeking the cheapest houses have difficulty in getting local authority mortgages. This is partly due to the use of surveyors who evaluate dwellings according to the more conservative principles of building society lending. In part it is also due to explicit policies. Some inner-city areas were denied local authority mortgages in the early 1970s because it was thought that the buildings would be demolished. Local authorities did not want to lend in areas where comprehensive redevelopment was planned. When the plans failed to materialize the areas still had problems in getting loans.

The support lending scheme Local authority mortgage lending was severely curtailed in 1975 as part of wider public expenditure reductions. To sweeten the bitter monetarist pill the Labour government sought to fill the gap left by the withdrawal of local authority mortgage lending. The societies agreed. They had been watching the local authorities lending moving up market into their traditional areas. Under the agreement the largest 200 local authorities could refer to building societies, applicants to whom they would have granted a mortgage given more funds. Regional offices of the Building Societies Association were involved in matching local authorities and societies. In the year 1975–6 £100 million had been set aside for this purpose, but this scheme was slow to get off the ground and by February 1976 only £18 million had been allocated. The scheme involved the creation of new links at the local level between housing departments and building societies; in some cases smooth working relations had yet to be achieved. The scheme did pick up and by July 1976 £64 million had been approved under referral mortgages. Further cutbacks were announced in local authority lending in July 1976 by Peter Shore, then Secretary of State for the Environment, and the building societies were asked to allocate a larger total for the support lending scheme. It was agreed by the government and building societies that £176 million should be allocated for 1977/8 and £300 million for 1978/9. Only two-thirds of the £176 million was taken up, though most of the £300 million allocated was in fact loaned in 1978/9.

Under the referral scheme the normal lending requirements still applied. So although more building society mortgages were going to lower-income applicants purchasing older property in the late 1970s, this was not a change from the previously more restricted lending. Under the referral scheme, as the building societies association noted, 'societies have undertaken in the *normal course of their business* many mortgages that would otherwise have gone to local authorities' (BSA, 1980, p. 54).

The support lending scheme did not fill the gap at the lowest end of the market formerly served by the local authorities. The scheme did not involve the reappraisal of those applicants whose income, proposed accommodation or future neighbourhood fell below the societies' requirements. The late 1970s saw a diminishing number of local authority loans going to the poorer inner areas of the city, and a further restriction on the housing opportunities of marginal owner-occupiers.

Insurance companies and banks

Insurance companies and banks are far less important in providing housing finance than building societies. Although they were important in the early 1960s, and in 1961 they jointly accounted for 26 per cent of all mortgages allocated, they became less important as the building societies grew and local authorities expanded their operations. In the late 1970s they contributed jointly less than 5 per cent of all mortgages.

They are important in certain sectors of the market. Insurance companies, for example, in contrast to the building societies, are more important at the upper end of the market, servicing the higher-income households purchasing more expensive property with shorter-term, higher-interest-rate mortgages. Almost a third of the value of insurance company lending takes the form of top-up loans to a building society mortgage. A typical example is of the household seeking to buy a £30,000 house: they have £5000 from the sale of their previous house, they get a building society mortgage of £20,000 and an insurance company top-up of £5000. Top-up loans are used by mortgage brokers because they get a commission from the insurance companies and they are enabled to spread their building society mortgage quota. Much of insurance company business in the housing market is in the form of endowment schemes used in conjunction with mortgage endowment policies. It works like this: the borrower pays off the interest to a building society and makes regular payments to an insurance company for an endowment policy which lasts for the same length as the mortgage. On maturity the endowment is used to yield a capital sum to the borrower and pay off the capital debt to the building society. In 1977, almost a quarter of all mortgages were of this endowment type. In general, insurance companies concentrate on the upper end of the market, acting as secondary mortgage lenders, providing second mortgages, topping-up-loans and providing endowment policies.

Banks serve the two extremes of the housing market. At the upper end they provide loans for higher-income customers. They are also involved in short-term bridging loans, which take two forms: either the bank provides all the money required to purchase another dwelling before the household's previous dwelling is sold and the mortgage is arranged, or the bank provides the 10-per-cent deposit required by solicitors on signature of the house purchase contract. More recently, in the late 1970s, the large clearing banks have been moving into more mainstream mortgage lending, after years of looking on from the sidelines at the lucrative trade in building society mortgages. In 1981, for example, Barclays Bank increased their 1981 quota for mortgage lending from £200 million to £500 million. The banks initially provided the larger loans for the more expensive properties, typically between £15,000 to £25,000 (the average building society loan in 1979 in comparison was £11,000). Their more recent relative success in moving down market derives from the higher interest rates of the late 1970s. As bank rates increased, building societies increased their mortgage rates in line with the higher rates afforded to investors to ensure continued inflow of savings. In the first half of 1981, for loans over £15,000, building societies were charging rates similar to or greater than those provided by the major banks. However, in January 1981, for example, when a £25,000 mortgage from the Halifax Building Society had an interest rate of 14.5 per cent, a similar mortgage from Citibank was only 14 per cent. In general, as house price inflation pushes up the mortgage loan required, more and more households are forced to pay the building societies higher rates for larger loans, at which point bank lending becomes very competitive. Unless the societies adjust their policies the banks will successfully move into the upper-middle and middle end of the market, and the building society growth of the 1970s may become a slight downturn in the 1980s.

At the lower end of the market some clearing banks and finance companies have been providing mortgages. During the early 1970s the banks moved into this area, offering short-term loans at high interest rates to purchasers of older property. Although the banks are less active at the lower end of the market, finance companies such as the Julian Hodge company still operate in certain inner-city areas, providing short-term loans with even higher interest rates. Table 6.4 provides a comparative picture of interest rates in Saltley, Birmingham, in 1974. The fringe banks and finance companies can be seen as lenders of the last resort, providing mortgages for households unable to obtain building society finance or local authority support. The punitive interest rates lead to high repayment costs for households, which may necessitate reductions in repair and maintenance expenditure and /or taking in lodgers to meet high outgoings. Both of these things may lead to a further deterioration in housing quality, greater difficulty in obtaining building society finance and thus a reliance on finance companies . . . and so the vicious circle is complete.

Table 6.4 Mortgage lending in Saltley, Birmingham, 1974

Mortgage source	*Interest rate (%)*	*Repayment period (years)*	*Average payment (£ per month)*
Building society and local authorities	11	15–25	20
Clearing banks	16–18	5–10	34
Fringe banks	17–28	5–10	47

The financing of owner-occupation

The post-war years have seen the rise of owner-occupation. This has been financed partly by private savings and partly by public subsidies. The level and method of financing owner-occupation has a number of repercussions with possible effects beyond the confines of the owner-occupied housing market. Three points can be made. First, the absolute level of financing is enormous. In 1976, a £6000 million gross fund was needed to finance house purchase loans, and in 1986 it is estimated that £9000 million will be needed (at constant prices). As owner-occupation has spread and the price of housing has remained high, there has been a growing, almost insatiable, demand for more funds. This raises a problem: can the private institutions meet the demand? Under present arrangements, they can do so only if they provide a competitive rate of return. In the case of the building societies this will involve a continuation of the privileged position afforded by the government, but now there is mounting pressure from the banks and from others for this position to be changed.

There is also competition from the government itself. In 1980 the National Savings Bond Scheme offering good inflation-proofed returns to the over-fifties raised £2000 million from the same pool of personal savings from which the building societies seek to obtain deposits. In this case there is direct competition between the government fiscal policy and its housing policy. The huge amounts of funds involved and the competition from other sources make the continuing financing of large-scale owner-occupation a problematic concern. Second, and this is directly related to the first point, is too much money being diverted to owner-occupied housing? There are two separate themes here:

(a) It has been argued that there is too much subsidization of owner-occupation. In the financial year 1978/9, tax relief on mortgage repayments amounted to £1100 million, and relief on capital gains cost the exchequer £1500 million in lost revenue. In total, therefore, £2600 million of revenue was lost in a year when the public sector borrowing requirement was £9100 million. To get the scale of the thing, if the government had an extra £1000 million it could allow a 2 pence in the pound reduction in the basic rate of income tax. Housing subsidies have been cut as part of public expenditure reductions, but only subsidies to the public housing sector; subsidies to owner-occupation have remained relatively unscathed.

(b) It has also been suggested that the amount of finance directed towards owner-occupation diverts resources from industry. On the surface the argument seems plausible. For while investment in manufacturing has fallen in real terms, coinciding with the declining world share in exports, the building societies are continuing to pull in money. But all the evidence we have (especially that reported in the Wilson committee) suggests that the lack of investment in industry reflects poor rates of return and little demand rather than an explicit diversion of funds. However, the contrast between the form and level of investments is striking: investors in building societies get good safe returns and borrowers receive loans to be paid over long periods, while entrepreneurs and manufacturing industry seeking cash can only receive high-interest loans over short periods.

Third, the form of the financing of owner-occupation has been regressive. Public subsidies of income tax and capital gains tax relief have helped owner-occupiers, who as a whole are richer than either council house tenants or tenants in the private rented sector. The distribution of subsidies to owner-occupiers and local authority tenants in different income bands is shown in Table 6.5. The table also shows that even within the owner-occupied sector the richer households have gained the most. The system of housing finance has given most to those who need it least.

Table 6.5 Distribution of subsidies★ by income and tenure

	Owner-occupiers	*Local authority tenants*
Income of household (£)	*Average tax relief and option mortgage subsidy (1974/5) (£)*	*Average total subsidy (1974/5) (£)*
Under 1000	59	166
1000–1499	73	180
1500–1999	91	180
2000–2499	104	144
2500–2999	101	147
3000–3499	129	154
3500–3999	129	148
4000–4999	148	164
5000–5999	179	156
+6000	369	154
All	141	162

★ Does not include capital gains tax exemption for owner-occupiers
Source: Housing Policy Green Paper, vol. 1, Tables IV34, IV35

THE HOUSEHOLDS

Who are the owner-occupiers?

The profile of owner-occupied households reflects the rules of access to the owner-occupied sector. The characteristics of owner-occupiers in relation to households in the other tenure categories are given in Figure 6.5, which shows that owner-occupiers in general tend to be richer than either council house tenants or tenants in private renting; and in Figure 6.6, which suggests that small family households predominate. The advertiser's image of the typical family – mother, father and two children – is met in reality most often amongst owner-occupiers. Although most middle- and upper-income households are in owner-occupation, and almost 90 per cent of professional workers and 80 per cent of employers and managers are in owner-occupation, it is not a tenure type solely for the professional classes. If we consider the distribution of the socio-

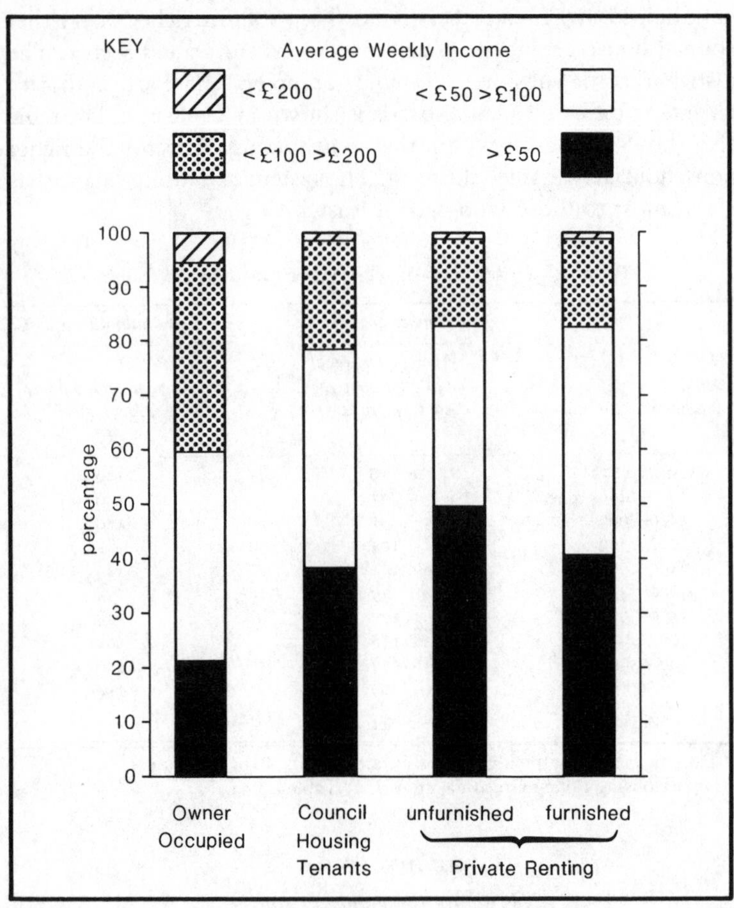

Figure 6.5 Tenure and income, 1976

economic group of the head of households by tenure, we can see that almost 41 per cent of owner-occupiers are manual workers. The category of owner-occupation is further broken down in Table 6.6 into outright owners and those with mortgages. A majority of households who are the outright owners of their accommodation are retired. Only a small proportion of those with mortgages are retired, and the comparison of those with mortgages and the distribution by socio-economic group for Britain as a whole reveals a marked bias towards non-manual households in general and the under-representation of the semi-skilled manual category in owner-occupation.

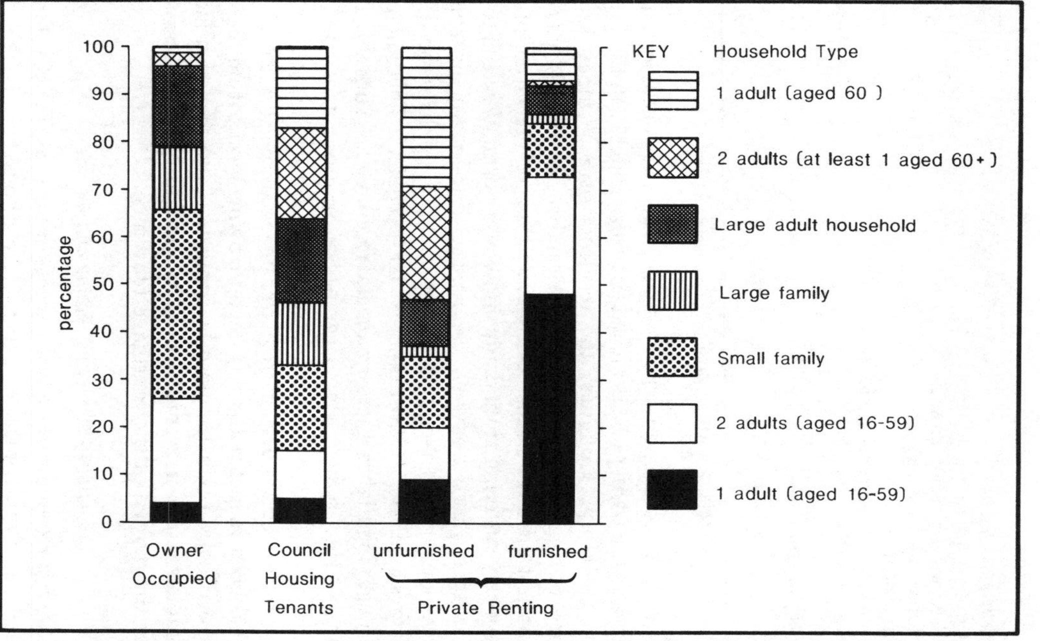

Figure 6.6 Tenure and household type, 1976

Table 6.6 Socio-economic status of owner-occupiers, 1978

Socio-economic category	*Outright owners*	*HHs with mortgages*	*GB total*
Economically active heads			
Professional and managerial	13	33	15
Intermediate and junior non-manual	9	21	13
Skilled manual and own-account non-professional	13	32	25
Semi-skilled manual, personal service and unskilled manual	8	9	13
Economically inactive heads	57	4	33
Total	100	99	99

Source: General Household Survey, 1978

There are, of course, owner-occupiers and owner-occupiers. The term covers the owner of a detached country residence in the green belt of the Home Counties, the residents of a Wimpey semi-detached paying off a large mortgage, and the household paying high interest rates for a finance-company loan on a terraced inner-city property suffering from damp and woodworm. We need to be aware of these distinctions. We can identify low-income occupiers of poorer-quality inner-city properties who do not share the fiscal advantages available to most other owner-occupiers. These households are paying higher interest rates and receiving less subsidy. The shift in housing policy from clearance to improvement has left behind many of the older private-sector houses in the inner city, demand for which has been particularly strong amongst Asians. The result has been an increase in low-income owner-occupation, but an owner-occupation which cannot be compared with that of affluent suburbanites either in terms of the size and nature of the housing asset or the burden of the mortgage repayments.

Owner-occupation, income and wealth

There are few expenditures which exceed the purchase of a dwelling. It is the largest single piece of expenditure a household is likely to make. Over the 1970s the average house price varied between 2.5 and 3.5 times the average annual income. The corresponding figures for a car were 0.5 and 1.0, and for a washing machine 0.08 and 0.12. Mortgage repayments themselves are a significant element in monthly budgets. At the beginning of a mortgage, repayments can constitute as much as one-third of household earnings. This is the so-called 'front-loading' problem: the heaviest burden of a mortgage being faced during the early years, often when incomes are low. Throughout the course of a mortgage, repayments decline as a proportion of income as the sum borrowed is paid off, with the rate of decline reflecting the rate of income inflation. The higher the rate of inflation, the less significant mortgage repayments become. When a change in interest rate occurs, if the change is relatively small the household often has the option of increasing payments or extending repayment periods. When the change is particularly large the mortgage institutions demand greater repayments. In November 1979, for example, the building societies recommended an interest rate increase from 12.5 to 15 per cent for new mortgages to be effective from January 1980. The usual monthly repayments on a £15,000 mortgage thus increased from £153.20 to £178.50. For the relatively affluent, old-established owner-occupiers this kind of increase is negligible, but for the new and lower-income borrower its magnitude impinges directly upon all aspects of the family budget. The rising interest rates of the late 1970s have prevented some households from taking out mortgages, as well as placing heavier burdens on those households with a mortgage (see Table 6.7). The pursuit of macro-economic policies, in this case the manipulation of interest rates, has had a direct effect on the budget of a large number of households.

Table 6.7 Building society interest rates for new mortgages

Month of recommendation	*Recommended interest rate (%)*
September 1945	4.0
July 1955	5.0
January 1965	6.75
April 1975	11.0
November 1979	15.0

When households make mortgage repayments they are paying for more than accommodation: they are purchasing property rights. We can make a useful distinction between the *use value* of a good and the *exchange value*. I shall use these terms in the following ways. The use value is the utility of a good – the use value of a car, for example, is the ability to drive around, the use value of a dwelling is the shelter it provides and the pleasure it brings. The exchange value of a good, in contrast, is the price we can get for it in the marketplace. The exchange value of a dwelling is the market price for which it can be sold. Owner-occupiers purchase both use value and possible exchange value, and in contrast with the other tenure types, owner-occupation can itself be a source of wealth.

In the post-war years dwellings have come to constitute an increasingly significant proportion of personal wealth as the level of owner-occupation has widened and deepened. In 1960 dwellings net of mortgages accounted for 17 per cent of total personal net wealth, and in 1975 this figure had increased to 37 per cent. The proportion of wealth in dwellings varied by income and Figure 6.7 shows how they are a significant proportion of the assets of the relatively affluent. For the very wealthy they are less significant. This distribution is not surprising. The rich invest in company securities and old masters while there are limits to housing consumption even for the wealthiest; indeed, the changing character of the times encourages relatively modest residences rather than the conspicuous consumption residences of the past. For the 'middle wealthy' range, however, the home is likely to be the main source of wealth. It has been possible to accumulate wealth by buying your own dwelling, because property has maintained and increased its value over the post-war years. Owner-occupiers have been able to purchase a steadily appreciating asset, with the rate of increase greater than the general level of price inflation. It has been one of the selling points of estate agents and building societies to lure first-time buyers: buying a house is an investment. An investment that, as Figure 6.8 clearly shows, has proved very successful.

There are four consequences of the exchange value element of owner-occupied housing.

(1) Because of the attractions of the investment many households have entered the owner-occupied sector. Although some commentators have seen this as a justification of the 'inherent' nature of the desire for private property, I prefer to see it as part of an investment decision. People, at least those who can afford it, have become owner-occupiers not simply because they have an innate desire to own a property but because it is a good investment. Given the fiscal character of the alternatives who would not choose owner-occupation? For existing owner-occupiers the fiscal attractions have led to a trading-up in the housing market, the purchase of more expensive housing in order to acquire a bigger asset. Before 1974, the larger the mortgage, the greater the tax relief, but since then the £25,000 limit has been imposed, a limit which has been maintained despite rapid house price increases. Nevertheless, it has paid owner-occupiers to move up-market, as the larger mortgage repayments have helped to reduce income tax and the greater repayments are

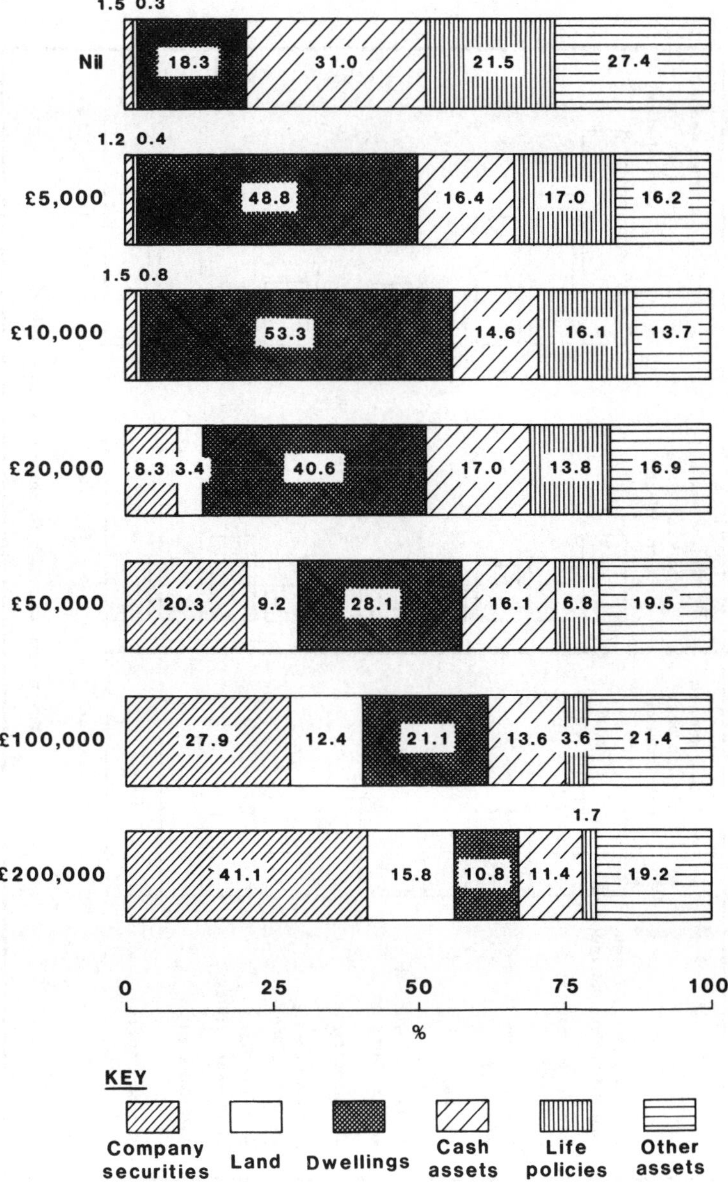

Figure 6.7 Asset structure by size of gross personal wealth (after Murie and Forest, 1980)

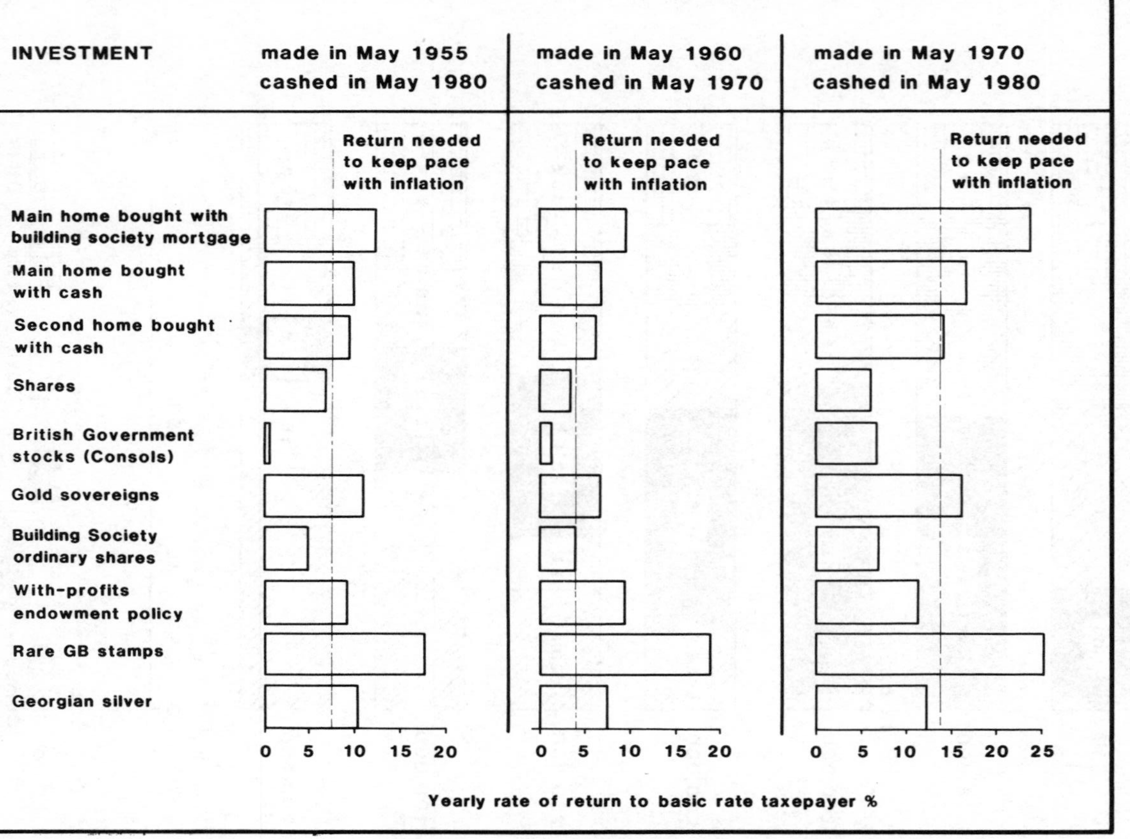

Figure 6.8 The relative return on housing compared to other investments (from *Which* 1980, p. 510)

offset, at least in the minds of the purchaser, by the larger assets being obtained. The order of the day has been for owner-occupiers to mortgage themselves to the hilt in order to buy the most expensive housing they can afford. Not all owner-occupiers have followed the logic of the financial arrangement of owner-occupation but a significant proportion have, to the extent that under-owner-occupation is an increasing phenomenon as more small households purchase large houses.

(2) Housing has and will become an important element in the transfer of wealth. In 1978 23 per cent of British households owned their property outright, and in the future this proportion is likely to rise. Outright owners have been and will be able to pass on their asset to their children in the form of legacies, and housing inheritance will become a significant element in the inter-generational transfer of wealth. Assume that parents leave a dwelling to their daughter. The transfer can take a number of forms: (a) the daughter could live in the house, thus saving mortgage repayments or rent payments; (b) she could sell the house and invest the proceeds; (c) she could keep the house and let it out, thus ensuring herself a regular income. If any of these strategies became dominant, then the following changes would occur. In the case of (b), households would have large capital sums at their immediate disposal either for investment in financial securities or for trading up in the housing market. The owner-occupied sector might become further segregated and a price division would occur, above which only those who had inherited housing wealth would be able to compete. Alternatively, if (c) became more important, then we might witness a revival of the private rented sector. What is certain is that the property inheritance would become a significant element in the transfer of wealth, overlying and often reinforcing the traditional divisions. An important distinction would emerge between households, based upon whether their parents were owners or non-owners. Property inheritance would become an important source of inequality as those not inheriting would become further constrained in their housing opportunity.

(3) There has been intense debate about the effects of owner-occupation on class structure and class-consciousness. Two positions can be crudely defined. First, there is the position which sets the primacy of social relations in the sphere of production. The basis of objective class position in this perspective is the ownership/non-ownership of the means of production. Owner-occupation may affect the perceived but not the objective class position. From

this standpoint the encouragement of owner-occupation is seen as an explicit state policy to provide a housing form which chimes in with the dominant ideology of private property ownership and to give a significant section of the population a stake in the present system. The encouragement of property-owning democracy is seen as an attempt to defuse sweeping social change. Ultimately, the effect is to obscure the real class relations behind the ideological fog of different tenure categories. A second alternative position has been advanced by Saunders (1978, p. 234) who argues,

> owner occupation provides access to a highly significant cumulative form of property ownership which generates specific economic interests which differ both from those of the owners of capital and those from non-owners. In other words I reject both the conservative argument that the spread of owner occupation constitutes the diffusion of capitalist property rights and the radical argument that it has resulted in a strengthening of false consciousness among the proletariat.

The first position is an assertion; the reality of the 'real' comes from the theory, not from empirical evidence or political action. The second position adopts too simplistic a division. As we have already noted, there are owner-occupiers and owner-occupiers. The term covers a variety of groups and dwellings, and owner-occupation is only a highly significant cumulative form of property ownership for the wealthier households. If both positions have their weaknesses they also have their strength. We can combine these in an alternative to the two extreme positions. In viewing the relationship between owner-occupation and class structure the following can be noted:

(a) Unlike the other tenure categories owner-occupation allows the realization of exchange value.

(b) Higher up the income and wealth scale housing is significantly more important as a form of accumulation.

(c) Class attitudes are formed by the totality of life experience. Experiences at work and at home can reinforce each other. If you are a factory worker you are unlikely to be the owner of a prestigious mansion. If you are screwed at work, the likelihood is that you are screwed in your housing construction. And being an owner-occupier does not compensate for living in a shoddily built, high-density box in the middle of a housing estate, with the dim prospects of a real gain at the end of your housing career.

(d) The political effects of owner-occupation seem to be most contentious to the middle class. Here an ambiguous position in relation to the means of production is superimposed upon a distinctive form of housing consumption.

Two contradictory processes have been at work in the post-war years. On the one hand, there has been the growing proletarianization of white-collar work. Many teachers, for example, now see themselves as state employees and members of a union fighting to preserve their job status rather than as élite members of a secure profession. Even university lecturers have a union affiliated to the TUC, and the talk in senior common rooms is more likely to be concerned with job security, fighting redundancies and bettering working conditions than with Wittgenstein, black holes, structuralism and post-modernist humour. On the other hand, it is precisely these self-same groups who have gained out of owner-occupation. With good access to building society funds they have been able to purchase a steadily appreciating asset at subsidized rates of interest. But while trying to keep council tenants out of their neighbourhoods the Association of University Teachers members, for example, may be combining with cleaners and laboratory technicians to fight against cuts in university education.

In conclusion then, owner-occupation has not significantly altered the *relative* distribution of wealth. It has been an important housing form for the growing number of white-collar workers, although the assertion that it is either a blinding of real interests or a new fracture of class divisions would seem to be too simplistic a statement for a complex phenomenon – a phenomenon bound up with the growth of the middle class. My contention is that while the work conditions of the middle income groups have drawn them into wider, work-based alliances, their housing consumption has distanced them from consumption-based alliances.

(4) The concern with the exchange value of housing has involved owner-occupiers in protecting property values in the constantly changing urban environment. All households are concerned to varying extents with what goes on in the neighbourhood as it impinges on their day-to-day life: the amount of play space, the character of the local schools, the nature of planning proposals for the locality are all matters of concern for all households, but for owner-occupiers there is an added interest. They tend to view such local events with particular attention to their effect on property values. In simple terms they want to protect their investment.

Indirect effects in the neighbourhood can take two forms. *Positive externalities* are the beneficial effects. A park, for example, provides positive benefits to nearby residences, and the creation of a new park may therefore increase property values. *Negative externalities* are the bad effects. A factory, for example, may generate traffic noise and pollution, all of which may lead to a reduction in property values. In the ever-changing urban environment owner-occupiers seek to manipulate the planning process through the form of political representation and informal lobbying, in order to increase positive externalities and reduce or stop negative externalities. Often the distinction is very fine. Access to local shops is an advantage, but being too close involves nearness to traffic. This ambivalence is also found with respect to schools and parks. There are, however, a number of widely agreed good and bad developments. For many owner-occupiers, the existence of nearby council housing estates is seen as a perceived negative externality. Similarly, new office or industrial development situated close at hand is seen as having a possible blight on property values. Even the construction of new owner-occupied housing is seen as a negative externality in the short term over the period of construction and over the long term if the new houses are cheaper than the existing dwellings. Much of local politics is taken up with owner-occupiers' mobilization against these developments. This involvement operates at a variety of scales. In London, for example, metropolitan housing politics have revolved around attempts of the 'owner-occupied' outer suburbs to resist the public rehousing programmes for inner-city residents, while within cities the councillors of owner-occupied wards have the responsibility of maintaining the exclusivity of their base. The process also operates in different places. In central city sites owner-occupiers have joined with renters to resist the encroachment of new office developments.

The local planning history of post-war British cities is essentially the story of urban renewal and the community response. At the edge of the city and in the exurban areas the story has been one of exclusion as owner-occupiers have sought to resist new residential developments which threaten their peace, quiet and property values. In the shire counties of the south-east the pressure of growth has resulted in the adoption of the politics of containment and exclusion by owner-occupiers' residents' associations as they have sought to stop new developments, direct them elsewhere or lessen their negative externalities. The process has been aided by changes in planning. Since 1968 the participation of the public has supposedly been an integral part of planning. The public is to be consulted about planning proposals before plans are implemented. In practice, public participation has been a partial thing, for those participating have been in general the articulate, the well heeled, those who can speak the planners' language and those with most to lose. By way of contrast we can compare the successful mobilization of wealthy rural owner-occupiers against the Third London Airport in the 1970s with the experience of low-income owner-occupiers fighting against the property development juggernaut in the central city areas.

For the very wealthy, direct action is rare. They live in the green belt, their property values are secured in the national interest. For middle-income owner-occupiers the position is different. They perceive dangers from below in the shape of new council estates, and above from builders and developers. Their success in dealing with these attacks on their property values depends upon their organizations, lobbying skills and resources. It is different again for the low-income owner-occupiers. With less resources and poor mobilization they have less power in manipulating the changing surfaces of externalities to their own advantage.

7

LOCAL AUTHORITY HOUSING

Local authority housing is housing provided by the local authorities (I shall use the terms council housing, local authority housing and public housing to mean the same thing). Its general story in post-war Britain has been one of a short period of initial expansion and then a longer period of downgrading to the role of a residual, though still important, tenure category. The period of expansion coincided with the first post-war Labour government and an increased demand for a higher social wage; council housing was an important element in the size and composition of the social wage. There was also a commitment by the first post-war Conservative government to build a record number of houses. From the mid-1950s onwards, however, owner-occupation was actively encouraged and less money was spent on council housing. The local authority housing sector was increasingly being used throughout the 1950s and the early 1960s to house special-needs groups, especially those rehoused in the process of comprehensive redevelopment. Local authority housing was becoming a residual category only suitable for those unable to afford owner-occupation.

The position of council housing as a second-class tenure category has a number of implications. It has meant that subsidies to owner-occupation have been seen as encouragement to market forces, while subsidies to council tenants are defined as handouts. It follows, then, that in times of financial stringency handouts should be reduced. To a tenure of failure, only the deserving should be admitted. Allocation roles, therefore, have to be established which distinguish between the deserving and the undeserving. Those undeserving existing tenants who are above certain income levels should be encouraged into entering their properly allotted tenure type. The carrots to do so have come in the form of physical incentives, and the stick has been one of higher council rents. The ultimate expression of post-war policy towards council housing is the sale of council houses.

This policy is predicated on the assumption that tenants should be liberated from their position. If they can afford it they should be able to buy their property and the natural order of things can then be restored.

There has been a convergence in the housing policies of the major political parties. Owner-occupation is now seen as the 'natural' tenure category. Council housing, in contrast, is seen as a second-class residual category, a tenure type which houses those who are unable to achieve owner-occupation. This social patronization turns into fiscal conservatism when economic crisis looms.

In this chapter the changing background to, and enfolding nature of, central state policies for the local authority housing sector will be examined. Since the policies are implemented by the local authorities I shall also examine the character of the local government response to central government directives. The relationship between the housing managers and the managed tenants will also be considered.

COUNCIL HOUSING AND STATE HOUSING POLICY

Chapter 2 has already provided an outline of the evolving story of post-war housing policies in Britain. It was shown that council housing played a key role in the deliberations. So as not to repeat all that exposition, I will thus represent the story in a different periodization, a classification of events which captures the essential story of council housing in post-war Britain.

Early encouragement (1945–54)

The Labour government which swept to power in 1945 had an electoral mandate for radical change. The war had proved a radicalizing experience, and the mass of people wanted social reforms and better housing. The Labour party met these demands, to some extent at least, in their manifesto for a new Britain. Housing was an integral part of the critical debate. In the 1945 election 41 per cent of the electorate sampled stated that housing was the most important issue, and only 15 per cent stated full employment. The nature of the political response was guided by the backroom planners. The desire for better social welfare provision was given substance by the civil servants. In the Ministry of Health a greater housing role was being planned for the local authority sector. In a planned society, local authorities were seen as responsive to planning signals whereas the private sector was not; the latter responded to profit, not social need or general social welfare.

The early legislation incorporated demands for better housing provision in the plans of the bureaucrats. Local authority housing was assigned a key role, and in 1946 local authorities were given the ability to purchase land for council house building, and the government subsidy for each council house was raised from £8.25 payable over forty years to £22 payable over sixty years. In 1949, local authority housing was to be provided for all the population, and was no longer reserved for special-need groups such as 'slum-dwellers' or the 'working class'. The result was impressive. Council housing completions increased from a negligible amount in 1945 to over 160,000 in 1948, and the proportion of households in council housing increased from 12 per cent in 1945 to 18 per cent in 1951. The quality of this housing was, in the light of later council housing, very good, because it was built to the relatively high standards laid down by the Dudley report.

The election victory of the Conservatives made little change to the council house building programme. If anything the programme was expanded as part of the Tories' election promise to build 300,000 houses a year. To meet this target the subsidy was raised in 1952 to £35.60 for each council house. Council house building increased and by 1954 it was running at over 200,000 completions per year. The role of the council house sector was, however, altered by the Conservatives. It was treated as a residual insofar as council house completions were to make up the difference between what the private sectors could complete for owner-occupation and the talismanic figure of 300,000. Local authority housing was to make up the difference. The quality standards were also reduced; in order to meet the high number of completions with the available funds, space standards were reduced. The Dudley report recommendations were not adhered to and the quality of the new council houses declined. Almost 100 square feet was lopped off the typical three-bedroomed house, and the average space fell from 1000 square feet in 1949 to just over 900 in the mid-1950s. Local authority housing was very gradually being transformed from a general-need, relatively good-quality tenure type to a much poorer-quality type.

Beginnings of a residual role (1954–70)

The pace of the transformation quickened in the mid-1950s. In 1955 the financing of local authority house building was altered. Previously, the authorities could borrow from the Public Works Loan Board at very low rates of interest. From the mid-1950s onwards the PWLB was only to be used as a last resort. Local authorities were thus forced to seek finance from the capital market, and local authority house building was made subject to fluctuations in commercial interest rates. As interest rates climbed, more of local authority housing expenditure was being used to pay off loans. By 1967–8 loan charges constituted 74.5 per cent of the expenditure of local authorities in England and Wales outside Greater London.

The residual role for local authority housing was mapped out by the 1956 Housing Subsidies Act. In this legislation central government subsidies for general-needs housing, i.e. housing to meet general demand, was abolished except for blocks of flats higher than four storeys. The subsidy was only paid for dwellings used to replace 'slums', again with the proviso that the higher the block of flats for rehousing former slum dwellers, the greater the subsidy. The local authority housing sector was further hit in 1957 as the response to emerging economic crisis was the now familiar tale of imposing limits on public expenditure. Local authority housing expenditure was immediately reduced by 20 per cent. The net result was that by the 1960s the quality of new council housing was low. As funds were turned off, the local authorities responded by reducing space standards. Subsidies to high-rise blocks were to begin the trend for local authorities to build high-density towers. In building unpopular poor-quality accommodation only for former slum dwellers, the local authority response was to strengthen the role of council housing as a second-class tenure category. It thus became easier for successive governments to see council house subsidies as essentially wasteful expenditure, a case of propping up the 'inadequates'. In the logic of this argument public expenditure reductions would naturally fall on the council house programme.

By 1960 council house building had fallen, primarily as a result of the expenditure cutback to under 100,000 completions per year. The 1960s marked something of a change. Council house building was stimulated in the early 1960s by the Conservatives, as part of an attempt to reflate the economy, and the 1961 Housing Act reintroduced general-need subsidies. Housing had also again become a political issue. The need to build more council housing was thus part economic and part political response. Public sector completions picked up from under 100,000 in 1961 to over 125,000 in 1964. Almost 40 per cent of these dwellings were in the form of blocks of flats of five storeys or more. This building form reflected the structure of subsidies, which in turn reflected the lobbying by the construction and design industries of central government and local authorities, and also the actions of local government members eager to point to gleaming concrete towers as a symbol of municipal *machismo*. The result was that, as more council houses were being built, more of them were in the form of tower blocks, and this unpopular building form was to stigmatize council housing even further.

When Labour came to power in 1964 they carried on with the Tories' building programme. The new government set out to build 500,000 dwellings by 1970, and the council house sector had a key role. To stimulate the local authorities the 1967 Housing Subsidies Act provided central government subsidies to counteract rising interest rates. The quality of new council houses was also improved by the setting down of minimum space standards and the phasing out of subsidies for high-rise blocks. Again, however, the local authority sector was secondary in importance. Labour had an historic and electoral commitment to council housing, but Labour's housing policy hinged upon spreading the benefits of owner-occupation to as many groups as possible and upon controlling the private rented sector. The expansion of council house building was seen only as a short-term necessity. In the long term, owner-occupation was to be encouraged. The acid test of Labour's commitment to council housing came in the wake of the economic crisis of 1967. Partial solutions to the crisis were seen in terms of reducing public expenditure, and the Treasury cast its fiscal eye on the local authority housing sector where costs were expanding because of high interest rates and the implementation of the much higher Parker Morris space standards. The Labour cabinet failed the test. Council house building was cut back and a new era was inaugurated in the British housing scene, a shift from new building to improvement. This shift not only involved a reduction in real resources, it also meant a greatly reduced role for local authority housing, since poor-quality houses in the run-down inner-city areas tended to be either in the owner-occupied or private rented sector. The improvement programme kept existing tenure arrangements intact.

A second-class tenure type (1970 onwards)

From 1970 onwards there has been a convergence in thinking between the major political parties concerning the broad outlines of their housing aims. For both parties owner-occupation is seen as a positive thing, something to be extended and encouraged. Council housing, on the other hand, has increasingly been downgraded as a peripheral tenure category, important in housing the poor but not a suitable tenure type for the majority of the population. Now there are some who would argue that the politicians have been merely reflecting the wishes of the people. Given the choice, it is true that most people would opt for owner-occupation. But this is not the point. The politicians and bureaucrats have created and maintained the conditions which make this choice all but inevitable.

The parties have, of course, differed in the specifics of the policies; the Conservative government of 1970, for example, took a direct line of attack against council housing, and their 1979 Housing Act reduced subsidies and will lead to increases in rent. Labour, in contrast, have had a different approach; they repealed the 1972 Act, increased subsidies, and tried to shield council house building from the ravages of inflation and spiralling construction costs. But they did little to change the basic operation of council house financing or the distribution of subsidies between the different tenure categories. Because local authorities had to go to the money market to obtain finance, the size of the loan charges reflected rates of interest, and increasing rates in the 1970s coincided with rising land and tender prices to increase costs dramatically. Table 7.1 shows the rapid increase in the early to mid-1970s. When the axe of public expenditure reduction was wielded in 1975 the council house sector was seen as a suitable and available neck. Local authority housing investment lost £646 million of its 1977/8 budget compared with 1975/6, almost a 25-per-cent reduction. In terms of the distribution of subsidies the then Secretary of State for the Environment, Anthony Crosland, set up the Housing Review to consider housing policy and housing finance. The report was published as a Green Paper in 1977. Those hoping for any real change were disappointed. The Report concluded that owner-occupation should be increased and no changes should be made to the existing pattern of subsidies. For the local authority sector the report suggested that a new block grant for housing investment should be introduced. Within this block grant,

Table 7.1 Average costs and borrowing rates of new local authority dwellings, England and Wales

	Average cost (£)	*Borrowing rate (%)*
1969/70	4190	9.1
1970/1	4560	8.5
1971/2	5140	7.0
1972/3	6130	8.5
1973/4	8360	12.8
1974/5	10,440	13.8
1975/6	11,960	12.1

Source: HPTV, Part III

the housing investment programme, the local authorities would have greater flexibility in spending money, but the size of the grant would be set by central government. While giving a measure of autonomy the new system was increasing central government control over local authority spending.

The Conservative government of 1979 took Labour's housing policies further along the same route, although to a much harsher conclusion. Both governments sought to reduce public expenditure in general, and local authority housing expenditure in particular, and both encouraged owner-occupation. Conservative policy, however, was wrapped up in Thatcherism – a mixture of economic monetarism and social Darwinism with a dollop of Christian redemptionism. The effects of Thatcherism were soon felt. The 1980 Housing Act extended central government control over local authority spending. Under the new financial arrangement, subsidies from central government to local authorities were based on the difference between costs, and income from rent and rate fund contributions. It was the Secretary of State for the Environment who was to judge reckonable cost. Here was the stick with which to beat spendthrift authorities who spent too much on council housing. The 1980 Act also gave tenants a statutory right to buy their council housing. Most tenants with three years' occupancy could buy at two-thirds of market value and the local authority also had to guarantee a mortgage.

There was also a direct attack on local authority housing programmes. Cuts were announced in June 1979, and in the 1980 White Paper on public expenditure housing expenditure was reduced from £5372 million in 1979/80 to £2790 million in 1983/4: a cut of almost 50 per cent. The White Paper budgeted for a total cut in spending up until 1983/4 of £3700 million, and reductions in housing expenditure constituted almost 70 per cent of this total. These cuts will mean the virtual collapse of council house building, the slowing down of improvement programmes and the demise of the local authority mortgage scheme. Estimates suggest that by 1983/4 there will be a shortfall of half a million dwellings. It was the largest attack on council housing in post-war Britain. The tragedy is that while local authority housing costs have been spiralling, this has not been due to building more houses. Between 1968/9 and 1977/8 the proportion of total housing expenditure used to build and improve dwellings has declined from 74 to 38 per cent. Almost two-thirds of the total expenditure went on loan charges. Thus, while the costs are those of interest repayments the cuts have been made in the capital expenditure programme of new house building and housing improvement. Between 1969 and 1974 the amount of interest paid to capital investors increased from £570 million to £1484 million, but the number of public sector completions declined from 150,000 to under 90,000. Interest continues to be paid but less houses are built.

THE MANAGERS AND THE MANAGED

Local authority housing is managed by the housing department of the local authority. This department is theoretically under the control of the housing committee of the local authority, although the level of control can vary from direct overseeing to minimal intervention. The housing department builds and designs the houses, sets rents and selects tenants, and allocates existing tenants to dwellings. There are strong central government guidelines for building and rent setting, but a much greater degree of freedom is afforded to local authorities in managing their housing programme. It is the local authority department, the housing managers, who determine the rules of access to council housing and allocate households to dwellings.

The context

The background within which housing managers operate is important in shaping the character of housing management. Four interrelated elements are important. The *political* context sets the size of their task. In Conservative-controlled authorities the local authority housing sector is small, rate fund contributions are kept low and the housing department is weak in relation to other local authority departments. In the large Labour-controlled authorities, local authority housing is an important element in the local housing market, rents are generally kept as low as possible and the housing department is one of the largest, most powerful departments in the local government bureaucracy. The *physical* context of the size and quality of the housing stock in relation to demand determines the difficulty of the task of the housing managers. When demand is low in relation to supply, the job is that much easier, and eligible households can be allocated acceptable dwellings; but when demand is high, applicants have to be graded according to some tight measure of need, and there is less slack for transferring tenants within the council house sector. In post-war Britain the general trend has been for demand to exceed supply. There are very few authorities that have had the luxury of supply exceeding demand. The precise nature of demand has often failed to mesh with the available supply. There is an overwhelming importance of three-bedroomed houses in the local authority housing sector, and over 45 per cent of all local authority dwellings are of this type. This structure operates against the entry of smaller families and one-person households into the local authority sector. In many of the larger cities the housing stock is dominated by flats. In the London boroughs 66 per cent of the stock is in the form of flats, with the proportion rising to 95 per cent in Camden and 93 per cent in Hackney. Yet this form of housing has proved to be very unpopular. Not enough council housing has been built and much of what has been built has proved unresponsive to demand.

The *ideological* context, by which I mean the set of ideas and beliefs that inform everyday life, determines the practice of council house management. Two elements are important. The first is the notion of council housing as welfare provision. We have already seen how the role of council housing has gradually been transformed into one of a residual function, housing those unable to get into owner-occupation. Translated into housing management and reinforced by the excess of demand over supply, this leads to the notion of council housing as a benefit, something given to the unfortunate that is not their right but a privilege. People, therefore, have to be deserving before they can get council housing. The housing department translates this notion of deserving households into a set of rules which seek to give clearcut guidelines in allocating dwellings. The second and related element is the atmosphere of paternalism which infuses council house management. Since council housing is seen as a benefit handed down to households rather than a basic right available to all households, the management of council housing takes on an authoritarianism which, as in other areas of social services, has probably done more to harm the cause of socialism than anything else. Most people have encountered the welfare state through frustrating experience with innumerable bureaucratic layers, whether in health, housing or education. In the council house sector this paternalism is very marked. Until 1980 tenants had no security of tenure and had a whole series of petty limitations placed on their occupancy of council housing. The 1980 Housing Act lifted some of these restrictions, but not the pervading ideology of local authorities as managers and tenants as the managed. For all intents and purposes tenants have had very little effective control over their accommodation.

Finally, there is the *temporal* context. In post-war Britain the precise role of local authority housing has varied. In the immediate post-war years council housing was meant to meet general needs. The housing department, therefore, had to deal with the wide range of applicants. From 1956 to the end of the early 1970s the local authorities embarked upon large-scale clearing schemes, and the housing departments were involved in rehousing many of the households whose accommodation was destroyed. During these years council housing was mainly for the special-need categories. Since the switch from clearance to renewal, the special-need function has declined and local authorities are now much more concerned with general needs.

These different contexts set the scene for housing managers. The most important elements in the housing manager's job are defining access to the local authority housing sector and allocating households to dwellings. We can consider each of these in turn.

Managing council housing

Those eligible for council housing include: (1) those in need of being rehoused as part of a clearance programme; (2) homeless households; (3) households in need.

(1) The eligibility for rehousing through clearance programmes is not automatic. Up until 1973 there was no legal duty for local authorities to house clearance families, and even after the 1973 Land Compensation Act the local authorities were given some measure of leeway in interpreting their duties. In general, most local authorities gave high priority to rehousing clearance families. In practice, the rehousing has given greatest priority to residents of long standing and to large families. Of those in clearance areas, young, small households, lodgers and families who have recently moved in have had the greatest difficulty in obtaining accommodation from the council. In most redevelopment schemes the councils have managed to rehouse almost 90 per cent of the residents, although this has involved a transfer of households from the inner city to the peripheral council estates as the overall densities of the replacement schemes were much lower than the original. This has often proved unpopular. In the Barton Hill scheme in Bristol almost 50 per cent of couples under forty were allocated accommodation in the outlying estates of the city, and of these households almost a half applied for a transfer back to Barton Hill after only a short period. The new rehousing schemes have often given people better housing in the wrong areas.

(2) Until the 1977 Housing (Homeless) Persons' Act local authorities did not have a statutory duty to rehouse the homeless. Some authorities did do so, but in others, like Bristol for example, the

social service department had responsibility and treated the problem by placing households without accommodation in bed-and-breakfast accommodation. In 1976 over 50,000 households applied for accommodation because they were homeless.

(3) In order to 'assess' need, households who apply for council accommodation are asked to fill in a questionnaire, and are interviewed at the council offices and/or in their home by a housing visitor of the local authority. The size of the household's housing need is then quantified by a points system which quantifies the unquantifiable. Points are gained for length of residence in the authority area, size of household in relation to space, the quality of the existing accommodation and related aspects such as ill-health. The points system varies by local authority, and Table 7.2 highlights the variation of the points system in six local authorities in the West Midlands. The number of points determines the position of the household on the housing waiting list, those with a large number of points receiving higher priority. The waiting list gives a semblance of rationality to the irrationality of the supply of adequate housing being less than the demand; it gives a sense of fairness to a basically unfair distribution of resources.

The points system and housing waiting lists have often been criticized for failing to deal adequately with housing need: the system requires households to apply – those who do not are obviously excluded; the points system adopted by a local authority will favour some groups at the expense of others; it is open to abuse insofar as persistent applicants and those who get medical evidence to support their case will push their way up the list. All these criticisms are true, but given the inadequate resources allocated to the council house sector it is difficult, barring a huge injection of funds, to think of a credible alternative. The main improvements could come from better advertising so that all households know their rights, easier forms to fill in so that no-one is dissuaded from applying, and free and ready access to information regarding the points system, priorities and positions in the waiting list.

Although different local authorities have varying points systems, there is a general picture of certain groups being excluded more than others from gaining high priority. Such groups include small, especially young, single-person households who cannot collect enough points in comparison with larger households, and recent immigrants who fail the length-of-residence qualifications. The explicit and implicit discrimination in council house allocation against blacks has also been well reported. Coloured households are under-represented in council housing as a whole, and those that are in the local authority housing sector are over-represented in the poorest-quality housing.

The housing managers allocate eligible households to available dwellings. Whether or not a household gets a dwelling depends upon its position in the waiting list and the availability of housing. The type of dwelling it gets depends upon household size and composition and again upon availability. The quality of housing depends upon the housing managers' assessment of the applicants. All would-be applicants and existing applicants seeking a transfer are interviewed by a housing visitor, who recommends the type of accommodation the household should be offered. The housing visitor's recommendation is based on his assessment of the applicant, an assessment which includes more than an analysis of housing need. Councils are concerned to find quiet, clean tenants who will pay their bills, maintain the property, keep the peace and not complain. The housing visitors' comments from Bedford and Hull shown in Table 7.3 demonstrate the type of assessment which occurs. This assessment is important in the type of accommodation offered to tenants. The data in Table 7.4 are taken from a study of local authority housing in Hull. The age of the local authority dwellings are taken as a surrogate of housing quality, and the table clearly shows the relationship between the local authority grading of tenants and the type of property offered; the better the grading, the better the accommodation.

Existing tenants move within the local authority housing sector by one of two ways. They can exchange their dwellings with another local authority tenant. If both parties are willing, the move would not result in overcrowding or under-occupancy and neither household has a poor record of maintenance or rent payment, then local authority sanction is generally automatic. Alternatively, households wishing to move can apply for a transfer. Transfers constitute an important element in council housing allocations, accounting for between a third and a half of all allocations in any one year. Transfers are administered by the housing managers, who award points for the need to move. Points are awarded for space deficiency, medical reasons and reasons connected with employment. A ranking takes place (Table 7.5 shows the system of ranking used by the GLC), which defines the position in the housing transfer list. The destination of the households successful in gaining a transfer is guided by the manager's assessment. The 'better class' tenants, defined in terms of the maintenance of their previous dwelling,

Table 7.2 Housing waiting list regulations in West Midland authorities

A Eligibility for consideration

Regulations	*West Bromwich*	*Warley*	*Wolverhampton*	*Halesowen*	*Stafford*	*Ludlow*
Residential qualification	None	Must live in county borough, or have lived in town for 2 years and not lived outside for more than 5 years, or have worked in Warley for 10 years	Must live in Wolverhampton	Must have lived or worked in municipal borough for all preceding 12 months, or have lived there most of life (restricted list less stringent – lived or worked in Halesowen, or born in town)	Must live or work within 10 miles of Stafford town centre	Must live or work in the Rural District
Other qualification	None	Single person without dependants, must be aged 25 or over	None	Over age 18, and have established a *prima facie* need for housing	None	None
Eligibility for consideration	Must have lived in county borough for past 12 months, or lived in town for 10 of the 15 years immediately prior to application	Applicant (or wife) must complete 2 years' residence in Warley	As above	As above	As above	As above
Other qualifications	Must be in housing need: –lodgers –overcrowded families	Must not be, or have been, in previous 3 years, an owner-occupier of self-contained	If a private tenant of self-contained premises, must establish specified evidence of housing	None; though an owner-occupier may have to accept a nominated tenant for his property as a	None	None

	–living in flat after 5 years –living in house without a bath after 5 years –ill-health	accommodation. Must not be tenant of adequate sized, self-contained accommodation with all amenities and in good state of repair	need. If an owner-occupier must have evidence of severe ill-health or social need	condition of rehousing

B Items included in points schemes

Item	*West Bromwich*	*Wolverhampton*	*Ludlow*
Date of application	★	★	
Bedroom deficiency in applicant's accommodation	★	★	★
Size of family	★		
Living in rooms as distinct from self-contained house or flat	★	★	
No separate living room	★	★	★
Bedsitting room only (with children)	★		
General overcrowding	★	★	★
Living apart because of accommodation	★	★	
Sex overcrowding in sleeping arrangements	★	★	
Ill-health or disability	★	★	★
Lack of amenities	★		
Service tenants where employer terminates employment or tenancy, or tenant resigns his job		★	
Sharing a kitchen			★
Unsuitable accommodation (conditions, location, etc.)			★
Discretionary points awarded by Tenancy Committee			★
Age (over pensionable age)			★
Suitability of applicant			★
Length of time in a flat			★

Source: Table 7.2A Niner, 1975

Table 7.3 Housing visitors' comments

Quotations from housing visitors in Hull

'Excellent tenant, suitable for new property.'

'Good type of tenant, every effort made, suitable for any property offered.'

'Good type of OAP. Suitable for new or post-war re-let.'

'Fairly good type – suitable for post-war re-let or pre-war property.'

'Poor type, will need supervision – suitable for old property . . . seems to have taken over the tenancy of this house and sat back until rehoused.'

'Condition of furniture good, applicant also in good order.'

'A good type of applicant – this is not a long-haired person. Suitable for a post-war re-let.'

Source: Gray, 1976

Quotations from housing visitors in Bedford

'She is obviously a very clean woman. Her standard would warrant modern accommodation.'

'They have refused Faraday Square. They really are too good for that area. They are two of the most courteous West Indians I have ever met. Their appearance and speech are excellent. I would think suitable for any new or good property in a good area.'

'Excellent standard of applicant. Ideal for Elms Farm.'

'Good standard, though all in one room. Accommodation is not suitable for young family. Mr G. suffers from reactive depression, precipitated by the overcrowding.'

'If Buckingham Palace became available she might accept.'

'I feel she is making a genuine effort. She has been registered since 1962 and should perhaps be considered for something slightly above blue cross standard' [blue cross properties are inner-area miscellaneous housing].

Source: Skellington, 1981

Table 7.4 Grading of tenants and local authority accommodation in Hull

	Local authority grading of tenant		
Age of dwellings occupied	*'Poor' or 'fair only' (n = 24)*	*'Fairly good' or 'good' (n = 137)*	*'Very good' or 'excellent' (n = 28)*
	%	%	%
1919–44	62.5	13.9	10.7
1945–65	29.2	38.0	28.6
Post-1965	8.3	23.4	17.9
New	–	24.8	42.9
	100.0	100.0	100.0

Source: Gray, 1976

overall behaviour and renting record, are allocated the better properties.

The meshing of allocation and transfer rules with the physical attributes of particular types of council housing produces a mosaic of different types of council housing areas. The local authority housing sector is not a homogeneous one. There are the good estates, where the well-tended gardens sit proudly one beside the other and the peace in the neighbourhood is rarely broken by the noise of rowdy

Table 7.5 Priority for exchange for GLC tenants

		% of GLC applicants
1	Council interest	0.3
Applicants with a recognized need to move		(63.0)
2	Bedroom deficiency	11.9
3	Too much accommodation	35.1
4	Health reasons supported by council's medical adviser	16.0
Applicants without a recognized need to move		(36.7)
5	Health reasons not supported by council's medical adviser	6.2
6	Reasons connected with employment	4.0
7–8	Personal and social reasons; applicants wanting a change	26.5

Source: Bird, 1976

children. These are the zenith of the council tenant's housing career, to be reached only after years of good service, regular rent payment and a commendation from the housing manager. Then there are the majority of the estates bordering around the average, containing a mix of young and old along with varying proportions of 'good' and 'bad' tenants. There is a direct relationship between the form of the building and the character of the estate; the 'best' estates contain the lowest-density or award-winning high-density two-storey good-quality housing. The most unpopular estates are the high-rise blocks and the poor-quality late inter-war housing.

An indication of the esteem of different estates can be gained from an examination of transfer requests. The good estates have few vacancies and they figure highly as the destination in many transfer requests, while the poor estates have many difficult-to-let vacancies, with a high proportion of the existing tenants seeking transfers. Then there are the problem estates. These are the nadir of the council housing sector, the headache for the housing managers and the source of stories sometimes bordering on the fantastic. Every town or city has its problem estate whose name immediately conjures up images of squalor, vandalism and trouble. The very name of these estates evokes an immediate response, usually dismissive or derogatory, from the local inhabitants. There are a number of factors behind the creation of such an image. Often the image was gained when the estate was first opened. Estates which housed outsiders from slum-clearance programmes were often stigmatized by the locals, and the stigma has stuck. But the problems of the problem estates are often more than those of image. The poor physical design of the dwellings, the lack of maintenance and heavy vandalism, the low pay of the inhabitants and the relatively high rents, and the social problems of the tenants in association with the policies of the housing managers, all combine to produce dump estates, areas where problem families are sent, good tenants try to leave and vacancies go unfilled. The problem for the housing managers is what to do with problem families who are noisy, dirty and do not pay their rent. Either the neighbours complain and ask the council to move them, or the managers review their case. A typical pattern has emerged for problem families to be dumped in these problem estates. This has its advantages and disadvantages. The advantages accrue to the problem families' former neighbours, while the disadvantages are felt by the households on problem estates whose address is a mark against them, an indication in the eyes of credit agencies and potential employers that they are shiftless and untrustworthy. This stigmatization becomes a self-fulfilling prophecy as people tarnished with the image of living on a problem estate find it difficult to move out, obtain credit or get a job simply because of their address.

The tenants

The characteristics of council tenants reflect the eligibility rules for access to council housing. Compared with owner-occupiers, for example, council tenants on average have lower incomes and contain a much higher proportion of semi- and unskilled manual workers. Larger families with more elderly households are also more important in the local authority sector than they are in owner-occupation. The local authority sector does not have all the elderly or all the poor households. It is not a residual sector in that sense. The private renting sector, especially the unfurnished sector, has a relatively higher, though absolutely smaller, number of elderly and low-income households (see Figures 6.5 and 6.6). The socio-economic status of local authority tenants is shown in Table 7.6. The figures reveal an over-representation of manual workers, especially semi-skilled and unskilled, and an under-representation of professional and managerial workers.

It has proved difficult to measure the changes in the characteristics of council house tenants in the post-war period. Definitions of family type and socio-economic status have varied over the different censuses, and the most useful source, the General Household Survey, has only been in operation since 1971. What we have is short-run data sources from which it is difficult to pick up long-term trends. What evidence there is suggests that the local authority sector is increasingly housing the poorer households (see Table 7.7). In the post-war period, council housing moved away from its original

Table 7.6 Socio-economic status of local authority tenants, 1978

Socio-economic group	*LA tenants*	*Great Britain*
Economically active heads		
Professional and managerial	3	15
Intermediate and junior non-manual	9	13
Skilled manual and own-account non-professional	27	25
Semi-skilled manual, personal service and unskilled manual	20	13
Economically inactive heads	40	33
Total	99	99

Source: General Household Survey

Table 7.7 Council housing tenants

	Tenants in lowest quartile of income distribution (%)
1953/4	16
1965	29
1976	43

Source: Family Expenditure Survey

position of providing general-needs housing to a residual role of providing housing for those unable to afford owner-occupation.

Council housing is a paternalistic housing type in which households are visited, selected and allocated dwellings by the housing managers, who set their rents, decide the colour of their doors and determine the rules and regulations which cover tenancy agreements. It was not until 1980 that council house tenants had any form of security of tenure. This relationship between decision-making managers and council tenants is occasionally overturned by the direct action of tenants' movements. Such movements tend to be locally based and concerned with particular issues. The journal *Community Action* provides a good coverage of such struggles and a forum for the exchange of information and tactics. Rent increases have a direct effect on a household's income, and the impact is immediate. If the increase is large enough, there is the possibility for mobilization by community activists. Households are also directly affected by the overall quality of their accommodation. Poor maintenance and the incidence of damp and mould are factors which impinge on a household's quality of life. In modern prefabricated high-rise dwellings there has been a persistent problem of poor-quality housing. Very little ventilation and poor design have all contributed to the damp problem of modern council housing. Much of the community action in the local authority sector has revolved

Table 7.8 Tenant–council relations

	Manipulation	*Informing*	*Persuasion*	*Consultation*	*Delegation*
Council	Total control of tenants as well as estates	Inform tenants	Retain control but want tenants' goodwill	Retain control but some power is declared	Retain core power but many peripheral areas of responsibility delegated to tenants
Tenants	Regulated	Informed	Persuaded	Consulted	Involved in working partnership

around tenants complaining about these problems. Tenants can take their complaints to the housing department and/or their local councillors. The extent of this lobbying is difficult to assess. It often takes place on an individual basis as households try to sort out their particular problems. Rent increases and quality of accommodation provide the possible basis for community action because they are felt by all households on the estate. There is no necessary relationship, however, between rent increases and tenants' action. Although felt by all, they are experienced by individual consumers. Between the cause and the social movement lies the commitment of the few ready to take on tasks of organizing and channelling individual discontent into some form of action. Often tenants' organizations are formed and disappear according to the entry and departure of a few key people who have the time and touch to organize action. The action can vary from simply setting up a tenants' organization to act as a focal point in mobilizing the tenants to demonstrations and rent strikes. Although difficult to organize and maintain, rent strikes can be and have been very effective.

Although statistics are negligible, reading the pages of *Community Action* suggests that tenants' organizations and associations have been growing. The growth reflects the increasing self-confidence of many council house tenants, the actions of community activists and the size of the perceived problems. Up and down the country there have been some successes, some small and some large, as not all tenants have accepted the passive role assigned to them by council house managers. The growth of associations has also reflected the operation of council house management. Initially treated with caution, if not outright distaste by managers, tenants' organizations have been incorporated into housing management schemes for tenants' participation. This partly reflects an acceptance of their existence and also represents an incorporation of potential protest as local authority housing departments seek to use tenants' associations as channels for disseminating the official line and controlling the estate. The range of possible tenant–council relations is shown in Table 7.8; moving from left to right there is an increase in tenants' participation and degree of power. Most actual participation schemes can be placed to the left. Participation does not necessarily involve a greater degree of power, as it can be used merely to inform or persuade tenants. But all participation schemes have a double-edged character. They may be used to incorporate protest or quell dissent, but they can also provide the platform for the exercise of real power.

8

PRIVATE RENTING AND MINORITY TENURES

PRIVATE RENTING

A story of decline

Over the course of this century the story of housing has been dominated by the decline of the private rented sector. Before the First World War almost nine out of every ten households rented accommodation from a private landlord. Even on the eve of the Second World War almost seven out of every ten were private renters. The pace of decline quickened in the post-war years and by 1978 less than two out of every ten households were in private renting (see Table 8.1). From 1945 to 1980 private renting changed from being the main tenure category to a minority tenure category.

Table 8.1 Number of privately rented dwellings in England and Wales, 1914–75

Year	*Dwellings (millions)*	*% of total housing stock*
1914	7.1	89.8
1938	6.6	57.8
1960	4.6	31.5
1971	3.3	19.3
1975	2.9	16.1

Source: HPTV, Part 1

The decline in absolute numbers reflects the response by landlords as capital investors to changes in the relative rates of return provided by the ownership of rented accommodation compared with alternative forms of investment. Before 1914, rented accommodation was one of the most profitable investments, providing returns almost double those from gilt-edged securities. By 1970 in contrast, landlords could only obtain an estimated 6 per cent on their investment compared with the 9 per cent available from long-dated government securities. For the small investor, who used to be the mainstay of the rented sector, the growth of building societies and other similar financial institutions has provided more attractive investment opportunities than the ownership of rented property. The relatively low returns on investment in private rented accommodation have been exacerbated by rent controls and methods of taxation. Rent control was first introduced in 1915 and, apart from two periods of decontrol, from 1923 to 1939 and from 1957 to 1964, rent controls of varying degrees of severity have been in operation ever since. The various rent control Acts have restricted the ability of landlords to set rent levels which cover loan charges and maintenance costs and which also provide an acceptable profit. Taxation policies have also played a part. Under the present arrangements landlords not only pay tax on their profit, but they cannot claim tax relief on mortgages, and any sums used to repay the mortgage are treated as taxable profit and are subject to capital gains tax when properties are sold. Compared with the owner-occupier, the landlord is not a privileged investor. Investment in rented property provides poor rates of return.

The landlord's response has been twofold. The main one had been to sell off properties. This disinvestment is the main reason for the absolute decline in private rented accommodation: between 1938 and 1975 landlords sold 2.6 million dwellings to owner-occupiers, almost a third of a million were sold to local authorities, and up to half a million units were converted to another use (see Table 8.2). Another response, for landlords who have not been able to sell their properties either through choice or lack of effective demand, has been to reduce maintenance and improvement expenditure. The landlord's profit is equal to the rental income less costs which include interest charges, rate and maintenance and improvement expenditure. The landlord's effective control over costs is limited to the level of maintenance and improvement expenditure, and landlords have responded to low fixed rents and rising costs by reducing such expenditure. The net effect is for a further deterioration in quality of the private-rental housing stock.

Table 8.2 Changes in the private rented sector, 1938–75

	Dwellings (millions)
Sales to owner–occupiers	−2.6
Sales to local authorities	−0.3
Demolition and change of use	−1.2
New building and conversion	+0.4
Net change	−3.7

Source: HPTV, Part III

The decline in the relative position of the private rented sector reflects the increasing importance of the other two main tenure categories. The post-war years have seen the emergence of owner-occupation as the dominant tenure type and the steady growth, at least in the first twenty-five years since 1945, of public housing. As these two tenure types have increased, private renting has declined. Between 1938 and 1975 only 40,000 dwellings were added to the rented housing stock, the bulk of which was in the form of conversions for the upper end of the housing market.

The pattern of disinvestment, the lack of improvement and the absence of new building had combined to produce a distinct character in the temporary housing stock. Private rented accommodation is older and of poorer quality than dwellings in the other two main tenure categories. The figures in Table 8.3 reveal the broad picture of an ageing housing stock of much poorer quality than either owner-occupied or local authority housing. In general, private rented dwellings provide the poorest form of accommodation in the British housing market.

Table 8.3 Housing quality by tenure category in England and Wales, 1976

	Owner-occupied	*Public housing*	*Privately rented and others*
% unfit dwellings	3.0	1.0	16.0
% dwellings lacking one or more basic amenities	5.0	6.0	26.0
% dwellings built before 1914	30.0	3.7	68.5

Source: HPTV, Part I

The legislative background

Against this background of decline the legislation specifically enacted for the private rented sector has followed a zigzag path of control, decontrol and the reimposition of control. The beliefs behind the measures are relatively simple. Rent control, it has been argued by those urging control, safeguards the rights of a tenant. Without them there is always the danger of exploitation, with unscrupulous landlords charging extortionate rents. The landlords and free marketeers take a different tack, arguing that rent controls strangle the supply of rented accommodation. Lifting the controls, they believe, will lead to higher returns and thus more property will appear on the market. These beliefs, often unsullied by empirical verification, have formed the basis of post-war legislation.

The first phase in the post-war years was one of rent control. The experience of the First World War had shown that at the time of sacrifice rent control was important to maintain social harmony and ensure the strength of the war effort: people would not be so willing to fight the enemy if they had to struggle with increased rents. At the beginning of hostilities in 1939, therefore, the Rent and Mortgage Interest Restrictions Act imposed rent control and froze rents at the 1939 level. Rent increases were only allowed in respect of rate increases or property improvement. The early post-war years strengthened the control mechanisms. A Rent Control Act of 1946 set up rent tribunals in certain areas to fix rents for furnished dwellings and provide security of tenure to tenants. The Landlord and Tenant (Rent Control) Act of 1949 extended these controls throughout England and Wales and empowered the rent tribunals to fix the rents of new lettings. These rent controls, effectively fixing rents at the 1939 level, were shaped by the climate of the times. A relatively radical Labour government had been voted in, housing was an important political issue and there were conditions of scarcity. All this combined to produce measures of control. Thereafter, the climate changed. The Tories came to power in 1951 committed to resuscitating the private sector, and the lobbying of landlords was sympathetically received by a government with a strong belief in the efficacy of market forces. The second phase, a period of decontrol, opened with the Housing Repairs and Rent Act of 1954. This legislation allowed rent increases when improvements to the property had been made. Landlords could increase rents after they had provided proof of recent repairs. This scheme was unwieldy and had little impact. More important was the Rent Act of 1957, which sought a much wider lifting of controls. This Act marked the zenith of decontrol and the belief in the beneficial effects of unbridled market forces in the private rented sector. Under the Act all dwellings with a rateable value of above £30 (£40 in London) were to be decontrolled. This criterion included 400,000 dwellings. For dwellings below this limit, decontrol was to occur when the existing tenancy expired. For dwellings still under control rents were increased between 50 and 75 per cent, with the average around 60 per cent. The 1957 legislation swung the balance of advantage towards the landlords; where housing was scarce the advantage was used.

The unfolding consequences of the 1957 Act were most vividly experienced in inner London. Here, redevelopment schemes and disinvestment had reduced the supply of accommodation, while the booming London economy had attracted workers from other areas, which led to an inflation in the demand for housing. In this tight market the 1957 legislation strengthened the hand of the landlords who could subdivide property and increase rents. The legislation also made it profitable to move out tenants with controlled tenancy arrangements, since control was lifted on change of tenant. With the most unscrupulous landlords this was an attraction which provoked harassment of tenants. Press reports highlighted some of the worst cases, but the picture was thrust firmly into the public gaze by the Rachman scandal and the Profumo affair. In 1963 it was revealed that a leading Conservative politician, John Profumo had been consorting with prostitutes. One of them, Mandy Rice-Davies, had also been a girlfriend of a London landlord, Perec Rachman. Here was the very stuff of public scandal: sex, possible corruption and treachery, a foreign, possibly Jewish landlord grinding the faces of the old and poor to pay for loose women and wild licentious parties. In amongst it all Rachman figures very large. He had died a year earlier and had ceased owning property in 1960, but his earlier exploits were vividly recounted. Rachman came to Britain from Poland in 1946 and from 1954 he began to acquire rented houses. By 1959 he was the owner of a considerable number of properties, especially in Notting Hill. Before 1957 Rachman persuaded tenants to sell to him their controlled tenancies; he then converted the properties to furnished accommodation which was not then subject to rent restrictions. Sometimes other methods were used, including physical and mental harassment. After the 1957 Rent Act many of his properties were automatically decontrolled, higher rents were charged and there was less security of tenure for tenants. Few repairs were ever done to his properties. By 1959 Rachman owned over 1000 properties. Tenants were beginning to fight back, and in the same year twenty-five of them occupied property and applied to the rent tribunal for a rent reduction. The affair involved the police and eventually the Inland Revenue. Rachman's activities came under closer scrutiny and he responded by selling off most of his rented accommodation by the end of 1960.

The Rachman case is interesting in two respects. First, it gave sensational coverage to the problems of private rented tenants. In the wake of the publicity a special committee was set up in 1963, under the chairmanship of Sir Milner Holland, to examine housing in Greater London. The report showed that over 190,000 households were in urgent need of better housing in Central London, while there were over half a million in the capital without even shared use of a bathroom. The problems were concentrated in the private rented sector, where the report showed that the lack of security of tenure caused real hardship, especially to low-income families with young children. Second, the Rachman affair has affected all subsequent debate. The spectre of a new Rachman or Rachman-type activities can be raised in debates about the lifting of rent control restrictions or security of tenure measures. The term 'Rachmanism' has passed into our vocabulary.

After the public concern and the evidence of the Milner Holland Committee the course of policy changed yet again. A phase of greater control was introduced. This third period was signalled by the 1965 Rent Act, which reintroduced security of tenure for most tenants in unfurnished accommodation and introduced a new system of rent regulation for tenancies not subject to control. This new system used the concept of a fair rent, which was to be fixed on application by either the landlord or tenant to an independent rent officer. The fair rent was to be 'what the value would be if there was no scarcity'. It was meant to be fair in the sense that tenants were to be protected from extortionate rents, while landlords could obtain a reasonable return on their investment. The Act froze rents at their 1965 value until a fair rent was assessed. From 1966 to 1970 almost 200,000 applications were received for the fixing of a fair rent. In the first year the vast majority of applications came from tenants seeking, in most cases successfully, to get their rent reduced. In the latter years landlords were applying for fair rent determination in order to get their rents increased. Over the whole period from 1966 to 1970, the Francis Committee found that of over 100,000 cases analysed 29.3 per cent of applications resulted in a decrease of rent, 8.7 per cent were unchanged and 62.0 per cent were increased. For the rents which were raised, in 40 per cent of cases the increase was greater than a half of the previous rent. The pattern of rent increases varied by type of accommodation. Table 8.4 shows the general trend for rent increases to be highest for houses and flats and lowest for rooms. In the case of London, the Francis Committee looked at 1142 rent determinations in the furnished sector and found that in 814 cases the rent was reduced.

Although the 1965 Act extended security of tenure it also allowed higher rents to be extracted. While causing hardship for some

Table 8.4 Rent increases by type of accommodation, 1969

	House	*Flat*	*Room*	*All types*
Average % of change in rent after registration	+35	+15	−14	+17

Source: Francis Committee, 1971

tenants, increases did little to halt the overall decline in private rented accommodation. Even with the higher rents given by fair rent registration, higher, safer returns could still be made elsewhere, and on obtaining vacant possession many landlords sold their property. The 1965 legislation also had the very specific effect of aiding the transfer of unfurnished let to furnished let. Landlords converted the properties because higher returns could be made from furnished accommodation. Moreover, from 1965 to before the 1974 Act tenants in furnished accommodation had more limited security of tenure than tenants of unfurnished accommodation. Landlords could evict tenants in furnished property more easily than those in unfurnished property. A common pattern therefore emerged for the landlords, on obtaining an unfurnished vacancy in a multi-occupied dwelling, to transfer the vacancy to a furnished let. By this method they hoped to increase the return and to overcome the problem of being burdened with tenants who could obtain security of tenure and whose presence limited their ability to sell the property.

Since 1965 rent policies have come and gone. In their 1972 Housing Finance Act the Tories sought to convert all controlled tenancies, approximately half a million dwellings, to regulated rents, with the highest rateable dwellings being converted first, followed by dwellings of increasing rateable value. This would have involved an increase in rent for tenants in controlled tenancies, but soon after taking office the Labour government's 1974 Rent Act halted the automatic transfer of controlled rent to regulated rent, and extended security of tenure and the rent regulation scheme to tenants in furnished accommodation; although this measure put the unfurnished and furnished sectors on the same footing it did little to halt the transfer of properties from unfurnished to furnished. Landlords still believed that rent officers determined much higher rents for furnished dwellings, even after taking the cost of furniture into account.

The latest legislation covering the rented sector was the 1980 Housing Act. In its second year of office under Mrs Thatcher the Conservative government sought to 'free' the housing market. The majority Tory belief was that landlords were not putting properties on the market because of the security of tenure afforded to tenants. They sought to change this by making it easier for the landlords to obtain possession, and this was achieved in the creation of a new protected short-hold tenancy. This new tenancy was to be for a fixed period of not less than one year and not more than five years. During this period the rent was to be registered, and at the end of the period the landlord was assured of receiving vacant possession. Whether this arrangement will halt the decline of the rented sector is difficult to say. It may encourage owners of under-occupied dwellings to let out part of their accommodation. However, it may have little effect on the relative rates of return afforded by the letting out of rented accommodation. If the returns fail to match those provided by other investments, then the decline will continue. The 1980 Act represents a slackening of controls and a shift in the balance of advantage towards the landlords. This legislation not only introduces a new form of tenancy but also allows rent registration after two years instead of three, and gives wider grounds for landlords to repossess their property.

The main problem of the private rented sector, and the one around which legislation has revolved, has been the conflict between tenants' interests and landlords' profit, which expresses the wider conflict between housing as a commodity and housing as a necessity. Successive pieces of legislation have not solved this dilemma – what they have done is to change the balance of advantage towards either the landlord or the tenant. Apart from a brief period from 1967 to 1975 the balance has been in favour of the tenant, and landlords have responded by selling their properties. The 1980 Housing Act represents a swing in the balance of advantage back towards the landlord.

The landlords

The term 'landlord' covers a variety of different types of individuals and companies. Although the desire for higher returns may be a common characteristic of these diverse groups, each of them has a different set of constraints and opportunities in achieving its goal. There are two sets of popular images concerning private landlords. These images roughly correspond with the different perspectives on rent control. On the one hand, there is the Rachman image of a greedy, unscrupulous landlord exploiting poor, unfortunate tenants. The picture is conjured up of helpless tenants unable to fight against greedy landlords without state help; on the other, there is the little old lady image of decent god-fearing people performing a public duty by letting out part of their property, only to be repaid by nasty tenants who smash the furniture, refuse to pay rent and enjoy continuous security of tenure. The images persist and are regularly trotted out to advance a particular case or general argument.

The reality is more prosaic. At the risk of over-simplification, two main types of landlords can be identified: the small-scale and the large-scale landlord. The typical landlord is a small-scale property

It's the tenants who have it good today

Figure 8.1 One image of landlords (from the *Sunday Times*, 15 October 1978)

owner. A number of studies have shown that the majority of landlords own very few properties and almost two-thirds of all private landlords own less than ten properties. A general profile of small-scale landlords would reveal that most of them are middle-aged to elderly, almost half of them have inherited their property, a great majority have medium to low incomes, and most of them receive less than £10 per week in rent. There are small-scale landlords who are just as much profit-maximizers as the largest property company, but for the small-scale landlord other goals are also important. For some, renting part of their house is a supplement to their income. Income from owning houses may be considered as a security for old age, a form of insurance, and for some being a landlord may be involuntary insofar as they have inherited an encumbrance rather than made an investment. For many immigrants, property ownership may be a symbol of status, of having arrived. There is no lack of new recruits for property ownership since it has a traditional image of a secure, safe investment, and for the middle and lower-middle class it combines a possible investment with the reinforcement of status.

The age, attitude and income of small-scale landlords suggests that they have neither the desire nor the ability to embark upon a large or, in some cases, even a modest programme of house maintenance and improvement. This has had obvious consequences for the quality of the private rented sector in general, and more serious implications for neighbourhoods dominated by accommodation owned by small-scale landlords.

Although they are a small percentage of the total number, large-scale landlords, including private individuals as well as property companies, own a considerable proportion of the private rented sector. Table 8.5 reveals the picture in Bristol, where landlords owning more than ten properties controlled more than four-fifths of all rented property. The Berger property empire based in London, for example, owns 11,000 units, and estimates of its value range from £50 million to £100 million.

The progression from small-scale to large-scale landlord is marked by increasing professionalism towards the mangement of rented property and greater sensitivity towards changes in investment opportunity. Large-scale landlords are very sensitive to any

Table 8.5 Tenancy distribution of landlords in Bristol

Size of holding	*No. of landlords*	*No. of tenancies*	*Tenancies (%)*
1–2 tenancies	35	51	3.7
3–9 tenancies	42	204	14.8
10+ tenancies	29	1118	81.5

Source: Short, 1979

decline in rates of return: small-scale changes are likely to be registered quickly and acted upon. In some cases, especially for the very large property companies, owning rented property may even be incidental to a wider market strategy. Such companies prefer to own complete blocks of flats, since they are interested in the asset value of the properties: if rents can be pushed up, asset value increases and large sums borrowed on the security of the building can be placed in profitable investments.

Contemporary landlords' investment yields relatively low returns. They have responded to this in two ways. First, they have sold their properties to owner-occupiers and to developers seeking suitable sites for property development. The break-up of blocks of flats in central London for sale to owner-occupiers, and the gentrification associated with sales of rented property to them, are only two of the more significant processes in the metropolitan housing market. In other cities, sales to owner-occupiers have been encouraged. This form of reduction in the private rented sector may be levelling off, because a large proportion of the remaining stock is of such a residual character that it is unlikely to attract building society mortgages. Second, since not all landlords can sell their properties – perhaps because they have controlled tenancies, because potential owner-occupiers cannot obtain funds or because the accommodation is on a site not suitable for commercial development – many of the remaining landlords have attempted to maintain and/or increase profitability by: (1) reducing maintenance and improvement expenditure; (2) by selecting short-stay tenants; and (3) by switching to furnished units.

(1) With low or fixed rents, on the one hand, and rising repair costs on ageing property, on the other, landlords have tended to reduce maintenance and improvement expenditure. Sixty per cent of landlords in a recent survey of landlords in Bristol stated that they were explicitly reducing repair and improvement expenditure in the face of rising repair costs (Short, 1979).

(2) Given the excess of demand over supply in the private rented sector, landlords are in a position to allocate vacancies to certain types of household. Many landlords are now allocating vacancies to short-stay tenants, i.e. those who require accommodation only for a limited period of time. A typical short-stay tenant would be a student household. Such tenants are selected because landlords feel that they are unlikely to go to the rent officer to get a fair rent or, even if they do, they imply a continual turnover of tenants, allowing regular rent increases to be made on change of tenancy. In a time of

rapid inflation the ability to raise rents quickly is highly valued by landlords. Having short-stay tenants has the added advantage that obtaining vacant possession for subsequent sale is assured, at least in the medium term. Vacant possession is essential for landlords selling to owner-occupiers and an added bonus to those landlords contemplating sale to property developers, since sitting tenants can reduce the value of a property from about a third to a half.

(3) Finally, there has been a pronounced switch in recent years from the unfurnished to the furnished sector. Since the 1965 Rent Act and before the 1974 Rent Act, tenants in unfurnished accommodation could obtain security of tenure on application to the rent officer. The tenants of furnished property had a more limited security of tenure. During this period, then, there was a differential of security of tenure afforded to the two sectors of the rental market, and a common pattern emerged for the larger-scale landlords on obtaining an unfurnished property to transfer the vacancy to a furnished vacancy. In Bristol, for example, where households in private renting fell from 50 per cent in 1961 to 28 per cent in 1971, the respective figures for households in furnished accommodation increased from 3.8 to 7.2 per cent. The conversion of tenancies has continued even after the 1974 Act, which gave equal security of tenure to tenants of furnished property. From the same survey of landlords and property managers in Bristol it was found that there was a strong belief that higher rents could be obtained in the furnished category. The converse to this switch to short-stay tenants/furnished units is that low-income families are finding it increasingly difficult to obtain accommodation because they generally require unfurnished accommodation for long periods. The net effect was to make it much more difficult for those trapped in the private rented sector to obtain accommodation.

The tenants

In the private renting sector we can distinguish between the short-stay and long-stay (or trapped) households. The short-stay households include students, newly married couples, single-person households and others who move around with their job. These households use private renting as a temporary form of accommodation and as a stepping stone to either owner-occupation or local authority housing. Figures 6.5 and 6.6 and Table 8.6 show how these households are concentrated in the furnished sector. Private renting provides them with a housing form that is relatively easy to enter – there are no formal waiting lists or mortgage requirements to

Table 8.6 Socio-economic status of tenants in private rented accommodation, 1978

Economically active heads	*Unfurnished*	*Furnished*	*GB*
Professional and managerial	8	11	15
Intermediate and junior non-manual	11	26	13
Skilled manual and own-account non-professional	21	19	25
Semi-skilled manual, personal service and unskilled	11	14	13
Economically inactive heads	50	30	33
Total	101	100	99

Source: General Household Survey

be fulfilled – and which does not prohibit future mobility. The longer-stay households include the more elderly lower-income households predominantly in manual occupations. These households are concentrated in the furnished sector. They are effectively trapped in the rented sector because they are excluded from the alternatives; this group includes those who cannot move into owner-occupation because of low incomes or poor credit rating, and those who cannot move into public housing because of the limited supply and their lack of sufficient points. The numbers in the different categories of the rented sector are shown in Figure 8.2.

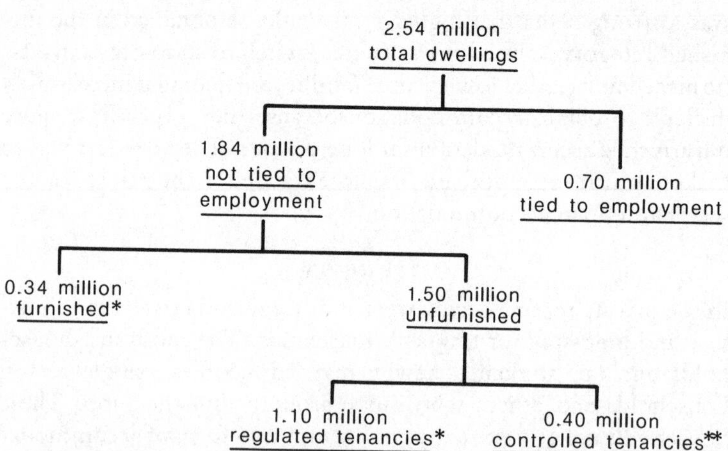

* Liable to pay fair rents fixed by rent officer
** Rents fixed in relation to 1956 rateable value and a proportion of the costs of certain subsequent repairs and improvement

Figure 8.2 Estimates of dwellings in the private rented sector in England and Wales, 1976

Private-sector tenants get a raw deal in comparison with either owner-occupiers or tenants in the public sector. The accommodation is of much poorer quality; prior to 1972 the only form of subsidy was the rent control measures; and even up until 1974 this did not apply to the furnished rented sector. Since 1972 rent allowances have been introduced, initially only for unfurnished tenancies; the rent allowance scheme incorporated tenants of furnished accommodation only after 1974. The system is complex. In general, it works on the principle that households with low incomes and high rent should be subsidized up to a certain level. In 1977, for example, the maximum allowance was £13 in London and £10 elsewhere. The impact of the subsidy in the early years is highlighted in Table 8.7. These figures need to be treated with some caution because they do not include furnished tenancies, since the rent allowance scheme did not operate in this sector until after 1974. It must be borne in mind that the figures average across each tenure category; they provide a rough guide and nothing more. They do, however, point to the inequitable distribution of subsidies. Tenants of uncontrolled unfurnished dwellings received much lower subsidies than local authority tenants or owner-occupiers, and even though tenants of controlled dwellings received similar levels of subsidy, notice the difference in average income shown in Table 8.8. The medium- to high-income owner-occupiers were receiving the same subsidy as the much lower-income tenants in controlled tenancies. It is difficult to escape the conclusion that the housing subsidy system is regressive – to them that have shall be given.

Table 8.7 Subsidies by tenure in 1973

	Subsidy (£ per annum)	*Average income (£ per annum)*
Local authority tenants	260–80	2021
Owner-occupiers	280	2432
Private renters		
–controlled unfurnished tenancies	260–80	1701
–uncontrolled unfurnished tenancies	170	1701

Source: Odling-Smee, 1975

The rent allowance scheme operates on the system of application. Tenants have to apply for an allowance, though this is not the case for tax relief to owner-occupiers or central exchequer subsidies to tenants of local authority tenures. A problem arises in the take-up of allowances. Between 1973 and 1976 take-up increased from 10 to 15 per cent of tenants to between 35 and 40 per cent, but this is still a low proportion. The problem of welfare in Britain is not that too many people are getting benefits but that so many eligible households are not receiving them.

As the private rented sector dwindles in size and thus in political importance, it is difficult to see an improvement in the position of the private rented tenant. There is powerful lobbying for the local authority tenant and even more powerful lobbying in the interests of owner-occupiers. The securing of the interests of owner-occupiers is an important 'constant' of British housing policy. Private rented tenants, in contrast, include the transients who only want to stay for a short while, those whose interests lie elsewhere, and the trapped who are economically weak and politically impotent. Improvement will only come about by our recognition of the inequitable nature of the subsidy system; but politics and policy-making rarely understands the calculus of charitable rationality.

HOUSING ASSOCIATIONS

Almost a million people in Britain live in homes provided by housing associations. In recent years they have expanded to become one of the most important of the minority tenure categories. To understand this growth it is important to place housing associations in some kind of historical context.

Housing associations are part of the voluntary housing movement, by which we mean the provision of housing on a rental basis by organizations run on a charitable foundation. They have a long history in the British housing market. Large organizations such as the Peabody Donation Fund, the Guinness Trust and the Joseph Rowntree Memorial Fund, which all provided reasonably good housing at reasonable rents, were small though significant elements in nineteenth-century urban housing markets. After 1919, with the beginning of public housing, there was less need for such organizations, and throughout the inter-war years and the immediate post-war years the voluntary housing movement was an insignificant though continuing part of housing in Britain. Housing associations, although they played an important part in the provision of housing for the homeless, the old and the disabled, had a negligible overall impact.

With the large-scale slum clearance and rebuilding schemes of the post-war period the relative and absolute position of public housing and private renting respectively increased and decreased. The increasing municipalization of the housing stock worried many Conservatives, who saw the rapid extension of public housing as an assault on the ethics of a market society, and the growth of a tenure category traditionally associated with voting for the Labour party. Consequently, in the late 1950s and early 1960s the Conservative government attempted to stimulate the private rental housing sector. This was tried in the 1957 Act, which introduced widespread decontrol, though very few people were willing to build new property specifically for private renting, and attention turned to the housing societies. These were organizations that provided accommodation essentially for the middle classes at rents which covered costs, in schemes that were termed 'cost-rent schemes'. Under the 1961 Housing Act housing societies were given access to exchequer loans at a cheap interest rate, and by 1963 thirty-nine societies advanced a total of eighty-eight schemes, and built 5540 dwellings. This brief flirtation with societies was considered a success, and there was growing Conservative support for a 'third arm' of housing, sandwiched between owner-occupation and local authority housing, which would replace the declining private rented sector. The 1964 Housing Act extended support to the housing societies and the cost-rent schemes by allocating more Treasury funds and securing agreements with building societies. The same Act also set up the Housing Corporation to act as a clearing house for government funds and to promote the overall development of housing societies. Between 1965 and 1972 the corporation financed the construction of 26,318 dwellings, subsequently let at cost rents. The housing societies were not housing the poor because their rents were too high for those households trapped in the private rented sector. During this period of expansion, housing associations did not have access to Housing Corporation funds and had to rely on subsidies from the local authorities.

With the return of the Conservatives in 1970 the search for alternatives to local authority housing continued. Private renting continued to decline, and in the early 1970s high interest rates ruled out the viability of cost-rent schemes. At the same time the local authorities were beginning to buy up the older property in the inner city as part of the switch from clearance to redevelopment. With housing societies now rendered useless, the Conservatives turned to housing associations to counteract the increasing municipalization of rented property in the inner city. In the 1973 White Paper the new role for housing associations, now given access to Corporation funds, was spelt out: 'The government will look to housing associations to acquire and manage property in Housing Action Areas and so preserve a wide range of choice in rented accommodation.'

In the hastily constructed 1974 Housing Act, initially prompted by the electoral promise to repeal the controversial 1972 Housing Finance Act, the Labour government endorsed the increased emphasis on housing associations. This action may seem strange, given Labour's historic commitment to local authority housing, but it is even stranger when we consider that many reports and studies had shown housing associations to be inefficient, some to be corrupt, and in general they provided no real basis for an attack on inner-city housing problems. Nevertheless, the 1974 Act increased the allocation of funds to the Housing Corporation and outlined the broad priorities of housing associations. These were threefold: (1) to support the drive to improve housing conditions, particularly in housing-stress areas; (2) to promote a substantial increase in new housing for rent, especially in high-demand areas; (3) to support the housing needs for special groups such as the mentally ill, physically handicapped, etc.

The course of legislation has been to give an extended role to housing associations, and this is reflected in the figures for dwellings completed. Between 1945 and 1965 housing associations completed 56,000 dwellings in England and Wales; but this represented only 2.6 per cent of all dwellings completed. The position since 1965 is highlighted in Figure 8.3, which shows the rapid rise in housing association activity. The general story is one of steady growth in the 1970s, with a huge expansion after the effect of the 1974 legislation

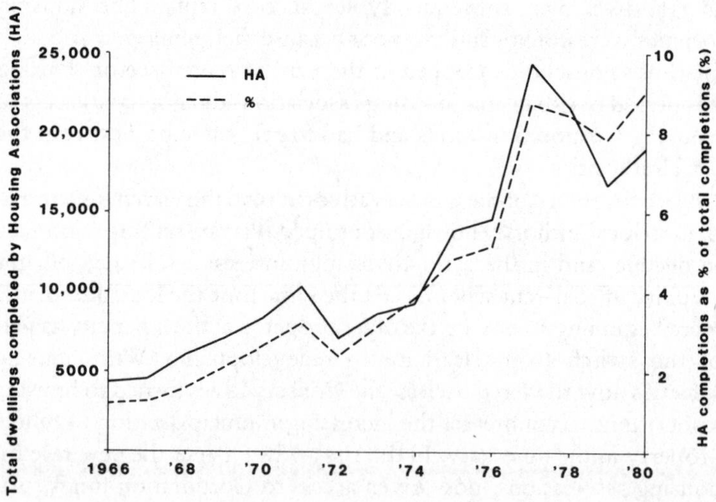

Figure 8.3 Dwellings completed by housing associations in England and Wales

had been felt. This legislation prompted housing associations to become involved in housing improvement schemes, and this is reflected in Figure 8.4 which shows the number of dwellings renovated by housing associations. Again there is a dramatic growth after 1974. Housing associations have been particularly active in inner-city areas, buying up property, modernizing it and letting it out to former tenants and households considered to be in real housing need. By 1980 the Housing Corporation was accounting for almost 20 per cent of all public-sector housing expenditure.

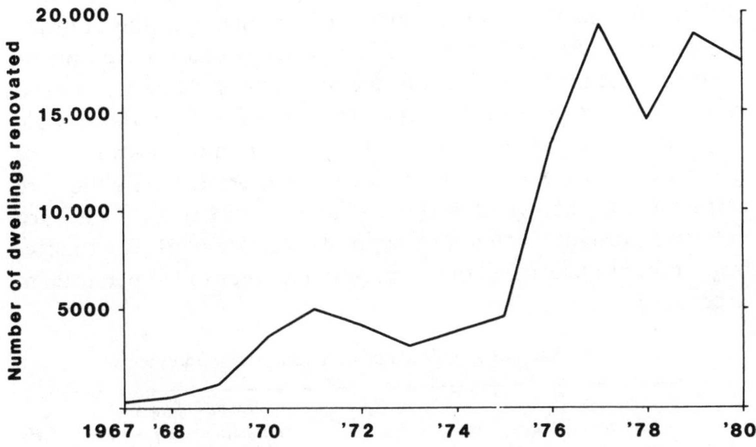

Figure 8.4 Housing association renovations in England and Wales

It has been claimed that housing associations have a more flexible approach to housing, insofar as they catch those households who slip through the local authority housing net. To an extent this is true. More than half of housing association tenants are over sixty years of age, almost nine out of every ten tenants earn less than the national average and a third have had previous experience of harassment or eviction. But nonetheless there are criticisms that can be made of the present arrangements. Four are important. First, there are a large number of separately run organizations. In 1978 there were approximately 2500 associations registered with the Housing Corporation, and this large number, given the lack of detailed guidelines, leads to the vitiation of a comprehensive housing policy. In Bristol, for example, three different housing associations in the inner city operate diverse policies. One attempts to rehouse existing tenants, another is attempting to introduce more 'respectable' families in order to 'balance' neighbourhoods, while the third simply wants to be a fair landlord. There is a real need for commonly shared objectives. Second, a large number of small associations obviously leads to diseconomies of scale. Housing associations working in the same local authority work at different offices, employ different staff and use their own waiting lists. The largest diseconomies of scale occur in the construction and conversion of property. To employ builders for small-scale, often one-off jobs is much more expensive than long-term contracts, and even more expensive than the use of local authority direct-labour organizations. Third, the housing associations are not accountable in their letting policy to anyone outside of the management committee and only nominally to the Housing Corporation. Although some housing associations have tenants on their management board this is not compulsory. Housing associations are in receipt of large sums of public money; either they should be made more publicly accountable, and/or more say should be given to tenants. Finally, the associations at present are obliged to charge a fair rent, which is the rent fixed by the rent officer; such rents are substantially higher than local authority rents. Rent allowances cannot make up all the difference since they only operate up to a certain level.

Table 8.8 Socio-economic status of housing association tenants

Economically active heads	*Tenants of housing associations/cooperatives*	*GB*
Professional and managerial	7	15
Intermediate and junior non-manual	13	13
Skilled manual and own-account non-professional	20	25
Semi-skilled manual, personal service and unskilled	14	13
Economically inactive heads	46	33
Total	100	99

Source: General Household Survey

Housing associations, and previously the housing societies, were originally stimulated by the Conservatives as part of an attack on local authority housing. There is now an all-party consensus on their use. The 1970s saw the largest extension of their powers and the most favourable of funding arrangements. Housing associations are now an important minority tenure category. In parts of the inner city they are one of the most important providers of accommodation. While giving a degree of flexibility to housing provision and an alternative to private renting and/or local authority, this resuscitation of the voluntary housing movement with its paternalistic ideology strengthens the concept of housing being dispensed as an act of charity. The use of charitable organizations, albeit funded by public monies, undermines the concept of decent housing as a democratic right.

TIED ACCOMMODATION

Tied accommodation is housing linked to employment. It is found amongst a number of occupations, including police, clergy, the armed services, the hotel and domestic sector, farm workers and masters of Oxbridge colleges. In 1976, almost a million households lived in tied accommodation; they included farm workers (130,000), service personnel (95,000), National Coal Board workers (100,000), and employees of hotel and catering establishments (70,000), while a very large number of firms held some accommodation for their workers. Tied accommodation varies in quality from masters' lodges to the generally poor quality of accommodation provided by hotels for their staff. It also varies in the way it is used by employers. Miners' housing, for example, does not constitute an important element in their relationship with the NCB, but the exercise of strong employer control is found across a range of occupational types. The single most important is the tied cottage system, whereby farm workers' accommodation is provided by the farmers, in most cases free of charge or for a nominal sum. The tied cottage system is an important strand in the employer/employee relationship, strengthening the employer's hand and the employee's dependency. The farmer can attract workers by the promise of housing, while keeping down wages. The system is implicitly used to discipline the work force while explicit use is also made – though rarely. Evictions have been running at about 1500 per year in the early 1970s. Since 1976 this power to evict has been stopped. The 1976 Rent (Agricultural) Act, which became effective from 1 January 1977, gave security of tenure to agricultural workers in the event of retirement, job loss or accident. The Act altered the explicit use of housing, but not its implicit use as an important strand in the farmer/farm worker relationship.

INSTITUTIONS

Not all persons live in private households. Public schoolboys, convicted criminals, people in hospitals, the disabled and the elderly in

Table 8.9 Persons in non-private establishments, 1971

Type of establishment	*Number of staff*	*Other persons*
Hotels, etc.	63,295	203,250
Educational establishments	27,135	191,440
Miscellaneous communal establishments	–	97,245
All other hospitals	63,515	246,320
Psychiatric hospitals	11,645	169,195
Homes for the old and disabled	14,025	149,430
Children's homes	10,750	31,445
Places of detention	27,135	191,440

Source: Census, 1971

homes, and others make up the population in institutions. The latest and most comprehensive survey of people in institutions was the 1971 census. The census figures shown in Table 8.9 show the position for one point in time only, freezing the continual movement of households into and out of hotels and the slower movement of people into and out of prisons and hospitals. Excluding staff and hotels, just over one million people live in institutions. The 97,245 people living in miscellaneous communal establishments include tepee settlements in North Wales, communes in the Lake District and Temples of Love in Balham.

9

HOUSING EXCHANGE

The amount of movement in the housing market is considerable. About 10 per cent of British households move house each year. Those with a greater propensity to move are younger households and private renters. In areas where these two characteristics predominate, population turnover is very high. More than half the population will have moved within the three years. In local authority and owner-occupied housing areas where the heads of households are older turnover is much reduced and it will take over ten years for half the population to have moved.

HOUSEHOLD MOVEMENT

People move house for many reasons, but the single most important is what we may term changing space requirements. Housing tends to be fixed in size and, although walls can be knocked down and new partitions erected, the amount of flexibility with traditional buildings is small. Yet a household's space requirements are constantly changing. A one-person household needs less space than a two-person household, and families with children need even more. We can construct a simple model of changing space requirements associated with the different stages of the life cycle. In Table 9.1 a five-stage cycle is presented to show how the different stages create different space requirements. Almost two-thirds of all household movement is generated by the early changes in the household life cycle. In terms of a model, stages (1) and (2) in Table 9.1 generate most movement, and the later stages generate least. Many households who change from the child-rearing to post-child status will not move house.

The model is a simple representation and not all households follow the pattern outlined. For those trapped in the private rented sector, the meshing of housing and space requirements may not

Table 9.1 The family life cycle model

	Stage in life cycle	*Space requirements/aspirations*
1	Creation of new household: pre-child stage (1 or 2 persons)	Relatively cheap flat or small house
2	Child-bearing (2 or 3 persons)	House with at least 2 bedrooms
3	Child-rearing (3, 4 or more persons)	Large house with at least 3 or 4 bedrooms
4	Post-child (2 persons)	Space needs reduced from (3)
5	Later life (1 person)	Institution/flat, live with relatives

occur, because of restricted housing opportunities. For those in the local authority housing sector the demand for new housing is mediated through the transfer scheme operated by the housing managers. Even for the lower-income owner-occupiers the first house purchased may be the only house lived in, and changes in the life cycle will be felt in terms of crowded living rooms and queues in the morning for the bathroom rather than changes in dwelling.

The moves associated with the different stages of the life cycle correspond broadly to tenurial moves. In terms of new households, some may enter local authority housing or owner-occupation, but the more usual pattern is for a new household to stay for a short time in private renting. This is the easiest sector of the market to enter, since it does not require proof of housing need, a large down-payment or the securing of a loan. For impecunious young households it provides relatively cheap accommodation without the ties which cling to living in the other two tenure categories. The period in private renting may be associated with a number of moves as households move from flat to flat. At this stage the population of new households breaks into three groups. First, there are those who continue to stay in the private rented sector either through choice – the single, the transient and the cosmopolitan rich – or through constraint. Those trapped in the private rented sector have the worst accommodation in Britain and receive less subsidy. Some may eventually move into local authority housing as they slowly advance up the housing waiting list. Then, secondly, there are those who move into local authority housing. They begin a housing career which can eventually lead to the tenancy of a sturdy home in a 'good' estate. The richer ones may eventually move into owner-occupation through buying their tenancy or through a move directly into the private sector. Finally, there are those who enter owner-occupation to begin a housing career which, for the few successful ones, may lead to that dream cottage in the countryside. For the rest, the great majority, a few more moves will occur, all of them within the owner-occupied sector until the very later stages of the household life cycle.

The absolute numbers involved in these terms are shown in Figure 9.1. Note the large amount of movement within the private rented sector and how this sector provides a temporary form of accommodation, a stepping stone for subsequent movement into the two main tenure types. Other movement takes place within each of these majority tenure categories; there is very little between owner-occupation and local authority housing in either direction. The most important changes within the post-war scene have been the increasing proportion of those moving straight into owner-occupation and those moving into owner-occupation from private renting. There has also been a steady increase in those moving from local authority housing into owner-occupation, in the form of council house sales, and through local authority tenants moving out and buying their own property. The fiscal advantages have redirected household movement towards owner-occupation.

There is a definite spatial pattern to residential mobility in Britain. Young new households move into the central city areas where accommodation in the private rented sector will be found. There

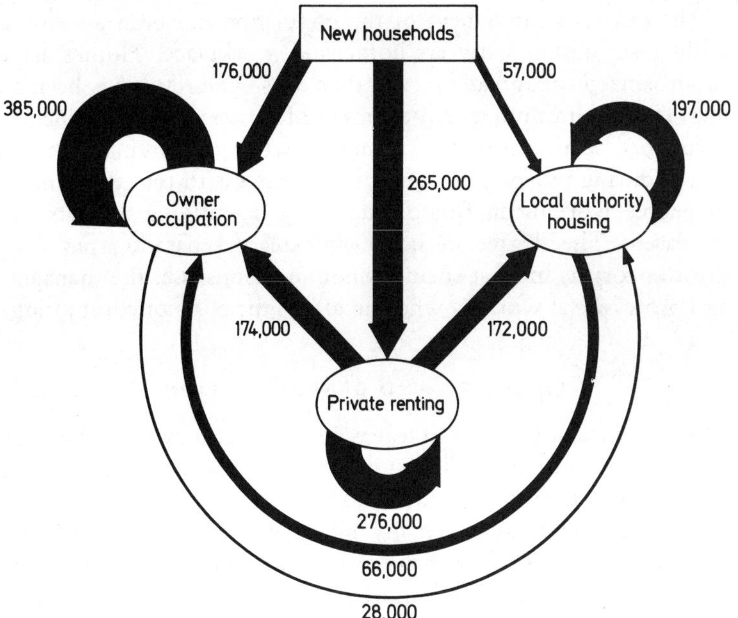

Figure 9.1 Household movement between tenure types, England and Wales, 1971 (from HPTV)

may then follow a period of movement within these inner-city areas as households seek better rented accommodation. Subsequent moves will take an outward trend as local authority tenants are directed towards the council housing estates on the periphery, and owner-occupiers move to the inner and outer suburbs. There is a centrifugal pattern of outward movement from the city centre. The aggregate trend is shown in Figure 9.2, which shows the population distribution by urban core, suburbs and non-metropolitan areas for 1960 and 1975. The diagram reveals the suburban and rural direction of population redistribution in Britain. Early results from the 1981 census suggest that the trend is continuing. There is also some evidence that this outward movement takes a definite sectoral pattern. Households do not tend to move from an inner-city area to a suburb on the opposite side of the city centre; rather they move outwards from where they are. There is a sectoral bias to the outward movement. Movement also takes place within areas of similar socio-economic status. Distinct channels of movement can be identified, consisting of streams of households of particular socio-economic status moving into particular areas of the city. These channels are the process structuring the pattern of socio-economic segregation in the city.

The outward movement of the population has been associated with a separation between home and workplace. Homes have suburbanized to a greater extent than jobs. The result has been an increase in commuting. An example of this trend is contained in Figure 9.3, which shows the journey-to-work patterns in the Bristol region during two periods. In 1971 compared with 1961 the number of people working in Bristol but living in outlying districts had increased. The degree of home–workplace separation has been greatest for the highest socio-economic groups, i.e. the managers and professional workers who can afford the costs of commuting.

FILTERING AND GENTRIFICATION

When a household moves, it leaves behind a vacancy. If the vacancy is filled by a household of lower income, the dwelling is said to have filtered down the income scale. This process of filtering has occurred in Britain, and there are many inner-city areas where the once fashionable houses of the rich have been subdivided into flats and bedsitters. Filtering is much more than a description of a process. It is often used as an argument for aiding the better-off. The argument goes as follows: by helping people to buy new houses, vacancies are

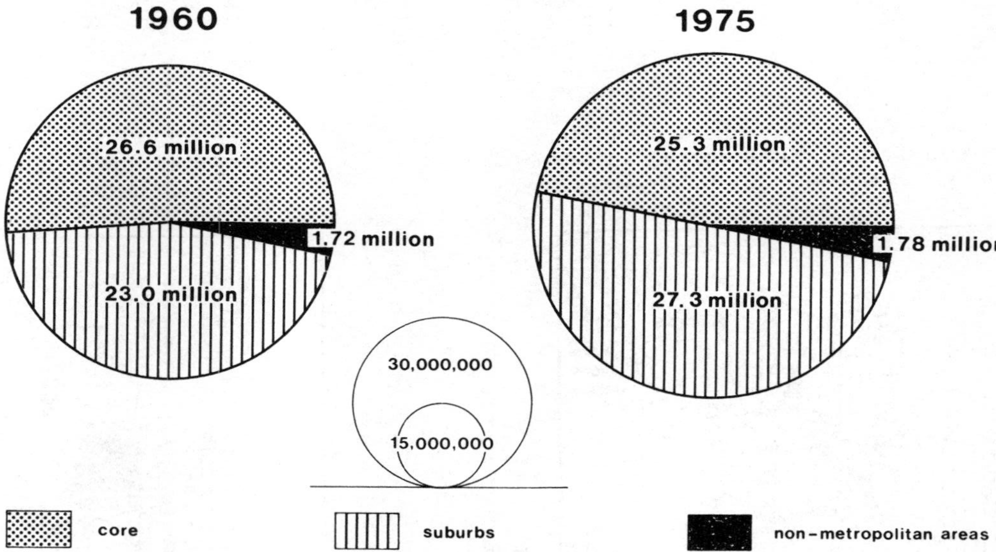

Figure 9.2 Population distribution in Britain, 1960 and 1975

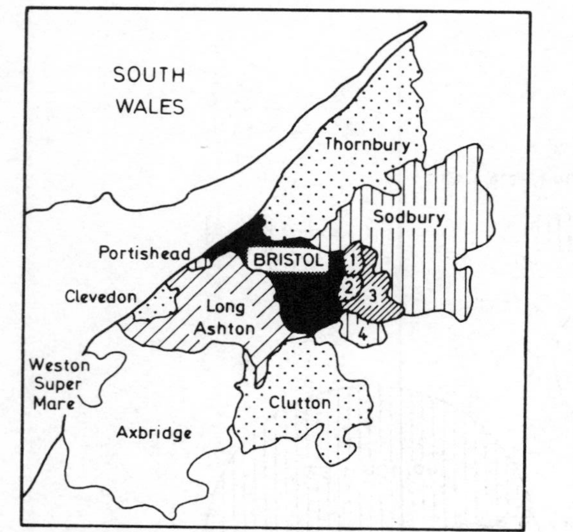

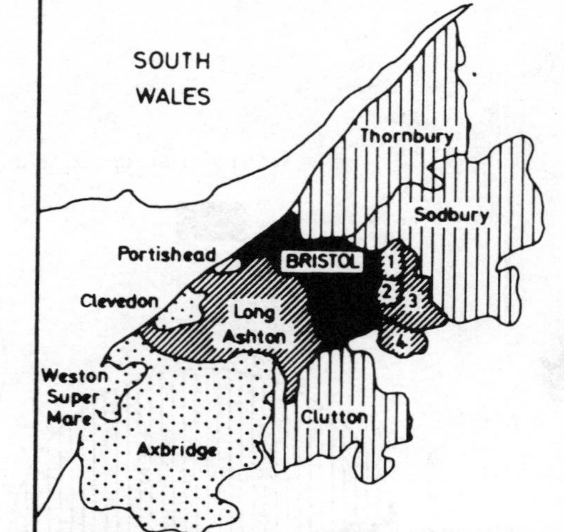

Figure 9.3 Suburbanization in the Bristol region

created which can be filled by the lower income groups, thus everyone benefits. The argument has been a powerful one in the past, and even today it is of some importance in American housing policy circles, the USA being one of those countries where welfare is created for the rich. In Britain, by contrast, an organized working class has fought for the provision of good-quality local authority housing, which negates the need for filtering. But as local authority housing is cut back we may see the apologists of expenditure reductions again returning to the filtering argument. It is an argument, although of perfect Benthamite credentials, lacking in any moral basis. Good housing is a right of every citizen, and the housing opportunities of the majority should not depend on the whim and actions of the minority.

When the vacancy is filled by a household of higher socio-economic status the dwelling is said to have filtered up the status scale. If this occurs with a lot of vacancies in an area, then the process is termed 'gentrification'. Gentrification has increased in certain inner-city areas as travel costs have increased and the suburbs hold out less attraction for a number of middle-income households. Islington in London is a prime example. The process has been lubricated, some would say initiated, by the estate agents, landlords and various financial institutions eager to profit from the consequent increase in turnover and the rise in house prices. Gentrification has so far affected only a few areas in selected cities. This is because certain preconditions are necessary: relatively large houses, good infrastructure and access to a range of facilities. Where any of these are lacking, only the hardiest of the middle-income, Habitat-buying, *Observer*-reading groups will dare to venture.

The movement of established households into new housing produces a chain reaction rippling through the housing market, creating vacancies in its wake. The chain ends when a vacancy is taken by a new household or when a vacant dwelling is demolished, not re-let or changed into non-residential use. Of new housing in Britain almost a quarter is taken up by new households who create no vacancies. Of the rest we have very little information. A study in Clydeside found that the average chain for a new owner-occupied dwelling was 2.09 compared to the 1.64 of the local authority dwelling. The relatively small chain length of the public sector dwellings reflected the fact that 55 per cent of chains terminated in the demolition of property. Studies from other cities with better housing conditions may yield different results.

THE EXCHANGE PROFESSIONALS

There are a group of agents directly involved in the exchange of housing. In the local authority sector the housing managers allocate dwellings to households, and in the private rented sector landlords and their agents are the gatekeepers. But it is in the owner-occupied sector that we can identify agents who are directly associated with servicing the exchange market.

Estate agents sell houses by linking up buyers and sellers. Their fees, payable by the seller, vary from 1½ to 3 per cent of the eventual selling price. Estate agents are now the biggest single source of information on housing vacancies; almost two-thirds of households obtained their present house through estate agents, and almost all buyers use them, which forces sellers, who are often unwilling to pay the fees, to use them. The role of estate agents can vary from passive coordination to active manipulation of the market. Agents can arrange mortgages, often at favourable rates to potential buyers, since they have arrangements with building societies. Because estate agents make their money from selling houses they benefit from increased turnover and rises in house prices. There is evidence from a number of case studies that estate agents have been influential in initiating the process of gentrification.

Surveyors are employed by buyers and the financial institutions to survey houses before purchase. It is impossible to get a building society mortgage without a surveyor's report, a report which the purchaser pays for but does not see. The cost of the survey can reach up to £75. Surveyors are important because their report decides the valuation of the property, which affects the amount of mortgage given by the building society or the local authority to the purchaser. Surveyors' reports also influence mortgage lending to different residential areas. Surveyors take the character of the immediate area into account in their report and if they assess the area to be poor, then a mortgage may be refused. The red-lining policies of building societies in part stem from unfavourable surveyors' reports. Surveyors are a conservative group since their professional competence and livelihood is at stake when they survey properties. Minimum lending in certain areas is as much a function of risk-minimization by surveyors as by building societies.

Solicitors: The transfer of ownership is a legal matter. The typical household uses a solicitor because it does not know any better or it lacks confidence in conveyancing firms or its own efforts. Conveyancing is an important source of income for solicitors, who obviously stress the enormous benefits gained from using them. In selling a £20,000 house and buying a £25,000 house the average solicitor's fees would reach £650.

The different exchange professionals are bound together in local housing markets by interlocking directorships. Threads of mutual interest tie together solicitors, estate agents, surveyors, mortgage brokers, banks, property companies and financial companies. Housing exchange is a lucrative business which attracts local business folk and people on the make.

THE COSTS OF MOVING

Because of all the agents involved and their often monopoly power, moving house can be an expensive business. Including estate agents' fees, solicitors' costs and the charge for the surveyors' report, it costs around £2000 to buy a house for £20,000 and sell for a similar price. There are also emotional costs. The house-buying system in England maximizes inconvenience, costs and uncertainty. It would be difficult to devise a worse system. Until the contracts are signed there is no formal sanction against households who back out of buying a property or suddenly raise the price before signing. Almost all owner-occupiers have their horror stories about moving, and most people emerge from buying and selling houses, hard bitten, world-weary and exhausted. Next to death, buying and selling housing in Britain is one of the biggest hassles a person is likely to experience.

The high financial costs of moving have resulted in the growth of conveyancing companies, who charge approximately half a solicitors' fees, and in do-it-yourself conveyancing. The high financial and emotional costs have also militated against movement within the owner-occupied sector. Households with decreasing space requirements in the latter stages of their lives are unlikely to brave the hazards or meet the costs of moving. The result is a high degree of under-occupation and overall a less than optimal use of the national housing stock. Households with expanding space requirements now find it as cheap to build an extension as to move house, and the inconvenience is probably less. The cost of exchange also operates against the movement of labour. The majority of skilled workers are now in owner-occupation, yet it is in the skilled sector that labour shortages are most keenly felt in regional and sub-regional labour markets. The large housing costs in the expanding areas of the south-east, where there is a demand for skilled labour, in association with the large costs of moving house, operate against the efficient flow of population. It is much easier to move within the private rented sector, but because of the present fiscal arrangements those with effective choice prefer owner-occupation. Yet the high costs of moving into and within the sector works against the easy flow of labour from declining to growing regions of the country. The operation of the housing market affects national economic performance.

10

HOUSING SUB-MARKETS

There is no such thing as the housing market. There is not an undifferentiated, homogeneous market; the production, consumption, allocation and exchange of housing takes place in a mosaic of sub-markets. In the public sector, council housing is commissioned and managed by the separate local authorities, which vary in the size of waiting lists and in the size and composition of their housing stock. These variations, which reflect need, past development and political disposition, are greater than the variations in demand. The result is that a household seeking council housing has a better chance of obtaining a good-quality house more quickly in some areas than in others. Where you are can be as important as who you are in determining access to housing.

Variations also exist in the private sector in terms of tenure distribution, quality of housing and other housing attributes. The sharpest distinction which can be drawn is price. The price of housing varies markedly through the country (see Figure 10.1). Income tends to be higher in the higher price regions, but for those on salaries assessed on a national basis the difference in house prices leads to varied housing experiences for those with similar incomes in different parts of the country. A civil servant in Yorkshire and Humberside is more likely to have a large house than a person with a similar job in Reading. These variations have important effects. Take the case of the £25,000 limit on the amount of loan eligible for income tax relief. In the cheaper housing regions of the country this limit affects relatively few people. In the pricier regions of London and the south-east in contrast, a higher proportion of housing is above this limit and therefore more households are affected. Location and space combine with socio-economic status to determine a household's position in the housing consumption stakes.

The data in Figure 10.1 are crude aggregate figures. They refer to coarse-grained regional divisions, but the private housing market

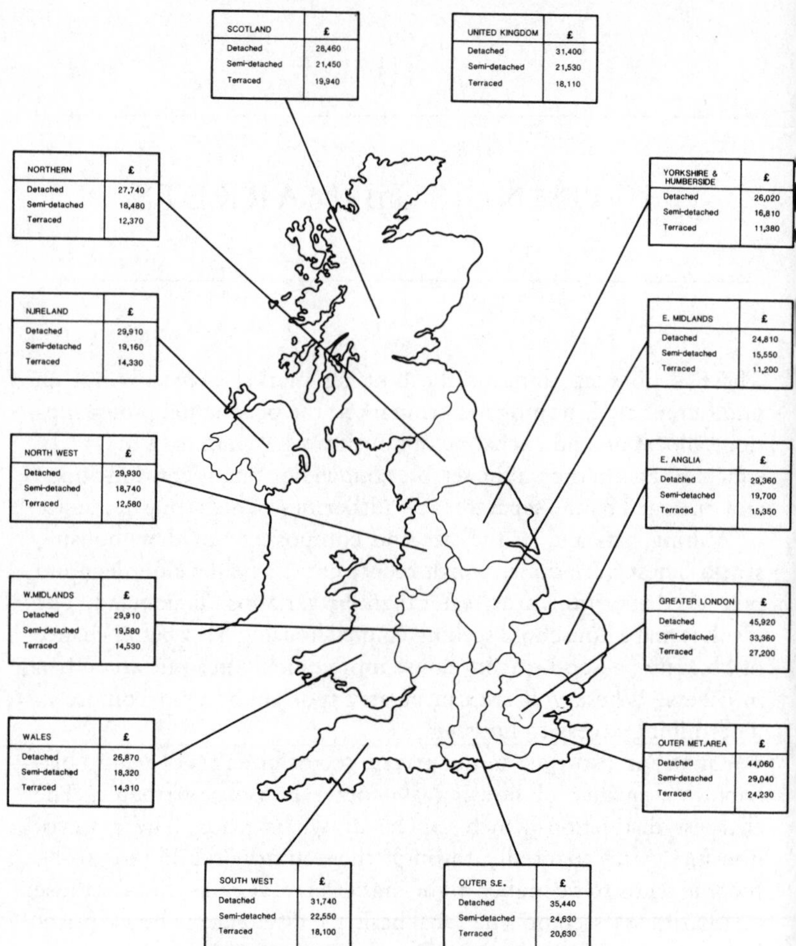

SCOTLAND £
Detached 28,460
Semi-detached 21,450
Terraced 19,940
UNITED KINGDOM £
Detached 31,400
Semi-detached 21,530
Terraced 18,110
NORTHERN £
Detached 27,740
Semi-detached 18,480
Terraced 12,370
YORKSHIRE & HUMBERSIDE £
Detached 26,020
Semi-detached 16,810
Terraced 11,380
N.IRELAND £
Detached 29,910
Semi-detached 19,160
Terraced 14,330
E. MIDLANDS £
Detached 24,810
Semi-detached 15,550
Terraced 11,200
NORTH WEST £
Detached 29,930
Semi-detached 18,740
Terraced 12,580
E. ANGLIA £
Detached 29,360
Semi-detached 19,700
Terraced 15,350
W.MIDLANDS £
Detached 29,910
Semi-detached 19,580
Terraced 14,530
GREATER LONDON £
Detached 45,920
Semi-detached 33,360
Terraced 27,200
WALES £
Detached 26,870
Semi-detached 18,320
Terraced 14,310
OUTER MET.AREA £
Detached 44,060
Semi-detached 29,040
Terraced 24,230
SOUTH WEST £
Detached 31,740
Semi-detached 22,550
Terraced 18,100
OUTER S.E. £
Detached 35,440
Semi-detached 24,630
Terraced 20,630

Figure 10.1 House prices by region, 1980

does not operate at this scale. The sub-markets in the private sector are what we may term city regions. These are regions comprising both an urban core and a commuting hinterland. A system of metropolitan and non-metropolitan regions has been constructed for Great Britain using the 1971 census. It is these regions, shown in Figure 10.2, that constitute the local housing markets.

The point I am making is that there are variations in housing markets across the country. There are a series of housing sub-markets defined by local authority boundaries and the limits of city regions. These boundaries overlap and sometimes diverge. The

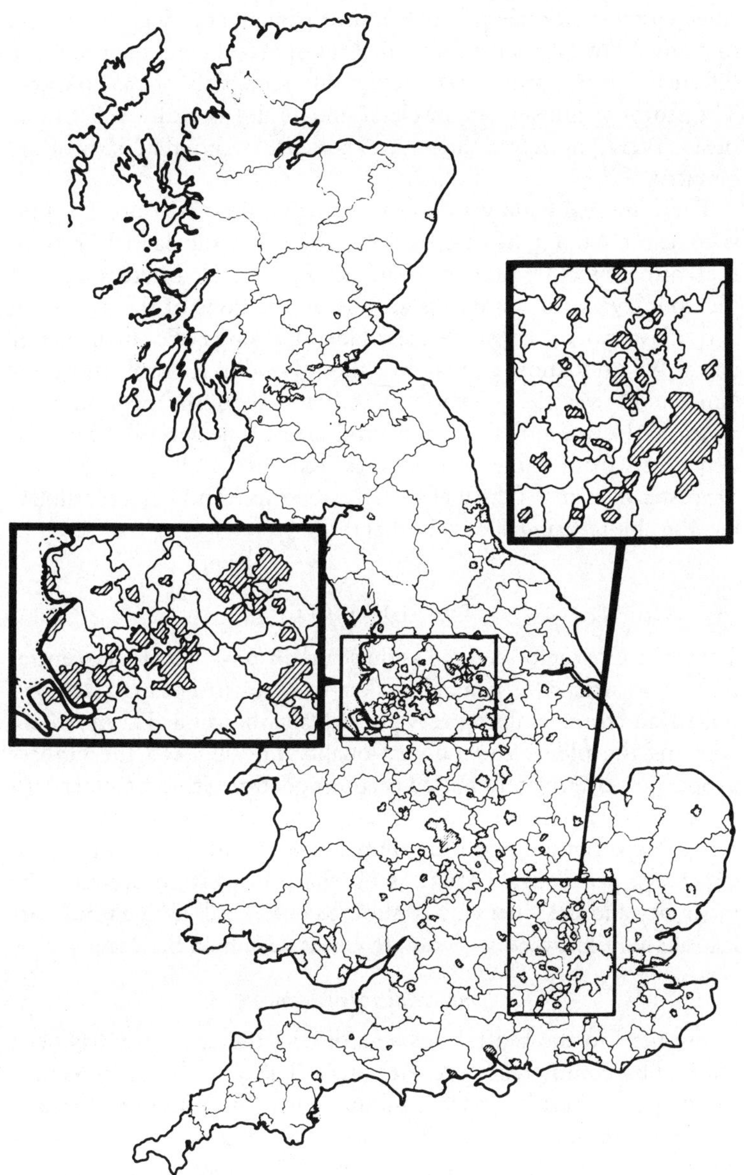

Figure 10.2 Urban regions in Britain (from Hall and Hay, 1980)

sub-market is the scale at which house prices and the degree of access to council housing is determined. An important consequence is the difference in housing experience in different parts of the country. The story of housing in England and Wales is really a fictitious mean, averaging across the wide experience of different parts of the country.

There are two main ways of summarizing this variation. The first is to select a range of case studies. There is a substantial body of literature now emerging on the housing market in different parts of the country; most numerous are the descriptions of the evolution and analyses of the consequences of local housing policy in the major cities. We now know a great deal about London, Bristol, Birmingham and Newcastle. We know slightly less about the medium-sized cities, and even less about the rural areas. The second way is to generalize from these case studies and discuss housing market processes in terms of distinct spatial categories. This latter method is used in the remainder of this chapter.

THE INNER CITY

The inner city can be defined as those urban areas around the central business district. It is generally taken to be an area of high-density, mixed land use containing very poor-quality housing. The inner city contains the oldest and poorest-quality housing and the highest proportion of privately rented accommodation. In some inner-city wards private renting constitutes over 60 per cent of the housing stock. Here can be found the slum dwellers and the inhabitants of expensive penthouses. There is no sharp distinction between the inner city and the inner ring of suburbs but like all difficult categorizations you know when you are either in one or the other.

Commercial redevelopment

Being next to the central business district the inner city has been affected by commercial redevelopment. The central business core is the area of highest land value and the centre for all kinds of speculative land-use development. The city-centre edges of the inner-area housing markets have been eaten away by various commercial and public schemes. From the private sector the inner-city areas have been affected by two phases of expansion in the commercial property sector. The first was in the period 1958 to 1965, when there was the construction of major shopping centres, especially in large provincial cities. The process was often aided by local authorities eager to attract rate-paying establishments. The property boom went hand in hand in many cities with public redevelopment schemes. The net effect was for the demolition of adjacent housing and the displacement of the local population. The second phase was the office property boom of the early 1970s when easy credit and heavy demand for office space, especially in London, resulted in large-scale office construction. Again the effect was the same: housing was demolished, low-income residents were displaced and the few units of housing which were constructed were invariably very expensive ones for richer households. Since the rise and fall of the office boom, community organizations have grown in size and sophistication. The property developers no longer have it all their own way. Planning enquiries can give community groups a strong platform on which to mount their protest, and major commercial property developments involving displacement of residents or disruption of communities have been the scene of long wrangles as the community organizations seek to halt the developments and minimize the disruption. The Coin Street Development in London has been held up for two years by a combination of a change of the party in power in the GLC and a well-organized community protest at the planning enquiries. In London at least, the nature of the redevelopment along the banks of the Thames is not a foregone conclusion.

Housing policies and their impact

The inner-city areas have seen housing policies come and go. In terms of housing policies with direct effects on the inner city, two successive waves can be identified. The first was the slum clearance programme of the 1950s and 1960s, when large amounts of housing declared substandard were demolished and the inhabitants were offered accommodation either in peripheral council estates or in the high-rise blocks which arose from the dust of the municipal bulldozer. These high-rise blocks were to prove unpopular and, although they represented improved physical standards of housing, they were a design failure. They now constitute a serious problem for housing managers and even more serious problems for the people who have to live in them. The second wave was the swing away from such comprehensive redevelopment towards improvement policies. This switch, determined by cost-cutting considerations, was signalled by the 1969 and 1974 Housing Acts, which raised the level of the improvement grant and introduced respectively GIAs and HAAs. These area-based improvement schemes were implemented in the older housing areas of the inner city, and they can be identified by the pedestrianization schemes, the new roofs of the dwellings, the increased greenery and the general air of housing improvement. Although successful in improving particular blocks of housing, the scheme has still to meet the scale of the problem. The programme was hamstrung through a succession of expenditure reductions in the mid- and late 1970s. The take-up of improvement grants was an important theme of this second wave. The distribution of improvement grants, however, has not followed the distribution of greatest housing need. A series of studies of Huddersfield, inner London and Bristol have all pointed to the fact that the largest number of grants has gone to the better-quality housing areas of the inner city. In the period 1969 to 1973 the improvement grants fuelled the process of gentrification. Since then restrictions placed on improvement grants have limited the amount of private gain from public investment, although the level of improvement grant has failed to meet the steady rise in repair costs. There has been a fall-off in the uptake of improvement grants in the poorer-quality housing areas of the inner city. The housing improvement programme has failed to provide a solution to poor-quality housing.

If one walks round the inner-city area of a major British city the impact of these different policies can be seen on the ground. The high-rise blocks now stand beside GIAs, with newly constructed small in-fill sites of high-density low-rise housing completing the scene.

The inner areas have also been affected by policies not specifically designed for the inner city. The most important has been the continuing operation of rent controls which have made renting by landlords relatively unprofitable. The landlords have responded by selling off their property to owner-occupation and where this has proved difficult, by reducing maintenance and improvement expenditure and by selecting short-stay tenants whose continued movement allows frequent rent increases. The net effect is to lead to a deterioration in the quality of private rented accommodation and increased difficulty for households seeking longer-term accommodation; these households tend to be the lower income groups effectively trapped in the private rented sector.

One of the main features of the inner-city housing market in contrast to the more suburban residential areas has been the relative lack of building society financing of house purchase. Because of building society policy many inner-city areas are considered high-risk areas, and in some cases there is an explicit policy of minimum lending. This has been termed *red-lining*. This lack of building society finance was partly met by the local authority mortgage scheme, especially in the early 1970s. However, this scheme has been reduced as part of a general reduction in local authority spending, and the building societies have failed to fill the gap. The result is that finance companies and clearing banks are used much more for house purchases in the inner city than in its other parts. The mortgages of finance companies and clearing banks have shorter repayment periods and higher interest charges, and households with such mortgages have much larger repayments than households with similar-sized building society mortgages. Thus the lower-income house purchases in the inner city are further disadvantaged.

The emerging problem of the inner city

Throughout the post-war period the inner city has emerged as a problem area. It is in the inner cities that many residents suffer from unemployment, poor housing, low incomes and poor schooling. Poor-quality housing is just one of the strands that catch inner-city residents in a web of multiple deprivation. The inner cities have also emerged as the main location for settlement by people from the Indian sub-continent and the West Indies. The coloured population of Britain is essentially an urban-based population and even more an inner-city urban population. Two-thirds of black households in Britain live in the inner areas of our major cities. The problems for young black children of poor schooling, low educational attainment and few job prospects are exacerbated by overt and perceived racial prejudice amongst employers and police. And this perceived feeling of deprivation has provided the tinder for the riots of 1980 in St Pauls, Bristol, and the more severe cases of disorder in Brixton, Toxteth and Moss Side in 1981. Here deprivation was just one of the ingredients in an explosive cocktail whose mixture included perceived police harassment, youth alienation, racial prejudice, common or garden hooliganism, mob hysteria and police incompetence. Not all the inner-city areas are the same. There are the rows of terraced housing kept neat by the inhabitants and the gentrified areas where young middle-class households have improved the Victorian and Edwardian dwellings. But the abiding image of the inner city, and one reinforced by television coverage of the 1981 riots, is of areas where there is a concentration of black people living in areas scarred by years of neglect. If the riots have done anything they have forced a rapid re-evaluation of public policy towards the inner city.

THE SUBURBS

The vast mass of British urban housing is found between the edge of the inner city and the edge of the built-up area. These are the suburbs. The term covers inter-war and post-war housing of both the public and private sectors. Within the city boundaries the inter-war private-sector houses constitute over a third of the housing stock. In the cities of the south and the Midlands this proportion is much higher. The inter-war building boom has left a legacy of acres of bay-windowed, two-storey housing and, although perhaps lacking the architectural critic's seal of approval, it has proved to be very popular. In these predominantly residential areas the building societies provide the bulk of house purchase funds. The typical household is the well-established child-rearing household with either a skilled manual or a non-manual worker as head.

Surrounding these inter-war estates are the post-war council estates and the private-sector developers. On the periphery of British cities are the lower-density council estates built in the 1950s and 1960s to rehouse those on the waiting list and those affected by comprehensive redevelopment in the central areas. The housing is physically sound, although the estates vary in attractiveness according to the related factors of the character of the tenants and the precise style and quality of the buildings. Some of the badly built estates which have acquired a poor reputation have become the sink estates where the local authority housing managers pour their problem families. In the more favoured estates there has been a greater demand from tenants to buy their property, and in some of the better-quality estates between a third and a half of the housing stock is now owner-occupied. It is only the better-quality local authority housing which has sold. The long-term result is for a residualization of the council house stock to high-rise blocks, housing in estates with poor reputations, and poorer-quality housing. The reputation of council housing will thus continue to deteriorate.

The vast mass of post-war suburban private housing is high-density, two- to three-bedroomed, two-storey housing built by both large-scale and small-scale speculative builders. The actual physical quality is often of lower standard than the best council housing because there are no Parker Morris standards in the private sector. The small variations in design – the provision of garages, and the results of individual gardening and house-painting styles – give these estates a slightly different atmosphere from the suburban council estate. The private estates vary in size of house and overall density, and this variation is reflected in the composition of the inhabitants. At one extreme the low-slung, low-density, well-built bungalows house those who have made it, while the smaller cheaper housing accommodates those who are still trying to make it. This post-war suburban housing is variegated enough to accommodate most of the variations in the middle-income range.

Households find it much easier to buy newer housing. The building societies are keen to lend, often with more favourable arrangements in terms of length of repayment and size of down-payment in suburban areas than elsewhere, and builders of new property can often arrange mortgages for new buyers. The system of house purchase finance lubricates the process of suburbanization. Although many households find some pleasure in living away from the city centre with its noise and traffic, a problem of accessibility has emerged. Much suburban housing is located far from cultural, shopping, employment and entertainment facilities. While housing has suburbanized, employment, retail outlets and entertainment centres have moved out much slower, and there has been a growing separation between house and job, and house and shop. The result is a long journey to work, reliance on public transport and, for those without good transport facilities, a restriction of opportunities. Even individual members of households with cars may be denied access for long periods. Housewives, schoolchildren and the elderly often find themselves relying on poor public transport or are restricted to their own homes.

The built form of post-war Britain has been predicated on relatively cheap transport costs. The expanding cities and sprawling suburbs with their growing separation between jobs, houses, schools, shops and centres of entertainment have all meant longer journeys. With the OPEC price increases of 1974 the era of cheap fuel ended, probably for ever. However, the structure of cities reflects the cheap fuel era. As energy prices rise and transport costs grow, suburban life becomes increasingly expensive. The short-term responses to higher transport costs lie in conserving energy and in providing more efficient transport systems. The long-term response will be to reduce the separation between different activity centres and hence the amount of movement required. We can see the gentrification process as perhaps the beginning of a move back to the cities; it is not incidental that the largest increases in house prices in recent years have been in those residential areas close to city centres.

THE NEW TOWNS

Almost two million people live in the new towns which represent the single most ambitious planning experiment in post-war Britain. The idea of new towns first grew up in the atmosphere of the nineteenth century when rapid unplanned urbanization resulted in sprawling, unhealthy towns, which some feared provided the basis for social disorder and societal chaos. In Hobsbawm's phrase, 'the city was a volcano'. There had already been a number of pamphlets published and experiments tried before Ebenezer Howard published in 1902 his *Tomorrow: A Peaceful Path To Real Reform*, but none had the same impact. In this book, first published in 1898 with the title *Garden Cities of Tomorrow*, Howard argued that the benefits of urban and rural life should be fused in the creation of new towns, which were to be of approximately 32,000 people based in a circular type of city covering 6000 acres. The land was to be owned by the municipality, and any surplus from rent and rates should be used for the provision of municipal services. The idea is so simple that it has the mark of genius.

Howard sought to turn his ideas into reality, and in 1902 he founded the Garden City Pioneer Company which bought 4000 acres in Hertfordshire to found Letchworth, the first truly new town. F. J. Osborn joined the company in Letchworth in 1912 and he was to give administrative drive and political commitment to Howard's ideas. In 1920 more land was bought for the second new town of Welwyn Garden City. Throughout the inter-war years the Town and Country Planning Association (TCPA), the pressure group for new towns, was very active in promoting their cause both inside and outside government committees. Their activities proved successful. The post-war planning system built on the basis of the Barlow Commission and the Scott and Uthwatt committees all gave attention to the deliberations of the TCPA. The aims of low-density, low-rise housing and planned neighbourhoods zoned from industrial land use were incorporated into various proposals. The TCPA pressure group gave legislative form to the popular demands for change and improvement. The masses provided the weight, the pressure groups the direction.

In 1945 a new town committee was set up under John Reith, which included F. J. Osborn. The committee, not surprisingly given the views of most of its members, argued the case for the creation of new towns in which land should be vested in the hands of a development corporation. The committee's recommendations were incorporated in the New Towns Act of 1946.

Two types of new town can be identified. The mark 1 new towns were designated between 1946 and 1950; of the fourteen designated, eight were located around London and were part of the attempt to decentralize growth from the metropolis. The remainder were in the development areas (see Figure 10.3). The 1950s were a lean period for new towns, with only Cumbernauld being designated in 1955. The mark 2 new towns were a feature of the 1960s and early 1970s; they were located around the major conurbations as part of attempts to decentralize from major urban centres and to resuscitate in regional planning the economies of failing regions. We can make a further distinction between the green-field mark 2 towns of the early 1960s, which were new in the literal sense, and the expanded towns of the late 1960s and 1970s such as Warrington, Peterborough and Northampton, which were new towns grafted on to old-established urban centres. They were a product of cost cutting, since green-field sites were considered much more expensive.

By definition the housing stock in new towns is of recent construction. If they do not have the high-quality housing of the Addison Act, neither do they show the poor quality of the inter-war medium-rise. The housing in new towns is physically sound, and most of it, 100 per cent in the green-field towns, is in planned environments with lots of greenery, with the separation of vehicular and pedestrian traffic best exemplified in Cumbernauld. At their best the new towns have provided pleasant urban environments, free from congestion and traffic noise, with the advantages of open green spaces. But even at their worst the housing in new towns is not much worse than the housing in new local authority estates or in private-sector developments.

Most housing in new towns is controlled by the Development Corporations, who act very much like the local authorities in selecting tenants and allocating particular households to specific dwellings. There is one important difference. In the early days new towns were attracting and keen to attract footloose industry. To do so, they needed a pool of labour, and skilled labour in particular. Households relocating with their firms and households already fixed up with employment in the new town were at the top of the queue for housing. Unlike amongst the local authorities, emphasis was on employment and less attention was paid to housing need. The result was that skilled persons predominated, and even today there is an underrepresentation of unskilled and semi-skilled workers in new towns.

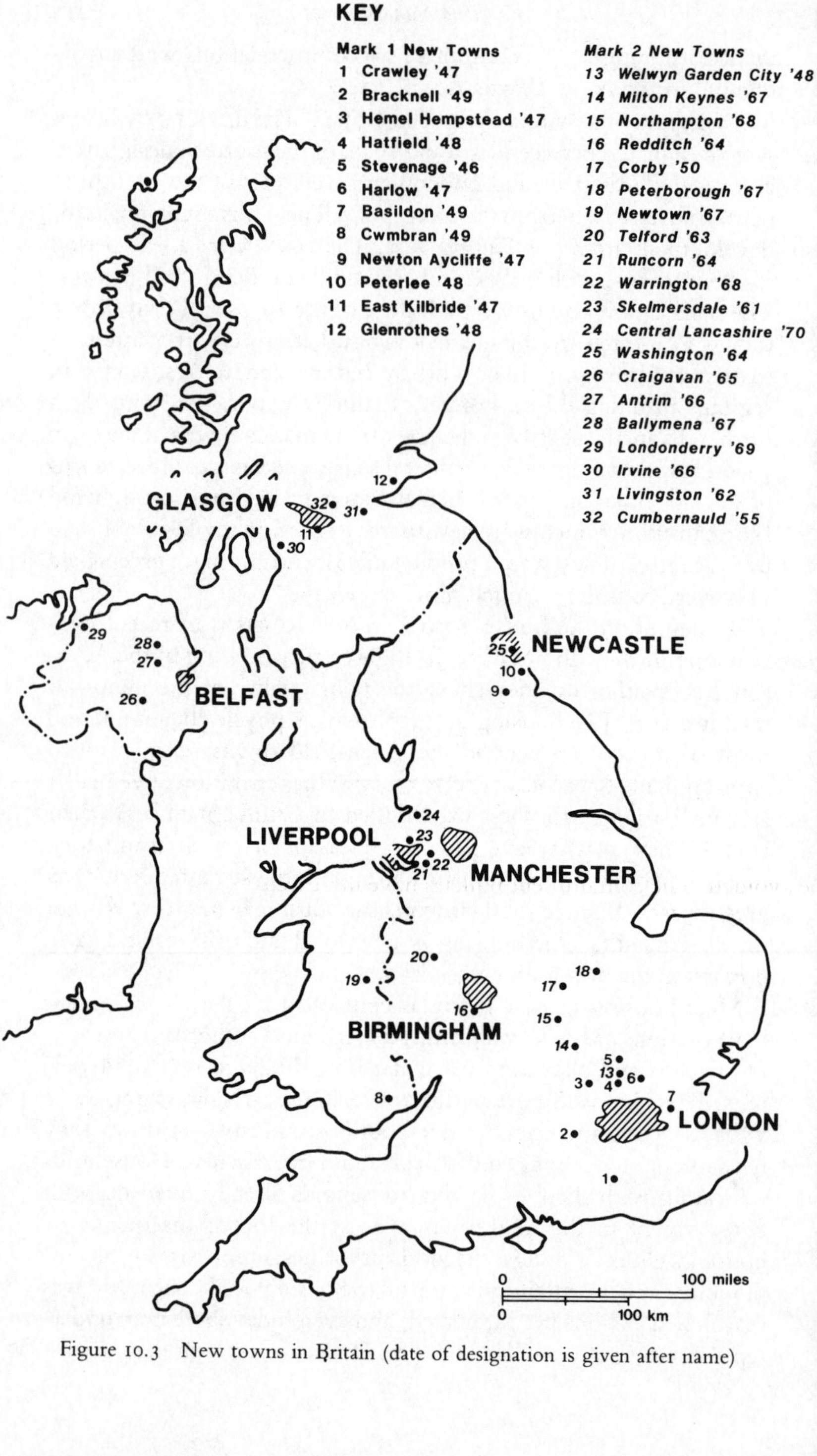

KEY

Mark 1 New Towns

1 Crawley '47
2 Bracknell '49
3 Hemel Hempstead '47
4 Hatfield '48
5 Stevenage '46
6 Harlow '47
7 Basildon '49
8 Cwmbran '49
9 Newton Aycliffe '47
10 Peterlee '48
11 East Kilbride '47
12 Glenrothes '48

Mark 2 New Towns

13 Welwyn Garden City '48
14 Milton Keynes '67
15 Northampton '68
16 Redditch '64
17 Corby '50
18 Peterborough '67
19 Newtown '67
20 Telford '63
21 Runcorn '64
22 Warrington '68
23 Skelmersdale '61
24 Central Lancashire '70
25 Washington '64
26 Craigavan '65
27 Antrim '66
28 Ballymena '67
29 Londonderry '69
30 Irvine '66
31 Livingston '62
32 Cumbernauld '55

GLASGOW
NEWCASTLE
BELFAST
LIVERPOOL
MANCHESTER
BIRMINGHAM
LONDON
0 100 miles
0 100 km

Figure 10.3 New towns in Britain (date of designation is given after name)

In terms of tenure, the corporation housing predominates (see Table 10.1). The amount of owner-occupation is highest in the expanded towns of central Lancashire, Northampton, Peterborough, etc., where the new-town designation was placed on an existing settlement. But even in these places there has been a relative fall in owner-occupation as more development corporation housing has been built. For the green-field new towns the general trend has been for an increase in owner-occupation, albeit on a small base. This has come about through the increasing sale of plots of land to speculative builders and the direct transfer of corporation housing to sitting tenants. In 1966 the government urged new towns to have at least 50 per cent owner-occupation; this has yet to be achieved,

Table 10.1 Percentage of owner-occupied dwellings in new towns

New town	*1972*	*1978*
England		
Aycliffe	8.7	21.4
Basildon	17.8	27.0
Bracknell	25.6	29.3
Central Lancashire	62.5	62.3
Corby	11.0	20.6
Crawley	37.5	42.8
Harlow	13.1	23.9
Hatfield	29.8	32.6
Hemel Hempstead	31.7	40.0
Milton Keynes	57.3	43.4
Northampton	59.2	55.6
Peterborough	54.8	48.2
Peterlee	4.2	11.3
Redditch	59.4	49.8
Runcorn	36.1	29.3
Skelmersdale	20.7	21.9
Stevenage	16.1	37.8
Telford	35.5	35.7
Warrington	55.1	56.8
Washington	24.8	28.2
Welwyn Garden City	27.2	28.3
Scotland		
Cumbernauld	9.0	18.4
East Kilbride	12.0	17.5
Glenrothes	8.1	13.8
Irvine	26.1	18.3
Livingston	3.4	8.1
Wales		
Cwmbran	18.6	21.2
Newtown	31.7	40.0

Source: Aldridge, 1979

although new towns were included in the Conservatives' 1980 Act, which gave sitting tenants the right to buy their accommodation. Sales of housing are likely to be proportionately higher in the new towns than in the local authority sector, because the former contain good-quality housing and well-planned environments which are likely to attract the interest of sitting tenants. Moreover, tenants of development corporation housing tend to have higher incomes than local authority tenants. There is therefore a greater effective demand.

The housing in new towns is much more expensive than local authority housing; on average the rent is half as expensive again as the typical rent of a local authority house. This arises because of the age distribution of new-town housing. Since much of it is relatively modern, there is less opportunity for the creation of a rent pool in which the rent for old, paid-off housing can be used to subsidize the rents of new housing which is still being paid for. The higher rents operate against the entry of lower-income households, and in association with the early allocation procedures this explains the under-representation of semi-skilled, unskilled and low-income households in new towns.

THE RURAL AREAS

Much of the foregoing discussion has been concerned with housing in urban areas. There is, however, a significant proportion of dwellings in rural districts. The term 'rural' is an administrative one, used in the sense of districts within county councils rather than metropolitan districts. In 1976, out of a total of just over seventeen million dwellings almost four million were located in the rural districts. Housing in rural areas differs from housing in the urban areas. In the first place, there is a higher proportion of owner-occupation and private unfurnished renting (see Table 10.2). The higher proportion of owner-occupation reflects the suburban spread of new housing; the large number of private rentings of unfurnished accommodation reflects the tied-cottage system. There has long been an antipathy against council housing in rural districts. The most powerful groups in the local political scene are the farmers and landowners, to whom local authority housing is an unwarranted expense on the rates and a form of housing which reduces the potency of the tied-cottage system. The relative lack of council housing has made this system more important: in 1948 34 per cent of farmworkers lived in tied housing, but by 1976 this figure had increased to 53 per cent. The

Table 10.2 Housing tenure in rural England, 1971

Tenure	% of dwellings	
	English rural districts	*England*
Owner-occupied	54.5	50.0
Local authority	21.1	28.0
Private renting (unfurnished)	20.9	17.1
Private renting (furnished)	3.3	4.7
Other	0.2	0.2
Total	100	100

Source: Dunn *et al.*, 1981

chronic shortage of council housing strengthened the farmers' hand as the tied house became more of an attraction. Council housing is a high burden on the rural rate because there are national standards for local authority housing, which when translated into the thinner spread of settlement in rural areas lead to higher costs. More recently, there have also been the objections against council housing developments by environmentalists seeking to halt urban encroachment, and existing owner-occupied rural dwellers who want to halt particular forms of residential development. The planning controls, with their bias towards urban containment and against housing developments in rural areas, have been used to create privileged areas free from further developments, while shifting the pressure to the key settlements. Most post-war rural planning has concentrated development in key settlements where the duplication of service provisions can be avoided. The containment policies have increased the desirability and cost of owner-occupied rural housing, while limiting the amount of housing for low-income households in rural areas. The net result has been to lead to severe housing shortages for the lower-income rural dwellers such as farm workers, and these poor housing opportunities in association with dwindling employment prospects have been the major causes of rural to urban migration.

As Table 10.3 shows, rural housing is of a relatively high standard. However, an important qualification needs to be made as there are pockets of poor-quality housing in rural areas. A survey of local housing by South Herefordshire District Council found that 15 per cent of housing was unfit and 12 per cent lacked one or more of the basic amenities. While the new owner-occupied estates drag up the average quality of rural housing, there are substantial remnants of older poor-quality housing. Along with low incomes, poor access to

Table 10.3 Housing quality in rural England, 1971

	% of total households	
	Rural England	*England*
Households living at densities greater than 1.0 person per room	4.4	6.0
Households lacking exclusive use of one or more basic amenities	13.8	17.6

jobs and facilities, poor-quality housing makes up the mix of rural deprivation suffered by the lower-income, and especially the elderly low-income, rural dwellers.

Nowadays, as a significant proportion of households can afford a second home, the pressure on the rural housing market increases. The pressure is greatest in rural areas fringing metropolitan centres and in areas of high landscape quality. Berkshire is an example of the former, and the Lake District of the latter. In the fringing rural areas, existing residents seek to contain and control new development. Planning controls are used to limit the size and reduce densities of new estates to exclude lower-income owner-occupied developments. The practice of local politics in the rural and suburban areas around metropolitan Britain is essentially the politics of exclusion. In the remoter areas of high landscape quality the councils have a different problem. Here the market in second homes can distort the price and availability of housing to the detriment of the locals. In some areas the scale of second homes is very large. In the Lake District as a whole, almost 10 per cent of the total housing stock is in the hands of second-home owners, while in specific districts the proportion can rise up to 50 per cent. The Lake District Planning Board has sought to limit new houses to local people, but this attempt was overturned by the Secretary of State for the Environment. In Wales the second-home issue was charged with nationalist sentiments as many second-home owners were English. In 1980 a series of arson attacks on English-owned cottages in Wales gave a new meaning to the advertising slogan, 'come home to a real fire'. As more people seek the rural escape, the pressures on the rural housing market will increase and housing opportunities for low-income rural residents will be further constrained.

PART 3

HOME SWEET HOME

11

THE HOUSING OF HOUSEHOLDS

THE QUALITY OF HOUSING

One of the most important features of post-war Britain has been the rise in standards of living. In 1980 the average household had a higher income, more consumer durables, more free time, better holiday arrangements and superior access to educational and health services than the typical household of 1945. The quality of housing has been a key element in this post-war phenomenon. People in Britain are now better-housed than they have ever been, and this is an important point which should not be forgotten. The three measures of physical quality shown in Figure 11.1 tell a story of sustained improvements. These improvements have come about through the clearance of slum housing, the improvement of existing dwellings and the construction of new, better housing. Rising housing standards are related to public policy implementation and growing private affluence.

Despite the general trend, housing problems remain. The most fundamental is the lack of a house. Homelessness is difficult to define and measure. A literal definition would encompass all households who do not have a home of their own, and this would include those living with in-laws, relatives and friends. Although such households may have accommodation, they face psychological pressures through lacking a place of their own. Official statistics on homelessness are only partial. The information in the housing and construction statistics only relate to households who have registered and been accepted as homeless by local authorities. This obviously excludes households who do not register and those who fail to meet the local authorities' criteria. A Shelter report published in 1981 also suggested that some local authorities were using a loophole in the 1977 Housing (Homeless Persons) Act to refuse to rehouse households they considered had made themselves intentionally homeless; over

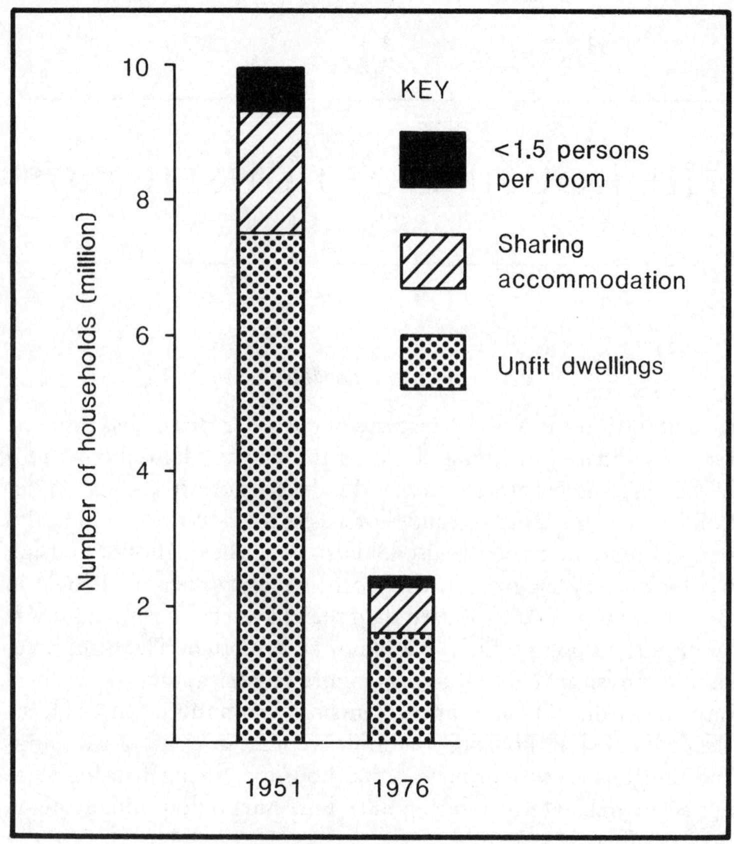

Figure 11.1 Housing quality in England and Wales, 1951 and 1976

2500 households were affected. For what they are worth the official statistics are shown in Table 11.1. They are a gross under-representation of the true level of homelessness. The official statistics also indicate the reasons for homelessness. Over 50 per cent of cases arise from the fact that parents, friends or relatives are no longer able or willing to accommodate the household; 15 per cent from a violent dispute with the spouse; 15 per cent from eviction from previous accommodation; while the remainder of cases arise from such varied reasons as mortgage arrears because of illness and being made homeless when a relative becomes ill. A combination of low income and family circumstances leads to homelessness.

There are also people still living in poor-quality accommodation. Even in 1976 over one-and-a-half million households were living in

Table 11.1 Homelessness in England: the official figures

	1978	*1979*	*1980 (first half)*
Homeless households accepted by local authorities	53,110	57,200	29,200

Source: HCS

dwellings considered unfit, and over half a million households were in shared accommodation. These poor-quality dwellings are found in the inner-city areas, and especially in the private rented sector. For the residents of the major cities poor housing is just one element in the cycle of disadvantage. Poor housing is particularly associated with ethnic minorities. A whole series of studies have pointed out that coloured households in Britain live in poorer-quality housing. This reflects discrimination, lower incomes and lack of access to better-quality housing. The position has improved slightly as length-of-residence qualifications become less important the longer coloured households live in the local authority, but they are still over-represented in poor-quality rented accommodation. Poor housing is just one problem in the festering sore of our inner cities, and high housing costs mean that minority households experience a greater degree of poverty than white households.

Recent trends also suggest a slight deterioration in housing. From 1971 to 1976 there was a 20 per cent increase in dwellings needing repairs costing (at 1971 prices) more than £500, and a 43-per-cent increase in dwellings needing repairs costing more than £1000. As the slum-clearance programmes have ended, and as public and private improvement schemes are hampered by lack of cash, the deterioration of housing is continuing apace. The process is particularly marked in the inner-city areas, where private landlords reduce maintenance and improvement expenditure, and low-income owner-occupiers are caught in the pincers of rising mortgage repayments on the one hand and steadily increasing repair and maintenance costs on the other.

The physical quality of housing has improved in post-war Britain; but housing must do more than simply keep out the wind and rain. It must provide the right environment for a full life. The most obvious design failure has been the high-rise blocks, which look good on architects' drawings but have failed the test of practical living. The dwellings themselves are often badly designed, leading to damp and mould, while the designs fail to generate any community feeling or neighbourhood control because of the lack of *defensible space*. Communities, like households, need demarcated boundaries to mark off their territory from public space; in lower-rise developments with walls, pavements and gardens, people can identify with their patch and the neighbourhood turf. The problem with the worst high-rise blocks is that outside your own door, everything is public space. There is no space which either the individual household or the residents can identify with, police or defend. There are obviously many reasons for the problems of vandalism and alienation which affect high-rise blocks, but the lack of defensible space is an important one.

There have also been the less dramatic failures. Much of post-war housing has been built with low space standards, poor internal layout and lack of sound insulation. Some of the poorest housing has been built by speculative builders for owner-occupation. Much of post-war housing stock consists of serried ranks of tiny boxes of housing in which there is little room to swing a cat and even less room for individual members of the household to pursue their own activities in privacy and quiet. As the basic physical standards are now taken for granted, households require housing which provides the proper environment in which to pursue a variety of actions from sleeping, watching television, reading and listening to music, all in separate private rooms. From this perspective, much contemporary housing is wanting in design and lacking in imagination. Our houses have yet to accommodate to the second half of the twentieth century; they relate to the picture of a household happily and quietly sitting in one main room with small bedrooms off for sleeping. As a society we have yet to provide better-designed quality housing at a reasonable cost for the mass of population.

THE COST OF HOUSING

Households now spend proportionately more on housing than on other items of expenditure. The growing proportion of housing expenditure is shown in Table 11.2. The increase reflects the rise in council house rents and the expense of owner-occupation. Housing costs vary by (1) income, (2) tenure, (3) age, and (4) place.

Table 11.2 Housing expenditure

	1953/4	*1960*	*1965*	*1970*	*1975*	*1978*
Expenditure on housing as a % of total household expenditure	8.8	9.3	11.7	12.6	13.1	14.8

Source: Family Expenditure Survey

(1) The poorest spend the highest proportion of their income on housing. In 1978, while those with an average weekly income of between £20 and £40 spent almost 23 per cent of their income on housing, those with average weekly incomes greater than £200 paid 13 per cent (see Figure 11.2). Housing is a necessity and, even with the poorest-quality accommodation, an expensive one. Housing costs figure largely in budgets of low-income groups, and any increase bites into their budgets more severely than for higher-income households because there is less monetary slack. Although rent and rate rebates can minimize the hardship, the schemes rely on people applying, and the take-up rate in the private-rented rent-rebate scheme is below 50 per cent of those eligible.

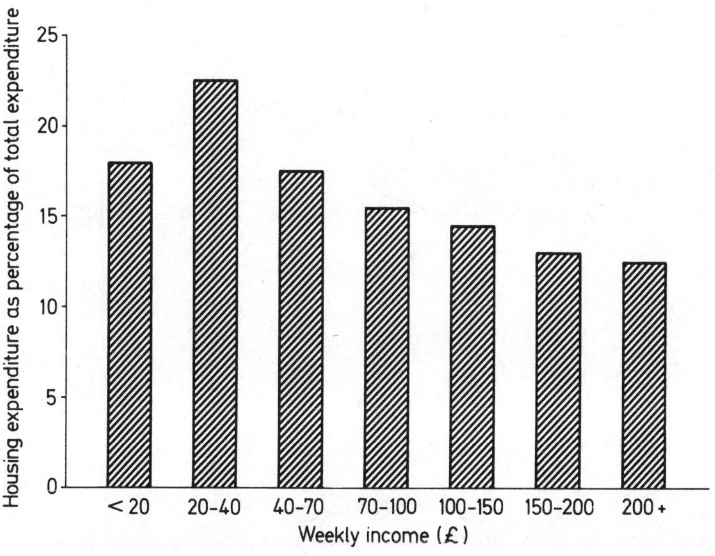

Figure 11.2 Housing expenditure by income

(2) We can also examine housing costs by tenure. Consider first the case of owner-occupation. The relationship between house prices and earnings is shown in Figure 11.3. There was a steady rise throughout the 1960s of house prices in relation to income, but the biggest change came in the early 1970s as house prices spiralled up to five times average earnings. The house price spiral subsided as quickly as it rose, and by the mid-1970s house prices were back to just over three times income, although the late 1970s have seen another, but less steep, rise in the ratio. This diagram charts the course of housing opportunity. When the ratio is low, more house-

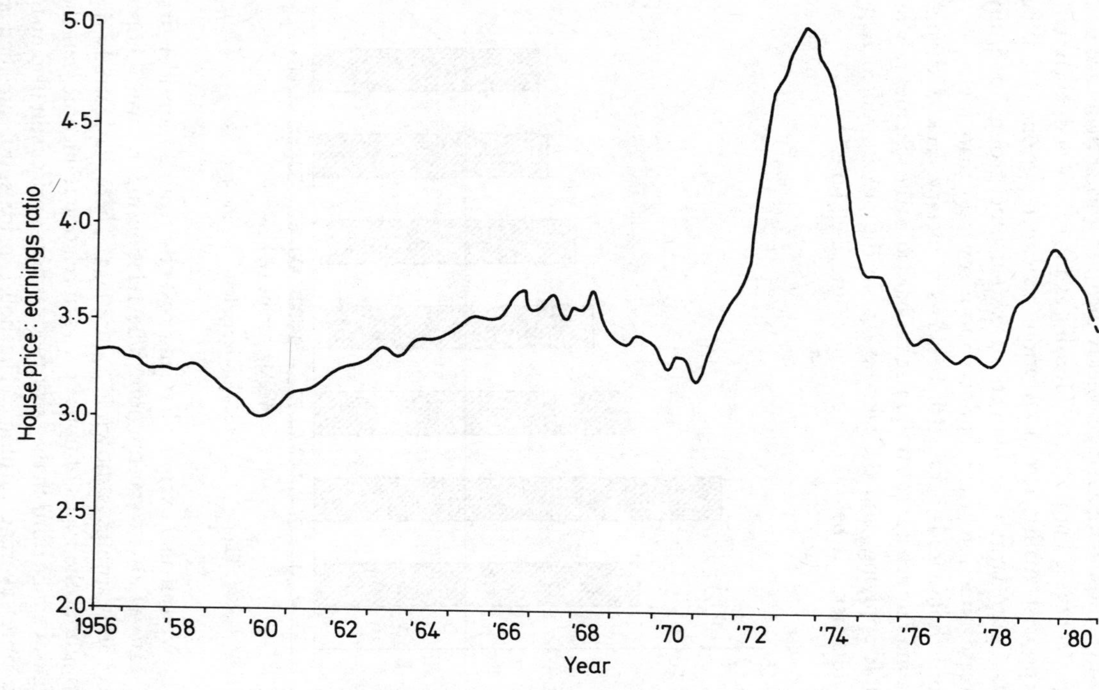

Figure 11.3 Ratio of house prices to income

holds can enter owner-occupation and can afford better-quality housing. When the ratio rises, households can afford less, they need to take out large mortgages in relation to their income, and lower-income households find it difficult to enter the owner-occupied sector.

Rent levels in the local authority housing sector are difficult to measure because there is such a large variation between the different authorities. Average figures tend to conceal as much as they enlighten; while the GLC average unrebated rent in April 1976 was £5.45 per week, this concealed the variation in rents charged by the GLC boroughs from Tower Hamlets charging £4.45 to the £8.65 charged by Kensington and Chelsea. The general trend of local authority rents in relation to average earnings is shown in Table 11.3. The high percentage in the financial year 1973/4 reflects the working through of the 1972 Housing Finance Act. Rents fell after 1974 initially because of the cancellation of further rent increases as part of a counter-inflation policy announced by the Labour government of 1974, and also because the 1975 Housing Act restored to local authorities the power to set rent levels. Many authorities reduced their rents. The 1980 Housing Act will reduce local authorities' autonomy and will lead to rapid increases in rent, which will be greater than increases in average incomes.

Table 11.3 Local authority rents and average incomes in England and Wales

	Average rent as % of average earnings
1946	7.0
1957/8	6.7
1963/4	7.3
1965/6	7.1
1967/8	7.9
1969/70	8.0
1971/2	7.9
1973/4	8.6
1974/5	7.8
1975/6	7.2

Source: HPTV

There is great variation in rent in the private rented sectors. Private renting provides some of the cheapest, though poorest accommodation, and also some of the most expensive. The majority of tenants in private rented accommodation pay low rents, and the average registered rent in 1979 for an unfurnished tenant was £483 per year, a little less than £10 per week. Rents are higher for tenants of housing association properties, and highest of all for tenants in furnished accommodation. The general post-war trend has been for rent increases, at least in the controlled and regulated tenancies, to be less than increases in general prices and inflation. For those sectors outside formal control, rents will be set according to the relative bargaining power of landlords and tenants, with rent being especially high in the right markets of central London (see Table 11.4).

Table 11.4 Average registered rents, England and Wales

	Mean registered rent (£)		
	Unfurnished tenancies	*Regulated furnished*	*Housing association*
1973	252 (358)	–	257
1974	258 (399)	–	323
1975	309 (419)	–	373
1976	343 (485)	–	399
1977	377 (546)	617 (783)	469
1978	433 (596)	679 (837)	524
1979	483 (688)	767 (929)	556

Note: figures in brackets refer to Greater London
Source: HCS

(3) Both income and housing costs vary through the life of a household. For manual workers peak income is reached at age forty years. For non-manual workers the peak is later, and higher, at just over fifty years of age. While household income tends to increase through time, the relative proportion of housing costs tends to decline, though perhaps rising in later years, especially for council tenants and private-rented tenants, as household income begins to decline after middle-age. The converse occurs in the owner-occupied sector, where the ordinary mortgage system ensures a front-loading of costs on to the early years of the mortgage. For the young first-time purchaser the total housing costs will constitute over a third and sometimes up to a half of total income. After ten years of a twenty-five-year mortgage, the mortgage costs will have fallen to less than 10 per cent of total income and less than 5 per cent after fifteen years, assuming a 15-per-cent inflation rate. The higher the inflation rate, the quicker the fall-off in relative housing costs. In contrast to everyone else, owner-occupiers want a stiff dose of inflation in the early years of their mortgage. The front-loading problem prohibits the easy entry of households into owner-occupation. Even small-scale changes in interest rates can make the difference between success and failure in the ability to enter the owner-occupied sector. Households who have extended themselves

financially to enter owner-occupation may face real difficulties if the mortgage rate increases.

(4) Housing costs vary across space. In the tighter market of London, for example, private renters can pay rents double those for similar occupation in provincial cities. Council tenants pay varying amounts, depending upon the disposition of their local authority, and for those entering owner-occupation house prices vary substantially across the country, with the most expensive housing in London and the south-east. The differing average incomes do not make up the disparity, and the result is difference in housing expenditure as shown in Table 11.5. Households in the south-east and the Midlands devote a higher proportion of their expenditure to housing than households in the other regions.

Table 11.5 Housing expenditure by region

	Housing as % of total expenditure during 1977/8
North	12.6
Yorkshire and Humberside	12.5
North-west	14.3
East Midlands	14.7
West Midlands	15.1
East Anglia	15.8
South-east	16.8
Greater London	17.2
Rest of south-east	16.5
South-west	15.4
Wales	12.5
Scotland	10.9
Northern Ireland	9.6

Source: Family Expenditure Survey

THE LOCATION OF HOUSING

Location is important, not only in terms of how much you pay for housing, but also in terms of access to employment, entertainment, shopping and other facilities. We can make a distinction between pre-war and post-war housing. Housing in post-war Britain has been built and planned according to certain principles. The most fundamental has been the belief in the efficacy of separating employment and residential areas. Most new housing has, therefore, been built in residential units separated from industrial areas and the result has been the home–workplace separation.

The local authority housing departments were primarily concerned with building houses, and in the early estates of the post-war period there was very little concern with the provision of community facilities or shopping precincts. Similarly with private-sector speculative housing, where there was often minimal provision of community and shopping facilities. Planning controls on industry, commerce, shopping and large entertainment facilities have operated differently from controls on residential development. Houses have suburbanized, the rest have not. The net result is that much of post-war housing built on the edges of British cities is far from essential services.

The built form and the evolving distribution of activities has been based on the speed of the fastest, namely people with access to a motor car. The problem is that not everyone has this. In 1977, only 260 households in every 1000 had a car, and even within households not all the members can drive or have access during work hours. The groups most affected by lack of accessibility are the low-income non-car-owning households, especially in rural and suburban locations, and even amongst car-owning families, when the wage-earner drives to work other members of the family are denied full access. The structure of the built form deprives some households while providing opportunities to others.

HOUSING AND THE FAMILY

Four out of five people in Britain live in families composed of married couples. Almost a half of them have one or two dependent children. The typical household in Britain consists of mother, father and two children. Housing in post-war Britain has reflected and to some extent reinforced this family structure. The bulk of housing is built to accommodate, separately, private households. This is so obvious that we need to consider the alternatives: one would be the provision of communal living arrangements for more than one family; another would be a kibbutz-type system where private households were merged in a collective. There are others, but the housing in Britain is, in contrast, individualized. To an extent this maintains the family structure. The basic structure has been further strengthened by the home-centred nature of much of our activities. Watching television, which takes place in the home, is the biggest leisure pursuit in Britain. As television diffusion has reached almost saturation level, the time spent in the home has increased. This orientation towards the home has also been strengthened by the weakening of old community ties, partly through population movement and partly as a function of rising real income and better employment protection. Many of the social ties in old-established communities were a form of protection against financial hardship in an uncertain and precarious job market. Better welfare provisions have lessened the need for such forms of community welfare insurance.

The orientation towards the home, and associated privatization, while partly maintaining family structure, also causes tension within households. The dwelling becomes the scene of family disputes and the house can echo, and sometimes amplify, household disputes. The lack of good insulation, in association with the noise-producing nature of much of our leisure pursuits, creates obvious tensions, especially between the generations. Another tension arises from the sexual division of labour. Individual houses require high inputs of work to service the place – make the beds, clean up, wash dishes, etc. – and this has traditionally been women's work. But new attitudes have emerged and there are now more women in the work force – 9.8 million in 1975 compared with 7 million in 1951 – over one-third of the total. A typical newly married couple now has both people working. Old modes of thought can clash with new economic realities. On the one hand, there is the old mentality that washing-up is women's work but, on the other, there is often a similarity in outside work experience and levels of take-home pay. Conflict is generated over the level and nature of individual housework, especially given the traditional divisions of labour. Family tensions are not caused simply by the nature of housing, and we have to be wary of a crude environmental determinism. But it is of some importance, and to ignore it would be an omission from a full understanding of sexual politics, personal relations and household structure.

HOUSING AND STATUS

A dwelling provides more than just shelter from the elements. The type and location of dwelling says who you are, where you are going and where you have been. Consider the case of tenure. Because of the nature of post-war housing policy, owner-occupation is the favoured tenure category. It provides a relatively safe investment but, more than this, because of the residualization of council housing, owner-occupation is a symbol of achievement. Council housing has been denigrated to the role of providing housing for those who cannot afford owner-occupation, and to become an owner-occupier is a mark of success, while to remain a council tenant is considered an admission of failure. The distinction is heightened by the definite differences in housing design; most people can identify a council estate by the layout and the whole look of the place. It is not incidental that the first thing people do when they have bought their council house is to paint their door differently, add a bay window, change the façade and anything which establishes in the eyes of the outside world a new status for the inhabitants. People want to become owner-occupiers not only because it is financially beneficial; it is an indication of success, an emblem of higher status.

There are differences within the two main tenure types. Council tenants, and indeed others, know the continuum of good and bad estates comprising the local authority housing stock, with the 'best-behaved' tenants at one end of the scale and the worst houses and the most 'difficult' tenants at the other. Within the owner-occupied sector there are subtle gradations between the different types of housing. The typical British household can see an old, solidly built, substantial house in the country as the zenith of its housing career. Along the path in ascending order of preference, would be a turn-of-the-century terraced house, a Wimpey box, a bigger Wimpey box, an inter-war semi with bay windows, and then a large house with a garden attached, all in a select residential area. A cosmopolitan may prefer a penthouse flat, a gentrifier an urban location, while the rich can miss out the early rungs altogether. The different types of house are so many markers on a route mapping social and economic advancement and decline.

The private rented sector plays a peculiar role in the housing status game. For those trapped there, it is a mark of failure. For the more transient households it is not so much a destination as a waiting room. It is difficult to put a tag on a shifting population. Private renting is a shadowy, ill-defined penumbra between the black and white of owner-occupation and local authority housing.

Where you live is as much a function as a reflection of who you are. The nuances of housing consumption overlie, reinforce and sometimes contradict status differences. Even within similar status groups there can be marked differences in housing consumption. The white-collar worker in the Wimpey box may have a different attitude from a similar worker who chooses to live in an inner-city terraced property. The variations in the private housing market allow some room for broad categories of preference to be realized, at least for the middle- and upper-income groups. The different residential areas emit different signals about the status and personality of their occupants. The residential mosaic is a pattern of messages.

Finally, we can return to the issue of the relationship between housing consumption and class. The arguments currently on offer are not particularly satisfactory. The argument that owner-occupation provides a bulwark against social change does not correspond with the reality. Encouragement of owner-occupation is a costly business and one which makes the everyday life of the majority of the population responsive to even small-scale changes of interest rate. The depoliticization argument is only consistent if low interest rates prevail, the exchange value of housing can be realized and house prices keep pace with inflation. Rather than a depoliticization, there has been the reverse as the existence of owner-occupation has had a profound effect on local land-use planning issues and central government fiscal policies. The alternative one of housing being a key element in the bag of communal goods and services termed collective consumption, and thus providing a basis for radicalization, is naïve in the extreme. Saunders' (1978) argument that the existence of owner-occupation provides a new source of differentiation into non-owners and owners is equally simplistic. As I sought to show in Chapter 6, there are owner-occupiers and owner-occupiers. There is as much differentiation within this sector as without, and the difference between low-income owner-occupiers and some council tenants is very small.

All three arguments posit a communality between housing and status as defined by occupation. This is too simple. Perceived status, or indeed class position, depend upon a whole range of factors; employment is, of course, the most important, but individual and collective socialization in the home, in the school, in the neighbourhood, all play a significant part. At the very lowest and highest ends of the income and status scales, there is a very clear correspondence among all these things. The very rich, for example, go to certain schools, live in certain areas, take holidays in certain resorts, and so on. For the vast group of people in the middle, however, the story of post-war Britain has been one of a fission in the communality of the separate items. While there has been a definite process of deskilling in the labour market for both manual and non-manual workers, leading to the obliteration of old occupational divisions and a growing homogenization in the work force, things have been different in the housing market. In the first place, there is the distinction between council tenants and owner-occupiers, and further differences in the lived experience of households in the same categories but in different housing positions. A household which bought a house before 1972 is in a markedly different economic position from a young household purchasing their first house in the current climate.

Similar trends can also be traced in the provision of education. In certain areas education has provided the escalator to better opportunities for working-class children, but elsewhere it merely slots them into an allotted task, or indeed sometimes fails to give them anything at all. The most extreme case is the difference between white and black households, often in the same jobs but living in very different areas with different housing costs, different educational and cultural facilities. The categorization of tenant or owner, manual or non-manual, alone fails to capture the lived experience, the consciousness or the subtleties in political disposition of different sets of households in different areas of the country. Housing is just one element in the reproduction of social life, social relations and political attitudes. There are others, and we should not assume that there is a simple linear relationship between patterns of housing consumption and the form of this reproduction. This is a theme that I shall take up in another book.

LIST OF ABBREVIATIONS

BSA	Building Societies Association
DLO	Direct Labour Organizations
FES	Family Expenditure Survey
GHS	General Household Survey
GIA	General Improvement Area
HAA	Housing Action Area
HCS	Housing Construction Statistics
HPTV	Housing Policy Technical Volume (1977 Green Paper)
PWLB	Public Works Loan Board
TCPA	Town and Country Planning Association

GUIDE TO FURTHER READING

GENERAL

There are a number of general texts on housing. Bassett and Short (1980a) consider the broad nature of housing and evaluate the general approaches to the study of housing. Darke and Darke (1979) provide a brief introduction, Cowley (1979) makes some interesting points and the CDP (1976a) pamphlet makes for lively reading. A general introduction to the British housing market is available in Murie, Niner and Watson (1976), while Burns and Grebler (1977) provide an international perspective.

HOUSING AND THE STATE

The early days

There are a number of books on nineteenth-century housing problems and policies. An excellent mid-century account is provided by Engels (1958 edition). Working-class housing is examined in Tarn (1971), Chapman (1971) and Gauldie (1974). A general introduction is available in Burnett (1978), and particular studies include Tarn (1973) on the five-per-cent philanthropy schemes, Wohl (1977) on the important role of London's housing experience in shaping national legislation, and Ball (1981) on the development of capitalism in eighteenth- and nineteenth-century housing provision.

The inter-war years

The most comprehensive study of inter-war housing policy is Bowley (1944). The immediate post-war period is covered by Swenarton (1981). Aldcroft and Richardson (1968) examine the boom in private-sector housing.

The post-war years

The effect of the war on immediate post-war policies is considered by Addison (1975). Foot's (1975) biography of Bevan, who was the first Minister of Housing, gives a feel for the immediate post-war housing scene, while Eatwell (1979) provides an assessment of the first post-war Labour government.

The politicians themselves are a handy source of information. Macmillan's (1969) autobiography gives an insider's view of the first Conservative government and its housing deliberations. Crossman (1975) was a key figure in the Labour government's housing dilemmas of the 1960s. Like the works of all politicians, they should be approached with caution.

General assessments of post-war housing policy can be found in Cullingworth (1979), Donnison (1967) and Berry (1974). Allaun (1972) has edited a useful book on Britain's housing failures as experienced by the victims. The three technical volumes of the DOE's (1977) Green Paper on Housing Policy provide a wealth of empirical material, and this is used by Lansley (1979) in assessing the distributional consequences of housing subsidy arrangements.

Duclaud-Williams (1978) compares British housing policy and politics with those of France.

'Socialist' critiques of housing policy can be found in CDP (1976a), while the 'free market' approach is given an airing by Barry (1977).

THE HOUSING MARKET

The land market

The creation of the post-war land-use planning systems is discussed by Hall (1975), while the most comprehensive assessment of the impact of the system is Hall *et al.* (1973). Lichfield and Darin-Drabkin (1980) provide a turgid account of British land policies, and Massey and Catalano (1978) discuss patterns of landownership. Best (1976, 1977) is a lively commentator on the extent of land conversion, while the land-availability debate is contained in Hooper (1979, 1980) and Humber (1980).

The construction of housing

Bowley (1966) provides an historical dimension and discusses the separation between design and construction, while Turin (1975) provides an economist's perspective. Ball (1978) examines the reasons for low productivity in the building industry, and the Direct Labour Collective (1978) provides a critique of the whole contracting system as well as a summary of the DLO's record. Cooney (1974) has a useful essay on high-rise buildings, and Bassett and Short (1978) discuss the distribution of grant-aided improvement work.

Owner-occupation

Kemeny (1981) and Pawley (1978) provide a general introduction to owner-occupation. The volume 8, number 3, 1980 issue of *Policy and Politics* is devoted to the sale of council houses. Boddy (1980) is the best introduction to building societies, and Kilroy (1979) to the whole field of the financing of owner-occupation. Bassett and Short (1980b) examine patterns of mortgage lending in the 1970s, while Murie and Forrest (1980) look at housing and wealth inheritance.

Local authority housing

Merrett (1979) provides the most comprehensive coverage of local authority housing; his book is an essential work. Also important is the CDP (1976b) report on council housing.

Private renting

Short (1979) provides a general introduction as well as a case study, but perhaps the best sources are the relevant government Select Committee reports; see Milner Holland Committee (1965) and Francis Committee (1971).

The inner city

Kirby (1978) provides a good general introduction to the inner city, while Short and Bassett (1981) consider the impact of housing policies, and Ambrose and Colenutt (1975) assess the impact of commercial redevelopment on the inner city.

The rural areas

Newby (1979) provides the overall rural context, and Dunn *et al.* (1981) is just one example of a growing literature on rural housing problems.

New towns

A critical assessment of the whole programme is provided by Aldridge (1979).

The exchange of housing

A case study of movement in the private sector is provided by Short (1978a). Short (1978b) reviews the general literature on residential mobility. Williams (1976) examines the gentrification process, and Boddy and Gray (1979) discuss the filtering argument.

Housing as lived experience

Allaun (1972) has edited an interesting collection of papers and excerpts. Newman (1972) discusses the concept of defensible space. Kirby (1979b) unravels some of the links between housing location and accessibility to various services. Issue 3 of volume 2 of *International Journal of Urban and Regional Research*, published in 1978, is devoted to examining women's role in the built environment. Some of the papers included expand upon themes only touched upon in this book.

Journals

There are a number of journals which publish items on housing. *Housing* is the publication of the Institute of Housing and gives an insight into the housing managers' problems. *Housing Review* publishes short general pieces. *Roof*, published by Shelter, is the most iconoclastic publication and, together with *New Society*, provides the best source of information for the general reader. The following academic journals regularly have papers on housing: *International Journal of Urban and Regional Research*, *Urban Studies*, *Environment and Planning A*, *Social Policy and Administration*.

REFERENCES

Addison, P. (1975) *The Road to 1945: British Politics and the Second World War*, London, Cape.

Aldcroft, D. H. and Richardson, H. W. (1968) *Building in the British Economy Between the Wars*, London, Allen & Unwin.

Aldridge, M. (1979) *The British New Towns: A Programme Without a Policy*, London, Routledge.

Allaun, F. (1972) *No Place Like Home*, London, Deutsch.

Ambrose, P. and Colenutt, R. (1975) *The Property Machine*, Harmondsworth, Penguin.

Ball, M. (1978) 'British housing policy and the house-building industry', *Capital and Class*, 4, 78–99.

Ball, M. (1981) 'The development of capitalism in housing provision', *International Journal of Urban and Regional Research*, 5, 145–77.

Barry, N. (1977) 'A political economy of housing', *CBI Review*, Spring, 3–15.

Bassett, K. A. and Short, J. R. (1978) 'Housing improvement in the inner city', *Urban Studies*, 15, 333–42.

Bassett, K. A. and Short, J. R. (1980a) *Housing and Residential Structure*, London, Routledge.

Bassett, K. A. and Short, J. R. (1980b) 'Patterns of building society and local authority mortgage lending in the 1970s', *Environment and Planning A*, 12, 279–300.

Berry, F. (1974) *Housing: the Great British Failure*, London, Charles Knight.

Best, R. H. (1976) 'The extent and growth of urban land', *The Planner*, 62, 8–11.

Best, R. H. (1977) 'Agricultural land loss – myth or reality', *The Planner*, 63, 15–16.

Bird, H. (1976) 'Residential mobility and preference patterns in the public sector of the housing market', *Transactions of the Institute of British Geographers*, New Series, 1, 20–33.

Boddy, M. J. (1980) *The Building Societies*, London, Macmillan.

Boddy, M. J. and Gray, F. (1979) 'Filtering theory, housing policy and the legitimation of inequality', *Policy and Politics*, 7, 39–54.

Bowley, M. (1944) *Housing and the State*, London, Allen & Unwin.

Bowley, M. (1966) *The British Building Industry*, Cambridge University Press.

BSA (1980) *Studies in Building Society Activity*, London, Building Societies Association.

Burnett, J. (1978) *A Social History of Housing, 1815–1970*, London, Methuen.

Burns, L. and Grebler, L. (1977) *The Housing of Nations: Analysis and Policy in a Comparative Framework*, London, Macmillan.

CDP (1976a) *Profits Against Homes*, London, Community Development Project Information and Intelligence Unit.

CDP (1976b) *Whatever Happened to Council Housing?*, London, Community Development Project Information and Intelligence Unit.

Chapman, S. (1971) *The History of Working Class Housing*, Newton Abbot, David & Charles.

Coleman, A. (1976) 'Is planning really necessary?' *Geographical Journal*, 142, 411–36.

Cooney, E. W. (1974) 'High flats in local authority housing in England and Wales since 1945', in Sutcliff, A. (ed.), *Multi-storey Living: the British Working Class Experience*, London, Croom Helm.

Cowley, J. (1979) *Housing for People or for Profit*, London, Stage 1.

Crossman, R. H. S. (1975) *Diaries of a Cabinet Minister*, vol. 1, London, Hamish Hamilton.

Cullingworth, J. B. (1979) *Essays on Housing Policy: the British Scene*, London, Allen & Unwin.

Darke, J. and Darke, R. (1979) *Who Needs Housing?*, London, Macmillan.

Davies, J. G. (1972) *The Evangelistic Bureaucrat*, London, Tavistock.

Dennis, N. (1970) *People and Planning*, London, Faber.

Dennis, N. (1972) *Public Participation and Planner's Blight*, London, Faber.

Direct Labour Collective (1978) *Building with Direct Labour: Local Authority Building and the Crisis in the Construction Industry*, London, Housing Workshop of the Conference of Socialist Economists.

DOE (1977) *Housing Policy – a Consultative Document*, Plus 3 Technical Volumes, Cmnd 6851, London, HMSO.

Donnison, D. (1967) *The Government of Housing*, Harmondsworth, Penguin.

Donnison, D. and Soto, P. (1980) *The Good City*, London, Heinemann.

Duclaud-Williams, R. (1978) *The Politics of Housing in Britain and France*, London, Heinemann.

Dunleavy, P. (1977) 'Protest and quiescence in urban politics', *International Journal of Urban and Regional Research*, 1, 193–218.

Dunn, M., Rawson, M. and Rogers, A. (1981) *Rural Housing: Competition and Choice*, London, Allen & Unwin.

Eatwell, R. (1979) *The 1945–51 Labour Governments*, London, Batsford.

Engels, F. (1958 edn) *The Condition of the Working Class in England*, Oxford, Blackwell.

Ferris, J. (1972) *Participation in Urban Planning: the Barnsbury Case*, London, Bell.

Foot, M. (1975) *Aneurin Bevan*, vol. 2, London, Granada.

Francis Committee (1971) *Report of the Committee on the Rent Acts*, Cmnd 4609, London, HMSO.

Gauldie, E. (1974) *Cruel Habitations*, London, Allen & Unwin.

Gray, F. (1976) 'Selection and allocation in council housing', *Transactions of the Institute of British Geographers*, New Series, 1, 36–46.

Hall, P. G. (1975) *Urban and Regional Planning*, Newton Abbot, David & Charles.

Hall, P., Gracey, H., Drewett, R. and Thomas, R. (1973) *The Containment of Urban England*, 2 vols, London, PEP and Allen & Unwin.

Hall, P. G. and Hay, D. (1980) *Growth Centres in the European Urban System*, London, Heinemann.

Hall, S. (1979) 'The great moving right show', *Marxism Today*, 23, 14–20.

Hooper, A. (1979) 'Land availability', *Journal of Planning and Environment Law*, 752, 56.

Hooper, A. (1980) 'Land for private housebuilding', *Journal of Planning and Environment Law*, 795–806.

House Builders' Federation (1969) *Land for Housing*, a discussion paper presented by a working party of the House Builders' Federation, London.

Humber, J. R. (1980) 'Land availability – another view', *Journal of Planning and Environment Law*, 19–23.

Kemeny, J. (1981) *The Myth of Homeownership*, London, Routledge.

Kilroy, B. (1979) 'Housing finance – why so privileged?' *Lloyds Bank Review*, 133, 37–52.

Kirby, A. M. (1978) *The Inner City – Causes and Effects*, Corbridge, Retail and Planning Associates.

Kirby, A. M. (1979a) *Towards an Understanding of the Local State*, Geographical Paper no. 70, University of Reading.

Kirby, A. M. (1979b) *Education, Health and Housing: an Empirical Study of Resource Accessibility*, Farnborough, Saxon House.

Lansley, S. (1979) *Housing and Public Policy*, London, Croom Helm.

Lichfield, N. and Darin-Drabkin, H. (1980) *Land Policy in Planning*, London, Allen & Unwin.

Macmillan, H. (1969) *Tides of Fortune 1945–1955*, London, Macmillan.

Massey, D. and Catalano, A. (1978) *Capital and Land: Landownership and Capital in Great Britain*, London, Edward Arnold.

Merrett, S. (1979) *State Housing in Britain*, London, Routledge.

Milner Holland Committee (1965) *Report of the Committee on Housing in Greater London*, Cmnd 2605, London, HMSO.

Muchnick, D. (1970) *Urban Renewal in Liverpool*, LSE Occasional Papers in Social Administration no. 33, London, Bell.

Murie, A. and Forrest, R. (1980) 'Wealth, inheritance and housing policy', *Policy and Politics*, 8, 1–19.

Murie, A., Niner, P. and Watson, C. (1976) *Housing Policy and the Housing System*, London, Allen & Unwin.

Newby, M. (1979) *Green and Pleasant Land*, Harmondsworth, Penguin.

Newman, O. (1972) *Defensible Space: People and Design in the Violent City*, London, Architectural Press.

Niner, P. (1975) *Local Authority Housing Policy and Practice*, Centre for Urban and Regional Studies, Occasional Paper no. 31, University of Birmingham.

Odling-Smee, J. C. (1975) 'The impact of the fiscal system on different tenure systems', in *Housing Finance*, Institute of Fiscal Studies Publication no. 12.

Pawley, M. (1978) *Homeownership*, London, Architectural Press.

Saunders, P. (1978) 'Domestic property and social class', *International Journal of Urban and Regional Research*, 2, 233–51.

Shoard, M. (1980) *The Theft of the Countryside*, London, Temple Smith.

Short, J. R. (1978a) 'Residential mobility in the private housing market of Bristol', *Transactions of the Institute of British Geographers*, New Series, 3, 533–47.

Short, J. R. (1978b) 'Residential mobility', *Progress in Human Geography*, 2, 419–47.

Short, J. R. (1979) 'Landlords and the private rented sector: a case study', in Boddy, M. (ed.) *Property, Investment and Land*, School for Advanced Urban Studies Working Paper no. 2, University of Bristol.

Short, J. R. and Bassett, K. A. (1981) 'Housing policy and the inner city in the 1970s', *Transactions of the Institute of British Geographers*, New Series, 6, 293–312.

Skellington, R. (1981) 'How blacks lose out in council housing', *New Society*, 55, 187–9.

Swenarton, M. (1981) *Homes Fit for Heroes: the Politics and Architecture of Early State Housing in Britain*, London, Heinemann.

Tarn, J. (1971) *Working Class Housing in the 19th Century*, London, Architectural Association.

Tarn, J. (1973) *Five Per Cent Philanthropy: an Account of Housing in Urban Areas between 1840 and 1914*, Cambridge University Press.

Townsend, P. (1980) 'Social planning and the Treasury', in Bosanquet, N. and Townsend, P. (eds.) *Labour and Equality: a Fabian Study of Labour in Power 1974–1979*, London, Heinemann.

Turin, D. (1975) *Aspects of the Economics of Construction*, London, Godwin.

Williams, P. R. (1976) 'The role of institutions in the inner London housing market, the case of Islington', *Transactions of the Institute of British Geographers*, New Series, 1, 72–82.

Wohl, A. (1977) *The Eternal Slum*, London, Edward Arnold.

NAME INDEX

SUBJECT INDEX